QUALITATIVE RESEARCH METHODS
FOR THE SOCIAL SCIENCES

THIRD EDITION

QUALITATIVE RESEARCH METHODS FOR THE SOCIAL SCIENCES

BRUCE L. BERG

California State University, Long Beach

Allyn and Bacon

Boston • London • Toronto • Sydney • Tokyo • Singapore

SERIES EDITOR: Sarah Dunbar
EDITOR IN CHIEF, SOCIAL SCIENCES: Karen Hanson
EDITORIAL ASSISTANT: Jennifer Muroff
VICE PRESIDENT, DIRECTOR OF FIELD MARKETING: Joyce Nilsen
MARKETING MANAGER: Karon Bowers
EDITORIAL-PRODUCTION ADMINISTRATOR: Annette Joseph
EDITORIAL-PRODUCTION COORDINATOR: Susan Freese
EDITORIAL-PRODUCTION SERVICE: Karen Mason
COPYEDITOR: Danny Marcus
COMPOSITION BUYER: Linda Cox
MANUFACTURING BUYER: Megan Cochran
COVER ADMINISTRATOR: Suzanne Harbison

Copyright © 1998, 1995, 1989 by Allyn & Bacon
A Viacom Company
160 Gould Street
Needham Heights, MA 02194
Internet: www.abacon.com
America Online: keyword: College Online

Library of Congress Cataloging-in-Publication Data

Berg, Bruce Lawrence
    Qualitative research methods for the social sciences / Bruce L. Berg. — 3rd ed.
        p.   cm.
    Includes bibliographical references and indexes.
    ISBN 0-205-26475-1
    1. Social sciences—Research—Methodology.   I. Title.
H61.B52   1998
300′ .72—dc21   96-49934
                                                                          CIP

Printed in the United States of America

10 9 8 7 6 5 4 3 2 1   02 01 00 99 98 97

CONTENTS

4 A Dramaturgical Look at Interviewing 57

Focus Group Interviewing 100

Ethnographic Field Strategies 120

Case Studies 212

 An Introduction to Content Analysis 223

12 Writing Research Papers: Sorting the Noodles from the Soup 253

PREFACE

THE GOAL OF THE THIRD EDITION of *Qualitative Research Methods for the Social Sciences* is the same as I intended in previous editions, to offer this book "as a handbook for anyone interested in but unfamiliar with qualitative research techniques." I continue to envision this book being used along with more general quantitative texts traditionally used in methods courses and as a stand-alone core text in courses on qualitative methods. As a supplement to other texts, this book offers students a basic look at qualitative research techniques and analytic strategies, not the lip service frequently found in most standard research methods texts. As a stand-alone text, *Qualitative Research Methods for the Social Sciences* offers students a solid grounding in many of the mainstream orientations commonly used in qualitative research today.

In this edition, I have again expanded and revised material in the text. The research style presented in this edition remains chiefly sociological. The application of data-gathering and -analytic strategies, however, is not designed exclusively for students of sociology or for sociologists. In fact, a growing number of my readers have come from the disciplines of English, nursing, education, and business, besides the more traditional social sciences such as psychology, anthropology, and criminology.

The book's central purpose remains a desire to instruct inexperienced researchers in ways of effectively collecting, organizing, and making sense from qualitative data. This edition also seeks to demystify the research process. I believe that what makes the research process frightening for some is merely a fear of the unknown. When novice researchers learn how a process or technique works, it becomes comfortable, relaxed, and—dare I say it—easy!

In keeping with my general pedagogical style, this edition of the book continues to move readers beyond the point of collecting data without knowing what to do with it. The goal is to get fledgling researchers to design, collect, and analyze data and then to present their results to the scientific community. This third edition also focuses on current issues in the world of researchers, which include a serious concern about ethical behavior and protocols in research and a more reflexive and sensitive role for the researcher. Toward this end, I have moved the subject of ethics to the third chapter, rather than discuss it near the end of the book, as in previous editions. My intention in doing so is to ensure that new researchers develop an appreciation for ethical concerns before they begin to study research collection, organization, and analytic techniques.

Furthermore, during recent years, I have begun myself to develop a more reflexive researcher role and to recognize the benefits of this orientation. In several places throughout this text, researcher reflexivity and researcher voice are explained and discussed. In fact, the use of the first person (*I, my,* etc.), which I began using in the last edition of this book, is a small example of my more reflexive researcher's role and voice. The orientation offered in this text does not fully embrace all elements of reflexivity but discusses several of the basic elements associated with this position.

As something of a traditionalist, I continue to believe that researchers learn their craft through a combination of trial and error and "getting their hands dirty" with data. I also believe this process works best when guided by a more experienced researcher—a mentor. Yet even this approach works more effectively when the apprentice has a firm understanding of the basic elements of the research process. This book is designed especially for accomplishing this purpose.

As was true in the first edition of this book, my personal bias as a symbolic interactionist guides my choices and explanations. Once again, I admit that all the techniques presented have been grounded in that theoretical approach. However, I continue to believe that the various techniques and strategies offered in this book can be equally effective when grounded in other theoretical perspectives, as well. Inexperienced researchers should thus take my presentation as suggestions and recommendations toward establishing a research foundation and not as the only methodological orientation available to them.

Finally, it is my deepest hope that after reading this book, students will think about research in a positive and even playful manner. Research can be extremely enjoyable when undertaken in the proper frame of mind. Even a trip to Disneyland can be ruined if you focus too much on the costs, the congested traffic, or the long lines. Many people go to Disneyland and never even notice these inconveniences. Research can be like a trip to Disneyland: It can be exciting, interesting, and rewarding. But first, you must open your heart and mind to the research process.

ACKNOWLEDGMENTS

My thanks, again, begin with my family: my wife, Jill, and our two children, Kate and Alex. Their support and confidence have continued to allow me time and opportunities to think and to write. Additionally, I want to thank my students. I have long viewed my methods classes as proving grounds for the material in this book. My students, in fact, have been both my ardent critics and greatest allies in developing elements used in each edition of this book. I thank them for their honesty, their patience, and their instruction.

I would also like to thank Peter Adler (University of Denver), Robert Benford (University of Nebraska), Thomas G. Blomberg (The Florida State University), and James A. Pearsol (The Ohio State University), who reviewed earlier drafts of this book for Allyn and Bacon.

INTRODUCTION

MANY BOOKS DISCUSS A VARIETY OF social scientific research methods; thus, you may reasonably question why anyone would bother writing another text. However, a close examination reveals that although a great many texts have been written about such abstract concerns as research design and sophisticated statistical procedures for tabulating quantitative data, few books have concentrated on how to do qualitative research and analysis.

Several fundamental texts were in vogue during the late 1960s and 1970s, but now many of these classic qualitative texts have been permitted to go out of print (such as Becker, 1970; Bogdan, 1972; Bogdan & Taylor, 1975; Denzin, 1978; Filstead, 1970; Glaser & Strauss, 1967; Schwartz & Jacobs, 1979; Webb et al., 1966, 1981). During the 1980s, several publishers began pressing books with qualitative orientations. Sage Publishing is responsible for a great many of these works. For example, they developed a string of short works, the Sage University Papers Series on Qualitative Research Methods. By 1989, the year the first edition of this text was published by Allyn and Bacon, Sage had published 16 books in their Qualitative Research Series. Also in 1989, Sage came out with several slightly lengthier works on qualitative methods in their Applied Social Research Methods Series (e.g., Denzin, 1989; Fetterman, 1989; Jorgensen, 1989).

A flutter of other qualitative reference works on methods arose during the 1980s (e.g., Berg, 1989; Kirby & McKenna, 1989; Strauss & Corbin, 1989; Van Maanen, 1988). Yet, even with these spurts of qualitative research material, there remains a decided imbalance in the literature on research methods in the academic community. While many quantitatively oriented research texts are published each year, only a few qualitative textbooks are available.

Ethnography saw a resurgence of sorts during the early 1980s, especially among educational researchers (e.g., Bogdan & Biklen, 1982; Bredo & Feinberg, 1982; Dobbert, 1982; Spindler, 1982). However, these books, like

1

most of those published in the various Sage series, often were limited to single techniques. In 1987, Anselm Strauss produced an excellent text on qualitative analysis, yet even it began with the tacit assumption that data already had been collected or that the researcher at least knew how to go about the task of gathering data.

In contrast, this text focuses on innovative ways of collecting and analyzing qualitative data from natural settings. It is centered on mainstream strategies, even though various dynamic—perhaps even radical—qualitative innovations have emerged during the past 20 years. Rather than offering glossed definitions for these strategies or confusing novice researchers with simplified versions, this text omits these less commonly accepted procedures.

QUANTITATIVE VERSUS QUALITATIVE SCHOOLS OF THOUGHT

As Dabbs (1982) remarks, "Qualitative and quantitative are not distinct." Yet in many social sciences, quantitative orientations are often given more respect. This may reflect the tendency of the general public to regard science as related to numbers and implying precision. It is not the purpose of this text to argue against quantitative procedures. Instead, it demonstrates the fruitfulness and, often, the greater depth of understanding we can derive from qualitative procedures. Thus, the orientation of this book does not entirely either embrace or reject Kaplan's (1964, p. 206) statement that "if you can measure it, that ain't it!"

Certainly, qualitative methodologies have not predominated in the social sciences. After all, qualitative research takes much longer, requires greater clarity of goals during design stages, and cannot be analyzed by running computer programs. Qualitative research methods and analytic strategies are not associated with high-tech society in the ways quantitative techniques may be. Nonetheless, as Bogdan (1972) makes clear, qualitative research has left its mark conceptually and theoretically on the social sciences. The lasting contributions to social understanding from qualitative research, as well as the sheer number of contributing social thinkers, are significant.

Even though the virtue of qualitative research is seldom questioned in the abstract, its practice is sometimes criticized for being nonscientific and thus invalid. However, these critics have lost sight of the probability factor inherent in quantitative practices and have replaced it with an assumption of certainty. Of course, some qualitative research projects have been just as poorly conducted as have some quantitative studies, but one need not dismiss the entire qualitative school of thought just because some studies inadequately applied the paradigm and methods.

In his attempt to differentiate between quantitative and qualitative approaches, Dabbs (1982, p. 32) indicates that the notion of *quality* is essential to the nature of things. On the other hand, *quantity* is elementally an amount of something. Quality refers to the what, how, when, and where of a thing—its essence and ambience. Qualitative research thus refers to the meanings, concepts, definitions, characteristics, metaphors, symbols, and descriptions of things. In contrast, quantitative research refers to counts and measures of things. This distinction is illustrated in Jackson's (1968) description of classroom odors in an elementary school.

> [The] odors of the classroom are fairly standardized. Schools may use different brands of wax and cleaning fluid, but they all seem to contain similar ingredients, a sort of universal smell which creates an aromatic background that permeates the entire building. Added to this, in each classroom, is the slightly acrid scent of chalk dust and the faint hint of fresh wood pencil shavings. In some rooms, especially at lunch time, there is the familiar odor of orange peels and peanut butter sandwiches, a blend that mingles in the late afternoon (following recess) with the delicate pungency of children's perspiration.

It would be impossible to capture these odors as Jackson has with any type of count or measure. Clearly, certain experiences cannot be meaningfully expressed by numbers. Further, such things as smells can trigger memories long obscured by the continuing demands of life. Qualitative research strategies provide perspectives that can prompt recall of these common or half-forgotten sights, sounds, and smells.

Some authors associate qualitative research with the single technique of participant observation. Other writers extend their understanding of qualitative research to include interviewing, as well. However, popular qualitative research additionally includes such methods as observation of experimental natural settings, photographic techniques (including videotaping), historical analysis (historiography), document and textual analysis, sociometry, sociodrama and similar ethnomethodological experimentation, ethnographic research, and a number of unobtrusive techniques.

American colleges have become pragmatic places where students train to get jobs rather than to obtain educations. As a consequence, students and graduates of social science programs increasingly use the research of others and/or conduct research themselves. Thus, students must confront the myriad problems associated with understanding empirical results as well as the process of research itself. This book provides much needed assistance for all researchers, including the inexperienced, through a discussion of various qualitative research strategies, design development, data organization and presentation, and analysis procedures.

Like other texts on qualitative methods, this one emphasizes methodological strategies. However, methodology cannot be examined in a vacuum. Instead, the core substance of qualitative sociological practice, including method, theory, and substantive interests, is explored (Bogdan & Taylor, 1975; Denzin, 1978; Lofland & Lofland, 1984). Data-gathering techniques are intentionally coupled with theoretical perspectives, linking method to theory. Data gathering is not distinct from theoretical orientations. Rather, data are intricately associated with the motivation for choosing a given subject, the conduct of the study, and ultimately the analysis.

Advocates of such particular methodological styles of research as participant observation are frequently more concerned with asserting or defending their techniques than with indicating alternative ways of approaching the study subject. In contrast, this book describes in detail seven primary ways to collect qualitative data: interviewing, focus groups, ethnography, sociometry, unobtrusive measures, historiography, and case studies. These descriptions include an examination of the basic theoretical assumptions of each technique and advice on how to start each procedure and how to resolve various problems that may arise. In addition, the technique of content analysis is related to grounded theory and the use of narrative ethnographies. This book also considers the ethical dimensions of conducting research on humans.

This third edition of *Qualitative Research Methods for the Social Sciences* begins with the assumption that the reader knows little or nothing about the research process. Chapter 2, therefore, offers a basic description of how to design a research project.

TRIANGULATION IN RESEARCH

Most researchers have at least one methodological technique they feel most comfortable using, which often becomes their favorite or only approach to research. This might be why many previous qualitative research texts presented only a single research technology (participant observation, interviewing, or unobtrusive measures). Further, many researchers perceive their research method as an atheoretical tool (Denzin, 1978). Because of this, they fail to recognize that methods impose certain perspectives on reality. For example, when researchers canvass a neighborhood and arrange interviews with residents to discuss their views of some social problem, a theoretical assumption has already been made—specifically, that reality is fairly constant and stable. Similarly, when they make direct observations of events, researchers assume reality is deeply affected by the actions of all participants, including themselves. Each method thus reveals slightly different facets of the same symbolic reality. Every method is a different line of sight directed toward the same point, observing social and symbolic reality. By combining several lines of sight, researchers obtain a better, more substantive picture of reality; a richer, more complete array of symbols and theoretical concepts; and a means of verifying many of these elements. The use of multiple lines of sight is frequently called *triangulation*.

Triangulation is a term originally more common in surveying activities, map making, navigation, and military practices. In each case, three known points or objects are used to draw sighting lines toward an unknown point or object. Usually, these three sighting lines will intersect, forming a small triangle called the *triangle of error.* The best estimate of the true location of the new point or object is the center of the triangle, assuming that the three lines are about equal in error. Although sightings could be done with two sighting lines intersecting at one point, the third line permits a more accurate estimate of the unknown point or object (Berg & Berg, 1993).

Triangulation was first used in the social sciences as a metaphor describing a form of *multiple operationalism or convergent validation* (Campbell, 1956; Campbell & Fiske, 1959). In these cases, triangulation was used largely to describe multiple data-collection technologies designed to measure a single concept or construct (data triangulation). However, Denzin (1978, p. 292) introduced an additional metaphor, *lines of action,* which characterizes the use of multiple data-collection technologies, multiple theories, multiple researchers, multiple methodologies, or combinations of these four categories of research activities.

For many researchers, triangulation is restricted to the use of multiple data-gathering techniques (usually three) to investigate the same phenomenon. This is interpreted as a means of mutual confirmation of measures and validation of findings (Jick, 1983; Knafl & Breitmayer, 1989; Leedy, 1993; Mitchell, 1986; Sohier, 1988; Webb et al., 1981). Fielding and Fielding (1986, p. 31) specifically address this aspect of triangulation. They suggest that the important feature of triangulation is not the simple combination of different kinds of data but the attempt to relate them so as to counteract the threats to validity identified in each.

Denzin (1978) insists that the multiple-methods approach is the generic form of this approach. But triangulation actually represents varieties of data, investigators, theories, and methods. Denzin (1978, p. 295) outlines these four categories as follows:

(1) Data triangulation has three subtypes: (a) time, (b) space, and (c) person. Person analysis, in turn, has three levels: (a) aggregate, (b) interactive, and (c) collectivity. (2) Investigator triangulation consists of using multiple rather than single observers of the same object. (3) Theory triangulation consists of using multiple rather than simple perspectives in relation to the same set of objects. (4) Methodological triangulation can entail within-method triangulation and between-method triangulation.

The research literature continues to support Denzin's (1970, 1978) recommendation to triangulate during research. For example, Goetz and LeCompte (1984) describe its use as a means of refining, broadening, and strengthening conceptual linkages. Borman, LeCompte, and Goetz (1986) similarly stress that triangulation allows researchers to offer perspectives other than their own. Chava Frankfort-Nachmias and David Nachmias (1996, p. 206) suggest that researchers can "minimize the degree of specificity of certain methods to particular bodies of knowledge," by using "two or more methods of data collection to test hypotheses and measure variables; this is the essence of triangulation." Unfortunately, the practice of triangulation often does not move much beyond a single theoretical explanation or an alternative hypothesis (Fielding & Fielding, 1986; Hammersley, 1984). This cursory use of the triangulation strategy fails to capture the essence of what Denzin (1978, p. 28) describes as the "logic of triangulation":

> I conclude that no single method will ever meet the requirements of interaction theory. While participant observation permits the careful recording of situations and selves, it does not offer direct data on the wider spheres of influence acting on those observed. Because each method reveals different aspects of empirical reality, multiple methods of observations must be employed. This is termed triangulation.

In a manner similar to those of Denzin (1978) and Webb et al. (1981), this book stresses several discrete yet intertwined strategies and techniques involved in each of the seven primary research schemes. In fact, the decision to discuss field research strategies under the broad umbrella of *ethnography* ensures the inclusion of a wide combination of elements, such as direct observation, various types of interviewing (informal, formal, semiformal), listening, document analysis (e.g., letters or newspaper clippings), and ethnomethodological experimentation. Spradley (1979) calls this creating "an ethnographic record." Novice researchers are thus instructed in the use of research strategies composed of multiple methods in a single investigation. Denzin (1978, p. 101) also suggests that triangulation includes multiple data-collection procedures, multiple theoretical perspectives, and/or multiple analysis techniques. The use of multiple research strategies and theories increases the depth of understanding an investigation can yield (see also Miles & Huberman, 1983).

QUALITATIVE STRATEGIES: DEFINING AN ORIENTATION

A simplistic explanation of qualitative techniques might lead researchers to believe in the adequacy of any procedure resulting in nominal rather than numerical sorts of data. Such an assessment, however, fails to appreciate both the theoretical implications of qualitative research and the basic purpose of scientific research in general. We do not conduct research only to amass data. The purpose of research is to discover answers to questions through the application of systematic procedures.

Qualitative research properly seeks answers to questions by examining various social settings and the individuals who inhabit these settings. Qualitative researchers, then, are most interested in how humans arrange themselves and their settings and how inhabitants of these settings make sense of their surroundings through symbols, rituals, social structures, social roles, and so forth.

Research methods on human beings affect how these persons will be viewed (Bogdan & Taylor, 1975). If humans are studied in a symbolically reduced, statistically aggregated fashion, there is a danger that conclusions—although arithmetically precise—may fail to fit reality (Mills, 1959). Qualitative procedures provide a means of accessing unquantifiable facts about the actual people researchers observe and talk to or people represented by their personal traces (such as letters, photographs, newspaper accounts, diaries, and so on). As a result, qualitative techniques allow researchers to share in the understandings and perceptions of others and to explore how people structure and give meaning to their daily lives. Researchers using qualitative techniques examine how people learn about and make sense of themselves and others.

As Douglas (1976, p. 12) suggests, the methods used by social scientists fall along a continuum from totally uncontrolled (and perhaps uncontrollable) techniques arising in natural settings to totally controlled techniques of observation. It remains, then, for researchers to choose their procedures keeping in mind the problems that may arise in specific research settings, among certain research groups, and in unique research circumstances. The analysis of qualitative data allows researchers to discuss in detail the various social contours and processes human beings use to create and maintain their social realities.

This is not to suggest that qualitative methods are not without methodological rigor. As will be demonstrated in the chapters to follow, qualitative methods can be extremely systematic and thus can be described and potentially reproduced by subsequent researchers. Replication and reproducibility, after all, are central to the creation and testing of theories and their acceptance by scientific communities.

In some methodological situations, this may include the use of various descriptive or nonparametric statistics (frequency distributions, proportions, ratios, chi-square, etc.). On the other hand, the orientation presented in this text should not be understood as intentionally promoting stark positivism. Rather, the intention is to offer an introductory level of information about developing and conducting high-quality qualitative research. From my perspective, this means research that can stand the test of subsequent researchers examining the same phenomenon through similar or different methods.

Theoretically, this explanation of the general purpose of qualitative research derives from a symbolic interactionist perspective that is central to the concept of qualitative methodology presented here. *Symbolic interaction* is an umbrella concept under which a variety of related theoretical orientations may be placed. The theme that unites the diverse elements of symbolic interaction is the focus on subjective understandings and the perceptions of and about people, symbols, and objects.

FROM A SYMBOLIC
INTERACTIONIST PERSPECTIVE

Symbolic interactionism is one of several theoretical schools of thought in the social sciences. It involves a set of related propositions that describe and explain certain aspects of human behavior. Human beings are unique animals. What humans say and do are the results of how they interpret their social world. In other words, human behavior depends on learning rather than biological instinct. Human beings communicate what they learn through symbols, the most common system of symbols being language. Linguistic symbols amount to arbitrary sounds or physical gestures to which people, by mutual agreement over time, have attached significance or meaning. The core task of symbolic interactionists as researchers, then, is to capture the essence of this process for interpreting or attaching meaning to various symbols.

The substantive basis for symbolic interaction as a theory is frequently attributed to the social behavioral work of Dewey (1930), Cooley (1902), Parks (1915), Mead (1934, 1938), and several other early theorists, but Blumer is considered the founder of symbolic interactionism. In fact, he coined the term *symbolic interaction*. In articulating his view of what symbolic interaction is, Blumer (1969) first establishes that human beings account for *meaning* in two basic ways. First, meaning may be seen as intrinsically attached to an object, event, phenomenon, and so on. Second, meaning may be understood as a "psychical accretion" imposed on objects, events, and the like by people. Blumer (1969, p. 5) next explains:

> *Symbolic interactionism . . . does not regard meaning as emanating from the intrinsic makeup of the thing, nor does it see meaning as arising through psychological elements between people. The meaning of a thing for a person grows out of the ways in which other persons act toward the person with regard to the thing. Their actions operate to define the thing for the person; thus, symbolic*

interactionism sees meanings as social products formed through activities of people interacting.

Blumer thereby suggests that meanings derive from the social process of people or groups of people interacting. Meanings allow people to produce various realities that constitute the sensory world (the so-called real world), but because these realities are related to how people create meanings, reality becomes an interpretation of various definitional options. Consequently, as Thomas states, "It is not important whether or not the interpretation is correct—if men define situations as real, they are real in their consequences" (Thomas & Swaine, 1928, p. 572).

For instance, the first day of each semester, students walk into their classroom and see someone who appears to be the professor. This supposed professor begins to lecture, distribute syllabi, discuss course requirements, and conduct various other traditional first-day activities. Few, if any, students ask to see the professor's credentials. Yet the students, within certain limits, perform their roles as students so long as this professor continues to perform the role of instructor. Suppose that several weeks into the semester, however, the class is notified that the person they assumed to be a professor is really a local dog catcher who has no academic credentials. The question then becomes whether the reality of the classroom experience during the previous weeks is void merely because the dog catcher was incorrectly interpreted as a professor. Although it would remain to be seen whether any information conveyed by the dog catcher was accurate, certainly, the classroom remained a classroom and students continued to perform their expected roles. From Thomas's perspective, these youths had defined the reality as a class, and it became one for them.

Symbolic interactionists tend to differ slightly among themselves regarding the relative significance of various aspects of an interactionist perspective. Several basic elements, however, tend to bind together even the most diverse symbolic interactionists. First, all interactionists agree that human interactions form the central source of data. Second, there is a general consensus that participants' perspectives and their ability to take the roles of others (empathy) are key issues in any formulation of a theory of symbolic interaction. Third, interactionists agree with Thomas (Thomas & Swaine, 1928) concerning "definitions of a situation": How inhabitants of a setting define their situation determines the nature and meaning of their actions as well as the setting itself.

Objects, people, situations, and events do not in themselves possess meaning. Meaning is conferred on these elements by and through human interaction. For example, the videocassette recorder (VCR) in a college classroom may be defined by the professor as a teaching device to be used for showing educational videos. For the student using a VCR in his or her dormitory to view rented movies, this instrument may be seen as a source of entertainment and pleasure, and for the inmate held in a maximum security prison who watches home movies sent from his or her family, it may be considered a window to the outside world. The meanings that people attach to their experiences and the objects and events that make up these experiences are not accidental or unconnected. Both the experiences and the events surrounding them are essential to the construction of meanings. To understand behavior, one must first understand the definitions and meanings and the processes by which they have been created. Human behavior does not occur on the basis of predetermined lockstep responses to preset events or situations. Rather, human behavior is an ongoing and negotiated interpretation of objects, events, and situations (Bogdan & Biklen, 1992). For the researcher to understand the meanings that emerge from these interactions, he or she either must enter into the defining process or develop a sufficient appreciation for the process that understandings can become clear.

Although social roles, institutional structures, rules, norms, goals, and the like may provide the raw material with which individuals create their definitions, these elements do not by themselves determine what the definitions will be or how individuals will act. In essence, symbolic interactionism emphasizes social interactions (action with symbolic meaning), negotiation of definitions, and emphatic role-taking between humans (Gecas, 1981; Turner, 1978).

WHY USE QUALITATIVE METHODS?

Many researchers believe that the social sciences have depended too much on sterile survey techniques, whether or not the technology is appropriate for the problem. For instance, nurses, when encouraged to do research at all, are strongly urged to use scientific strategies of quantification over more sociologically or anthropologically oriented ones considered less scientific. Unfortunately, clinical settings in which nurses are likely to conduct their research fail to meet most quantitative requirements for representativeness and sufficiency of sample size to allow statistically meaningful results.

For instance, let us say the average number of beds in a critical care unit varies between 8 and 12. Even when there are multiple units (such as in a medical intensive care unit or a cardiac intensive care unit), typically fewer than 40 cases are available at any given time. With regard to research strategy, such a situation should preclude most quantitative investigations. On the other hand, 40 cases would prove ample for a number of qualitative strategies. In fact, as Chapter 8 describes, a setting such as a hospital would provide researchers with numerous opportunities to implement unobtrusive measures.

It is also important to examine the reasons for the charge that qualitative methods are nonscientific. As Schwartz and Jacobs (1979, p. 4) point out, "There are many, in both qualitative and quantitative sociology, who advocate and bask in the value of science." Further, Borman, LeCompte, and Goetz (1986, p. 51) have argued that criticism of qualitative approaches arises out of an "erroneous equation of the term 'empirical' with quantification, rather than with any real defect in the qualitative paradigm itself." Although various technologies may be used by different researchers, it turns out that everyone is doing science, provided that *science* is defined as a specific and systematic way of discovering and understanding how social realities arise, operate, and impact on individuals and organizations of individuals.

Scientific researchers may thus emphasize a more positivist view or may be primarily interested in individuals and their so-called life-worlds. In the case of the former, positivists utilize empirical methodologies borrowed from the natural sciences to investigate phenomena. Quantitative strategies serve this positive-science ideal by providing rigorous, reliable, and verifiably large aggregates of data and the statistical testing of empirical hypotheses.

In the case of life-worlds, researchers focus on naturally emerging languages and the meanings individuals assign to experience. Life-worlds include emotions, motivations, symbols and their meanings, empathy, and other subjective aspects associated with naturally evolving lives of individuals and groups. These elements may also represent their behavioral routines, experiences, and various conditions affecting these usual routines or natural settings. As Schwartz and Jacobs (1979) suggest, many of these elements are directly observable and as such may be viewed as objective. Nonetheless, certain elements of symbolism, meaning, or understanding usually require consideration of the individual's own perceptions and subjective apprehensions.

A PLAN OF PRESENTATION

Having briefly outlined the basic assumptions and qualitative orientations of symbolic interaction, it is now possible to weave in various methodological strategies. Chapter 2 provides the basic information necessary for understanding the research enterprise. This chapter discusses the research process and proposes a spiraling model to follow when developing a research agenda. Chapter 2 also offers advice to the novice researcher about how to organize and conduct a literature review.

Chapter 3 considers a number of ethical concerns that are important for new investigators to understand before actually conducting research. Among the salient issues considered are covert versus overt research concerns, privacy rights, human subject institutional review boards, and informed consent in human subject research.

In addition to providing a general discussion of various forms and styles of traditional interviewing techniques, Chapter 4 uses a kind of symbolic interaction known as *dramaturgy* and suggests an effective research strategy for conducting in-depth interviews.

Chapter 5 also addresses the area of interviewing but moves toward a specialized style, namely, group interviews or focus groups. This chapter examines the early origins of focus-group interviews, their development during the past several decades, and their growing use in the social sciences.

Chapter 6 builds on the foundation constructed by Chapters 1 through 4 and extends the research process into the natural setting by examining ethnography. Along with interviewing, Chapter 6 discusses watching and listening, field notes, and a number of other field research concerns. This chapter examines ethnography both as a means of collecting data (what some call the *new ethnography*) and as an end in itself (narrative ethnographic accounts).

Chapter 7 considers an established yet underused data-collection and analysis strategy, namely, sociometry. The basic history of sociometry is offered, and procedures for its use are discussed. Several examples of settings and situations where sociometry might be effective are considered.

While Chapters 4, 5, and 6 separately address the concept of interviewer reactivity, Chapter 8 offers several strategies that avoid reactivity entirely: It explores the use of unobtrusive measures.

As foreshadowed slightly in Chapter 8, the use of certain unobtrusive data has grown quite specialized. Chapter 9 examines a specialized and systematic use of certain kinds of running records, namely, historiography. In addition to the use of records, Chapter 9 considers oral histories and life histories as variations in historiography.

Chapter 10 examines a technique used to study individuals in their unique settings or situations. This technique is commonly called the *case study method*. This chapter also discusses how case studies may be undertaken on communities and organizations.

Chapter 11, "An Introduction to Content Analysis," dovetails with each of the preceding chapters on research technique. Included in this chapter are recommendations for how novice researchers may organize their data and begin to make sense of what may be volumes of notes, transcripts, and trace documents and artifacts. Chapter 11 also briefly considers the use of computers to assist in this data-management scheme.

Chapter 12, the final chapter, offers recommendations for how novice qualitative researchers can disseminate their research findings.

"Trying It Out," a section at the conclusion of each of the data-collection technique chapters, offers suggestions for practicing each of the seven strategies.

REFERENCES

Becker, H. S. (1970). *Sociological Work: Method and Substance*. Chicago: Aldine.

Berg, B. L. (1989). *Qualitative Research Methods for the Social Sciences*. Boston: Allyn and Bacon.

Berg, B. L., & Berg, J. (1993). A reexamination of triangulation and objectivity in qualitative nursing research. *Free Inquiry in Creative Sociology 21*(1), 65–72.

Blumer, H. (1969). *Symbolic Interactionism: Perspective and Method*. Englewood Cliffs, NJ: Prentice Hall.

Bogdan, R. (1972). *Participant Observation in Organizational Settings*. Syracuse, NY: Syracuse University Press.

Bogdan, R., & Biklen, S. K. (1982). *Qualitative Research for Education*. Boston: Allyn and Bacon.

Bogdan, R., & Biklen, S. K. (1992). *Qualitative Research for Education* (2nd ed.). Boston: Allyn and Bacon.

Bogdan, R., & Taylor, S. J. (1975). *Introduction to Qualitative Research Methods*. New York: Wiley.

Borman, K. M., LeCompte, M. D., & Goetz, J. P. (1986). Ethnographic and qualitative research design and why it doesn't work. *American Behavioral Scientist 30*(1), 42–57.

Bredo, E., & Feinberg, W. (1982). *Knowledge and Values in Social and Educational Research*. Philadelphia: Temple University Press.

Campbell, D. T. (1956). *Leadership and Its Effects Upon the Group*. Columbus: Ohio State University Press.

Campbell, T. T., & Fisk, D. W. (1959). Convergent and discriminant validation by the multivariate-multimethod matrix. *Psychological Bulletin 56*, 81–105.

Cooley, C. H. (1902). *Human Nature and the Social Order*. New York: Scribner.

Dabbs, J. M., Jr. (1982). Making things visible. In J. Van Maanen (Ed.), *Varieties of Qualitative Research*. Beverly Hills, CA: Sage.

Denzin, N. K. (1970). *Sociological Methods: A Sourcebook*. Chicago: Aldine.

Denzin, N. K. (1978). *The Research Act*. New York: McGraw-Hill.

Denzin, N. K. (1989). *Interactive Interactionism*. Newbury Park, CA: Sage.

Dewey, J. (1930). *Human Nature and Conduct*. New York: Modern Library.

Dobbert, M. (1982). *Ethnographic Research: Theory and Application for Modern Schools and Societies*. New York: Praeger.

Douglas, J. D. (1976). *Investigative Social Research*. Beverly Hills, CA: Sage.

Fetterman, D. M. (1989). *Ethnography Step by Step*. Newbury Park, CA: Sage.

Fielding, N. G., & Fielding, J. L. (1986). *Linking Data*. Newbury Park, CA: Sage.

Filstead, W. (1970). *Qualitative Methodology: Firsthand Involvement and the Social World*. Chicago: Markham.

Frankfort-Nachmias, C., & Nachmias, D. (1996). *Research Methods in the Social Sciences* (5th ed.). New York: St. Martin's Press.

Gecas, V. (1981). Contexts of socialization. In M. Rosenberg & R. H. Turner (Eds.), *Social Psychology: Sociological Perspectives* (pp. 165–199). New York: Basic Books.

Glaser, B., & Strauss, A. L. (1967). *The Discovery of Grounded Theory: Strategies for Qualitative Research*. Chicago: Aldine.

Goetz, J. P., & LeCompte, M. D. (1984). *Ethnography and Qualitative Design in Educational Research*. New York: Academic Press.

Hammersley, M. (1984). The researcher exposed. In R. Burgess (Ed.), *The Research Process in Educational Settings: Ten Case Studies.* New York: Taylor & Francis, Palmer Press.

Jackson, P. W. (1968). *Life in Classrooms.* New York: Holt, Rinehart, & Winston.

Jick, T. D. (1983). Mixing qualitative and quantitative methods: Triangulation in action. In J. Van Maanen (Ed.), *Qualitative Methodology* (pp. 135–148). Beverly Hills, CA: Sage.

Jorgensen, D. L. (1989). *Participant Observation.* Newbury Park, CA: Sage.

Kaplan, A. (1964). *The Conduct of Inquiry.* Scranton, PA: Chandler Publishing.

Kirby, S., & McKenna, K. (1989). *Experience, Research, Social Change: Methods from the Margins.* Toronto: Garamond Press.

Knafl, K. A., & Breitmayer, B. J. (1989). Triangulation in qualitative research: Issues of conception, clarity, and purpose. In J. M. Morse (Ed.), *Qualitative Nursing Research: A Contemporary Dialogue.* Rockville, MD: Aspen.

Leedy, P. D. (1993). *Practical Research: Planning and Design* (5th ed.). New York: Macmillan.

Lofland, J., & Lofland, L. H. (1984). *Analyzing Social Settings* (2nd ed.). Belmont, CA: Wadsworth Publishers.

Mead, G. H. (1934). *Mind, Self, and Society.* Chicago: University of Chicago Press.

Mead, G. H. (1938). *The Philosophy of the Act.* Chicago: University of Chicago Press.

Miles, M. B., & Huberman, M. A. (1983). *Qualitative Data Analysis.* Beverly Hills, CA: Sage.

Mills, C. W. (1959). *The Sociological Imagination.* New York: Oxford University Press.

Mitchell, E. S. (1986). Multiple triangulation: A methodology for nursing science. *Advances in Nursing Science 8*(3), 18–25.

Parks, R. (1915). *Principles of Human Behavior.* Chicago: Zalaz.

Schwartz, H., & Jacobs, J. (1979). *Qualitative Sociology: A Method to the Madness.* New York: Free Press.

Sohier, R. (1988). Multiple triangulation and contemporary nursing research. *Western Journal of Nursing Research 10*(6), 732–742.

Spindler, G. (1982). *Doing the Ethnography of Schooling.* Prospect Heights, IL: Waveland Press.

Spradley, J. P. (1979). *The Ethnographic Interview.* New York: Holt, Rinehart, & Winston.

Strauss, A. L. (1987). *Qualitative Analysis for Social Scientists.* New York: Cambridge University Press.

Strauss, A., & Corbin, J. (1989). *Qualitative Research Methods.* Newbury Park, CA: Sage.

Thomas, W. I., & Swaine, D. (1928). *The Child in America.* New York: Knopf.

Turner, V. (1978). Foreword. In B. Myerhoff, *Number Our Days.* New York: Simon and Schuster.

Van Maanen, J. (1982). *Tales of the Field: On Writing Ethnography.* Chicago: University of Chicago Press.

Webb, E., Campbell, D. T., Schwartz, R. D., & Sechrest, L. (1966). *Unobtrusive Measures: Nonreactive Research in the Social Sciences.* Chicago: Rand McNally.

Webb, E. J., Campbell, D. T., Schwartz, R. D., Sechrest, L., & Grove, J. B. (1981). *Nonreactive Measures in the Social Sciences.* Boston: Houghton Mifflin.

DESIGNING QUALITATIVE RESEARCH

THIS CHAPTER CONSIDERS VARIOUS ways of thinking about and designing research. It includes a discussion of the relationships among ideas and theory, concepts, and what I have long believed is the most diffi-cult facet of research—namely, operationalization. This chapter further offers a strategy for conducting literature reviews and explains the impor-tance of carefully designing and planning research in advance. Let's begin with some thoughts about ideas and theory.

IDEAS AND THEORY

Every research project has to start somewhere. Typically, this starting point is an idea. Sometimes this idea originates because of a particular problem or situation one actually experiences. For example, a nurse might observe a coworker coming to work under the influence of alcohol and begin to think about how that influences nursing care. From this thought, the idea for researching impaired nurses could arise. A counselor at a delinquency detention center might notice that many of her clients have been battered or abused prior to their run-ins with the law. From this observation, she might begin to think about how abuse might be linked with delinquency and how she could investigate this linkage. Or an elementary school teacher might notice that the most disruptive children in the class eat large amounts of sugary junk food during lunch. The teacher might begin to think about the possibility that junk food is in some way related to children's behavior and might wonder how he or she could test such an idea.

In some situations, ideas move from information you hear but may not actually experience yourself. For instance, you're sitting at home listening to the news, and you hear a report about three youths from wealthy families who have been caught burglarizing houses. You begin to wonder, Why on earth do they do something like that? What motivates people who don't need money to steal from others? Or you read in the newspaper that a man living around the corner from you has been arrested for growing marijuana in his garage. You start thinking back to times when you passed this man's house and smiled a greeting at him. Or you begin to wonder, Why didn't I realize what he was up to? Who was he going to sell the marijuana to, anyhow? From these broad curiosities, you might begin to think about how these questions could be explored or answered and how you might research these phenomena.

The preceding examples serve two important purposes. First, they point out how ideas promote potential research endeavors. But second, and perhaps more important, they suggest a central research orientation that permeates this book. This orientation is the attitude that the world is a research laboratory, that you merely need to open your ears and eyes to the sensory reality that surrounds all of us to find numerous ideas for research. In fact, once you become familiar with this orientation, the biggest problem will be to filter out all the many possible researchable ideas and actually investigate one!

Most experienced qualitative researchers will agree that if you drop a qualitative investigator into any neighborhood, he or she will manage to identify a research idea, develop a research plan, and be thinking about potential research findings. This notion is likely to contrast dramatically with the inexperienced researcher's fear that he or she cannot even think of anything worthwhile to research. There may be considerable truth to the optimistic view of experienced researchers. This does not mean, however, that all research ideas will be equally easy or interesting to research.

Some ideas will be more difficult to investigate than others. This is because those who control access to a given location—what the literature calls *gatekeepers*—or the subjects themselves may be reluctant or resistant to cooperate. Gatekeepers are discussed in greater detail in Chapter 6. Also, some ideas may initially seem extremely interesting, but become rather plain or uninspiring upon further investigation.

So, you begin with an idea. But how is this related to theory? For that matter, what is meant by theory? In a formal sense, social scientists usually define *theory* as a system of logical statements or propositions that explain the relationship between two or more objects, concepts, phenomena, or characteristics of humans—what are sometimes called *variables* (Babbie, 1992; Denzin, 1978; Polit & Hungler, 1993). *Theory* might also represent attempts to develop explanations about reality or ways to classify and organize events, describe events, or even to predict future occurrences of events (Hagan, 1993).

There are some who argue that ideas and theory must come before empirical research. This has been called the *theory-before-research model* (Nachmias & Nachmias, 1992, p. 46). This orientation has been nicely described by Karl Popper (1968), who suggests that one begins with ideas (conjectures) and then attempts to disprove or refute them through tests of empirical research (refutation).

In contrast to the theory-before-research proponents, there are some who argue that research must occur before theory can be developed. This orientation, *research-before-theory*, can be illustrated by a statement from Robert Merton (1968, p. 103):

> *It is my central thesis that empirical research goes far beyond the passive role of verifying and testing theory; it does more than confirm or refute hypotheses. Research plays an active role: it performs at least four major functions which help shape the development of theory. It initiates, it reformulates, it deflects, and it clarifies theory.*

In other words, research may suggest new problems for theory, require theoretical innovation, refine existing theories, or serve to verify past theoretical assumptions.

The approach offered in this book views theory-before-research and research-before-theory as highly compatible. Often, methods texts and courses describe the research enterprise as a linear progression. In this progression, you begin with an idea, gather theoretical information, design a research plan, identify a means for data collection, analyze the data, and report findings. This may be diagramed as follows:

Idea → Theory → Design → Data Collection → Analysis → Findings

For the most part, this orientation resembles the theory-before-research model. But it could also be drawn as the research-before-theory model:

Idea → Design → Data Collection → Theory → Analysis → Findings

In either case, you have the feeling that each of these components is a distinct and separate successive stage, that you first derive an idea and then move on to either theory or design and so forth. In essence, it seems that you complete various necessary tasks of each stage and then move forward, leaving the completed state behind.

In this chapter, I argue for a different model for the research enterprise, a model that encompasses both the research-before-theory and theory-before-research models. This is possible because the proposed approach is conceived as spiraling rather than linear in its progression. In the proposed approach, you begin with an idea, gather theoretical information, reconsider and refine your idea, begin to examine possible designs, reexamine theoretical assumptions, and refine these theoretical assumptions and perhaps even your original or refined idea. Thus, with every two steps forward, you take a step or two backward before proceeding any further. What results is no longer a linear progression in a single, forward direction. Rather, you are spiraling forward, never actually leaving any stage behind completely. This spiraling approach may be drawn as follows:

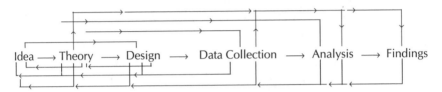

In order to make things easier to follow as individual elements of this model are discussed, let's redefine the stages slightly, as follows:

	Literature			Data Collection	Analysis		
Idea →	Review	→	Design →	and Organization	→	and Findings	→ Dissemination

As shown here, you begin with some rough *idea* for a research study. The next stage in this process is to begin thinking and reading about this topical idea. This is accomplished as you begin the literature review.

LITERATURE REVIEW

After developing a rough idea for research, you begin to examine how others have already thought about and researched the topic. Let's say an idea for some research begins with an interest in alcohol use by male college students. You might formulate a rough question for research, such as: What is the relationship between college and drinking among American males? This rough statement already shows elements of refinement. It has been limited to consideration only of American males. The next step is to visit the library to get started on a literature review. To begin, you can consult any of a number of available cumulative indexes. These indexes contain many thousands of journal and monograph references, indexed by both authors' names and subject topics. In some cases, you will find these as bound texts in the reference section of the library. In other cases, these indexes may be computer based and require both some assistance and a small charge to use.

In many larger public libraries and in a growing number of colleges and universities, these cumulative indexes have been placed in CD-ROM format. If you have never used one of these indexes or are unfamiliar with the use of computers, you might want to consult the reference librarian at your library.

The next task is to begin to creatively think about cryptic subject topics related to your rough research idea or question and to search for these topics in the indexes. For the example above, you might begin making a list, such as "alcohol use," "collegiate alcohol use," "alcohol on campus," "drinking," "males and alcohol," "Americans and alcohol," "social drinking," "substance abuse in college," "campus problems," and so forth. It is important to develop a number of different subject areas to search. Some will be more fruitful than others, and perhaps some will yield little information. This is because both the paperbound versions and computer-based versions of indexes are created by humans. Because of this, they unavoidably suffer from the problem of terminological classification bias. In other words, even though these indexes are cross referenced, if you do not use the same term or phrase used by the original indexer, you may not locate entries he or she has referenced.

For instance, several years ago, I became interested in the idea of doing research about women in policing. More directly, I was interested in the effect of policing on female officers. I asked my graduate student to see if she could locate some material about female police officers. When she returned the next day, she reported that there was virtually nothing in any of the index databases on the topic "female police officers." I asked if she had tried "women in policing," or "women police officers," or even "minorities in policing." Sheepishly, she explained she had not thought to do that and returned to the library. The next time she returned to my office, she carried a list of literally dozens of references for me to consider. The lesson to be learned from this is that you must not be too restrictive in your topics when searching for reference materials in indexes. In fact, most CD-ROM-based indexes provide users with a thesaurus to assist them in locating subject terms used to index material on the CD-ROM.

Avoid becoming too computer dependent during your literature search. Again, since computer listings are limited by the way they have been indexed, not all the information that is relevant for a study may be recognized in a computer-based search. While revising this book, I asked my graduate assistant, a bright first-year doctoral student, to locate some recent material on "active informed consent." This ethical concern is discussed in Chapter 3. My graduate assistant is very well versed in computers and surfing the Internet. Naturally, he sought an answer to my request by diving right into the Internet.

I waited several days before asking him if he had located any recent articles or chapters on this subject. He informed me that there were none. I asked if he had gone to the library and looked up "informed consent," "passive consent," "active consent," or any similar topics. With a note of anger in his tone he informed me that he had done better. He had checked with various Internet information sources. I then asked if he had gone to the library and physically looked through the last several years of such journals as *Journal of Ethics,* or *Social Problems,* or any educational, nursing, or medical journals. With even more anger, because I was questioning his work, he informed me he had not. He also naively insisted that if he couldn't find it through the computer, it wasn't there!

I suggested we take a trip to the library together. (In fact, I literally took him by the hand and walked him to the library.) Together we scoured the library, and within fifteen minutes had located about four potentially usable items. My graduate assistant admitted that these items had not shown up in any of his computer searches.

The moral to this story is simple. Computer searches and the vast information available via the Internet are wonderful places to begin. They can provide enormous amounts of information. Frequently, however, there is no absolute replacement for simply physically thumbing through journal indexes.

You have now presumably located the relevant reference indexes for the research idea and have used cryptic subject terms to locate a list of references. The next task is to locate several of these pieces of literature and begin reading about the topic. You also will need to continue trying to expand this literature search. You can do this by locating several fairly recent articles and consulting their reference pages. Frequently, this search will yield additional pieces of information that were not generated by the original index search.

As you are doing all this literature searching, keep records on which pieces of literature you have obtained and notes about what each one says. There are numerous ways you can keep records and notes during a literature review. What follows, the *two-card method*, is a long-standing albeit very time-consuming strategy. Inexperienced writers and researchers may want to try using it fairly precisely. More experienced investigators may decide to make variations on it. In any event, it provides a means for developing an extremely systematic literature review.

The Two-Card Method

As indicated by the name, this strategy requires you to create two types of 4 × 6-inch index cards. The first is the *author card.* Annotate each with the reference information for every article of literary material you locate and examine. Whenever possible, you should also include the library call numbers. Several of my students in recent years have preferred to use electronic index cards, as provided in some computer software packages. Although any entry format on the card or electronic card can be used, I recommend that you use a consistent entry style (see Figure 2.1).

FIGURE 2.1   Author Card

```
[Author's Name]
 Berg, Bruce L.,

      [Date]       [Title of document and publication
       1992         information]

                    Law Enforcement: An Introduction to
                    Police in Society. Boston, Mass.:
                    Allyn and Bacon

[Library Call #]
```

Author cards should be kept in alphabetical order to ensure that you will always have complete information for citations and the ability to locate the document at a later time. Even fairly experienced writers have misplaced a document or returned it to the library, only to find they need it or the citation material later. Often, even with considerable effort, these writers are unable to locate the necessary information. Author cards provide a kind of insurance against not having the correct information when you need to write up references or check up on information. Also, should you continue researching in this area, you will have a head start on future literature reviews.

The second type of card is called the *topic card*. Topic cards also should follow a consistent pattern and include the author's name, the date of the publication, a brief topical label, and a short verbatim excerpt (see Figure 2.2).

FIGURE 2.2   Topic Card

```
            [Topic Label]   Police Detective
       [Author's Name]
        Berg, Bruce (1992:p83)

            [Verbatim Quote]

Detective, as a noun, makes its first appearance in lay
parlance in the 1840s in order to identify the police
organizational position of an investigator (Klockars,
1985, Kuykendal, 1986, 175). The central function of
early detective work in police organizations was
apprehension.
```

Since the author cards contain all the title and publication information, duplicating those details on the topic cards is not necessary.

Many students have either been taught or have developed similar note-taking strategies. In some cases, these other strategies call for the use of legal-length note pads. This technique, however, inhibits your ability to sort through or organize the excerpts, short of cutting sheets into pieces. Additionally, these other strategies usually ask you to paraphrase the material you take down as notes. Certainly, paraphrasing is somewhat less tedious to accomplish than the verbatim annotation of excerpts, as promoted in my plan. However, there are several critical reasons why I recommend the use of verbatim quotes on these topic cards.

First, it reduces the physical amount of material you will ultimately use when you get down to writing reports about the research. Anyone who has undertaken a large writing project, even a term paper, should relate to the problem of having stacks of photocopies and piles of books cluttering the room. Trying to find some specific piece of information under such circumstances is quite burdensome.

Second, you can very quickly sort the topic cards into their categories (e.g., placing all the cards about police detectives together). In this manner, you can assemble the piles into an organized sequence that will reflect how you plan to write the report or paper. This allows you to read through the relevant materials for each section rather than repeatedly reading through all the material in order to write a single section.

Third, topic cards allow you to assess whether multiple authors actually have made similar statements about issues or situations. In turn, you are able to make strong synthesized statements regarding the work or arguments of others. For example, "According to Babbie (1992), Frankfort-Nachmias and Nachmias (1996), and Leedy (1993), design is a critically important element in the development of a research project."

If you, as an investigator, paraphrase material on the topic cards, it is possible that you might slant or alter meanings. Without intending to, you might have misread, misinterpreted, or poorly paraphrased material. When you go through the topic cards looking for agreement among authors, you might find paraphrased statements that *seem* to represent similar ideas but that actually do not accurately represent the sentiments of the original authors. Using verbatim excerpts ensures that this will not occur. Either the authors did say similar things or they did not.

The obvious question at this juncture is, How much should you annotate on the topic cards? While there are no hard and fast rules, I recommend only about two to four paragraphs. The purpose of these cards is to reduce the amount of material ultimately necessary for the writer-investigator. To completely transcribe works tends to defeat this purpose. Bear in mind that you might find three or four different topics in a short article, or you might find six or seven. Likewise, you might find 10 or 12 topics to excerpt in a book, or you might find only a single topic worthy of excerpting.

Usually the excerpt will fit on a single card (front and back). However, on occasion, you might find it necessary to use a second or even a third card. It is important to number or letter subsequent cards in order to keep them in correct sequence. In the event that you find an enormous cache of simply wonderful material, you can make a note of this on the card. This is a better strategy than copying 10 or 11 cards. Simply excerpt the usual three or four paragraphs and then write something like "MORE GREAT MATERIAL!" In this case, you will want to have the source nearby when you write the paper.

Excerpting for topic cards can be fairly tedious. You should not plan on spending many hours at a time writing topic cards. Instead, plan to spend only an hour or so at each topic card writing session. Even small amounts of time, such as 10- or 15-minute intervals, can be successfully used for this purpose. Remember, what this strategy loses in excitement it gains tenfold in organization and effective writing later.

This strategy also is very portable. You can slip index cards into your pocket, bag, briefcase, or backpack along with a book or photocopy of some article. While waiting for a doctor's or dentist's appointment, you can easily be reading and excerpting material. Or you might do topic cards while riding a train or bus. The important thing to remember is that as you are reading and creating topic cards, you also should be thinking about the material.

Thoughts should begin to turn toward refinements of the original research idea or question. What are some specific research questions that need to be considered in the eventual research? How have others theorized about the topic? How have others researched the topic? What have others found in previous research? Is there an interesting angle or approach that would set your research apart from that of others or refine findings offered by past research? You also should begin to consider exactly how *you* will frame your research questions or problems.

FRAMING RESEARCH PROBLEMS

Research problems direct or drive the research enterprise. *How* you will eventually conduct a research study depends largely upon *what* your research questions are. It is important, therefore, to frame or formulate a clear research problem statement. Remember, the research process began with an idea and only a rough notion of what was to be researched. As you read and collect information from the literature, these rough questions must become clearer and theoretically more refined.

Let's return to our original research idea: What is the relationship between college and drinking among American males? After reading through some of the literature, you might begin to refine and frame this idea as a problem statement with researchable questions:

Problem Statement
This research proposes to examine alcohol drinking behaviors in social settings among college-age American men.

Research Questions
A number of questions are addressed in this research including (although not limited to) the following:

1. What are some normative drinking behaviors of young adult American men during social gatherings where alcohol is present?
2. How do some young adult American men manage to abstain from drinking (e.g., avoidance rituals) while in social situations where alcohol is present?
3. How do young adult American men define appropriate drinking practices?
4. How do young adult American men define alcoholism?

These questions did not just happen spontaneously. They were influenced by the literature about drinking practices among Americans. They resulted after the investigator began thinking about what issues were important and how those issues might be measured. This required the researcher to consider various concepts and definitions and perhaps to develop operationalized definitions.

OPERATIONALIZATION AND CONCEPTUALIZATION

When someone says, "That kid's a delinquent," most of us quickly draw some mental picture of what that is, and we are able to understand the meaning of the term *delinquent*. If, however, someone were to ask, "How would you define a delinquent?" we would probably find that some people think about this term differently from others. For some, it may involve a youth under the legal age of adult jurisdiction (usually between 16 and 18 years of age) who commits law violations (Bynum & Thompson, 1992). For others, a delinquent may be simply defined as a youthful law violator (Thornton & Voigt, 1992). Still others may require in their definition some notion of a youth who not only breaks a law but who is also convicted in court of this law violation (Siegel & Senna, 1988). In other words, there are a number of possible definitions for the concept *delinquent*.

If you, as a researcher, are interested in studying the behavior of delinquent girls, you will first need to clearly define *delinquent*. Because humans cannot telepathically communicate their mental images of terms, there is no way to directly communicate which possible meaning for delinquent you have in mind. To ensure that everyone is working with the same definition and mental image, you will need to *conceptualize* and *operationalize* the term. This process is called *operationally defining* a concept.

Operational definitions concretize the intended meaning of a concept in relation to a particular study and provide some criteria for measuring the empirical existence of that concept (Leedy, 1993; Frankfort-Nachmias & Nachmias, 1996).

In operatively defining a term or concept, you, as a researcher, begin by declaring the term to mean whatever you want it to mean throughout the research. While it is important for your readers to understand what you mean when, for example, you use the concept *delinquent*, they need not necessarily agree with that definition. As long as they understand what you mean by certain concepts, they can understand and appraise how effectively the concept works in your study.

Once defined, the concept needs some way to be measured during the research process. In quantitative research, this means creating some index, scale, or similar measurement indicator intended to calculate how much of or to what degree the concept exists. Qualitative investigators also need agreement over what a concept means in a given study and how that concept is to be identified and examined. How will the researcher gather empirical information or data that will inform him or her about the concept?

Consider, for example, the concept *weight*. As a researcher, you might define the concept *weight* as the amount of mass an object possesses in terms of pounds and ounces. Now everyone holds the same concrete meaning and mental image for the concept weight. How shall this concept be measured? Operationally, weight can be determined by placing an object on a scale and rounding to the nearest ounce. This operational definition clearly tells others what the concept is designated to mean and how it will be measured.

Unfortunately, not all concepts are as easy to define as weight or as easy to measure. Polit and Hungler (1993), for example, suggest that many concepts relevant to research in nursing are not operationalized simply. For instance, in nursing research, the quality of life for chronically ill patients may be defined in terms of physiological, social, and psychological attributes. If the nurse researcher emphasizes the physiological aspects of quality of life for chronically ill patients in his or her definition, the operationalized component may involve measuring white blood cell counts or oxygen output, assessing invasive surgical procedures or ventilation procedures, measuring blood pressure, and so forth.

If, on the other hand, quality of life for chronically ill patients is defined socially, the operationalized elements of the definition would need to measure family or social support, living arrangements, self-management skills, independence, and similar social attributes. Likewise, if the nurse researcher uses a more psychological conceptualization, the operationalized measures would be directed along the lines of the patients' emotional acceptance of chronic illness.

Let's try another illustration of defining and operationalizing. Say you are interested in studying to what degree or extent people are religious. To begin, you must define the concept *religious*. For this example, *religious* will be defined as how actively one is involved with his or her religion. Next, you must decide what kinds of information inform others about someone's active involvement in religion. After consulting the literature, you decide that you know how religious someone is by knowing whether that person believes in a divine being, attends organized religious services on some regular basis, prays at home, reads religious materials, celebrates certain religious holidays, readily declares membership in a particular religion, participates in religious social organizations, and contributes to religious charities.

In effect, you, the researcher, are saying, "I can't immediately apprehend a person's religiousness. But I can think about what elements seem to go into making up or representing observable behaviors I understand to mean *religious*." By obtaining information regarding the subset of observable attributes delineated earlier to represent religious, you can study religiousness. Again, as you are thinking about what observable attributes might make up some concept, you should be perusing the literature. By spiraling back into the literature stage, you can seek ways on how others have examined the concept of religious. You may borrow some of these previous attributes for religious, or you may create others.

In some forms of qualitative research, the investigator is not as rigorously concerned with defining concepts in operational terms as outlined here. This is because some forms of interpretative and phenomenological research seek to discover naturally arising meanings among members of study populations. However, in many cases of qualitative research, failure to define and operationalize concepts will spell disaster. If, as a researcher, you have not made clear what your concepts mean, your results may be meaningless in terms of explanatory power or applicability. If you have not thought about how data will be collected to represent attributes of the concept, it will be very difficult for you to determine answers to research questions. And if you have not worked with the literature in developing relevant meanings and measurable attributes, it will be impossible for you to see how eventual results fit into this extant body of knowledge.

Your next problem, then, is determining exactly how information about various attributes will be obtained. As you reach this point, you move one foot forward to the design stage of the research enterprise. Naturally, your other foot will remain in the literature stage.

DESIGNING PROJECTS

The design for a research project is literally the plan for how the study will be conducted. It is a matter of thinking about, imagining, and visualizing how the research study will be undertaken (DeBakey & DeBakey, 1978; Leedy, 1993).

The design stage of research is concerned with what types of information or data will be gathered and through what forms of data-collection technology. In doing research, you must decide whether to use one data-collection strategy alone or to combine several strategies (data triangulation). Will you undertake the study alone or with the assistance of others (multiple investigators triangulation)? You must consider whether the study will be framed by a single overarching theory or by several related theories (theoretical triangulation). How much will the project cost in time and money, and how much can you actually afford? What population will best serve the study's purposes? Are the data-collection strategies appropriate for the research questions being asked? What will the data look like once they have been collected? How will the data be organized and analyzed?

In effect, during the design stage, you, the investigator, sketch out the entire research project in an effort to foresee any possible glitches that might arise. If you locate a problem now, while the project is still on the drafting board, there is no harm done. After the project has begun, if you find that concepts have been poorly conceived, that the wrong research questions have been asked, or that the data collected are inappropriate, the project may be ruined.

Researchers in the social sciences typically conduct research on human subjects. The design stage is the time when you, the researcher, must consider whether ethical standards and safeguards for subject safety are adequate. You must make certain that subjects will be protected from any harm. Chapter 3 discusses issues of research ethics in detail. For now, regard the design stage to be the time when you appraise ethical proprieties such as honesty; openness of intent; respect for subjects; issues of privacy, anonymity, and confidentiality; the intent of the research; and the willingness of subjects to participate voluntarily in the research.

DATA COLLECTION AND ORGANIZATION

As you begin visualizing how the research project will "unfold, cascade, roll, and emerge" (Lincoln & Guba, 1985, p. 210), you also must imagine what the data will look like. Will raw data be audiotape cassettes that result from long interviews? Will data comprise dozens of spiral notebooks filled with field notes? Will they include photographs or video recordings? Will they entail systematic observational checklists or copies of files containing medical or criminal histories? May data actually be the smudges left on a polished counter or glass display case? Just what will the research data look like?

Furthermore, what will you do with the data to organize them and make them ready for analysis? That many students fall down at this stage of the research process and find themselves lost, even after taking several research courses, is interesting to note. While most research courses and textbooks are excellent at describing the basic structure of research, few move the student into the areas of data organization and analysis. What results are students who can come up with excellent ideas for research, conduct solid literature reviews, produce what sound like viable research designs, and even collect massive amounts of data. The problem arises, however, at this point: What do they do with this mountain of data once it has been collected?

If you were doing quantitative research, there might be an easy answer to the question of organization and analysis. You would reduce the data to computerizable form and enter them into a database. Then using one form or another of packaged statistics for the social sciences, you would endeavor to analyze the data. Lamentably, qualitative data are not as quickly or easily handled. A common mistake made by many inexperienced or uninformed researchers is to reduce qualitative data to symbolic numeric representations and quantitatively computer analyze them. As Berg and Berg (1993) state, this ceases at once to be qualitative research and amounts to little more than a variation of quantitative data collection.

How qualitative data are organized depends in part upon what they look like. If they are in textual form, such as field notes, or can be made into textual form, such as a transcription of a tape-recorded interview, they may be organized in one manner. If they are video, photographic, or drawn material, they will require a different form of organization and analysis. But regardless of the data form, you must consider this issue during the design stage of the process. Again, this points to the spiraling effect of research activities. If you wait until data have actually been collected to consider how they are to be organized for analysis, serious problems may arise. For example, you may not have planned for adequate time or financial resources. Or you might collect data in such a way that they should be systematically organized, coded, or indexed as they were collected and not after the fact. In any event, you must direct thought toward how data will be organized and analyzed long before you begin the data-collection process. Specific issues related to various aspects of data organization and analysis of qualitative data are discussed throughout this book.

DISSEMINATION

Once the research project has been completed, it is not really over. That is, doing research for the sake of doing it offers no benefit to the scientific community or to the existing body of knowledge it might inform. Research, then, is not complete until it has been disseminated. This may be accomplished through reports submitted to appropriate public agencies or to funding sources. It may include informal presentations to colleagues at brown-bag lunches or formal presentations at professional association meetings. It may involve publishing reports in one of a variety of academic or professional journals. Regardless of how the information is spread, it must be disseminated if it is to be considered both worthwhile and complete. Chapter 12 explains how you may go about disseminating your research results. For the purposes of designing research projects, it is important to bear in mind that this stage of the research process is integral to the whole.

TRYING IT OUT

There are a number of ways you can practice aspects related to the planning of research. What follows are only a few suggestions that should allow you an opportunity to gain some experience. While these are useful experiential activities, they should not be confused with actually conducting research.

Suggestion 1

Locate three or four different textbooks on juvenile delinquency. Look up the definition of *delinquent* either in the text or in the glossary. Remember, you might need to try looking under "juvenile delinquent," depending on how the term was indexed. Now consider the differences, if any, that exist between each text's definition, and write a single synthesized definition.

Suggestion 2

Locate the *Index to the Social Sciences* in a college or university library. Use this index to find 10 sources of reference material for a potential study on child abuse. Remember to be creative in developing topics to look up.

Suggestion 3

Identify six concepts and operationally define each. Be sure to consult relevant literature before terms are defined. Do not just make up definitions. When operatively defining how each concept will be measured, be certain these operations conform to both relevant literature and the qualitative paradigm.

REFERENCES

Babbie, E. (1992). *The Practice of Social Research* (3rd ed.). Belmont, CA: Wadsworth Publishing.

Berg, B. L., & Berg, J. (1993). A reexamination of triangulation and objectivity in qualitative nursing research. *Free Inquiry in Creative Sociology 21*(1), 65–72.

Bynum, J. E., & Thompson, W. E. (1992). *Juvenile Delinquency: A Sociological Approach.* Boston: Allyn and Bacon.

DeBakey, L., & DeBakey, S. (1978). The art of persuasion: Logic and language in proposal writing. *Grants Magazine 1,* 43–60.

Denzin, N. K. (1978). *Sociological Methods: A Source Book* (2nd ed.). New York: McGraw-Hill.

Frankfort-Nachmias, C., & Nachmias, D. (1996). *Research Methods in the Social Sciences* (5th ed.). New York: St. Martin's Press.

Hagan, F. E. (1993). *Research Methods in Criminal Justice and Criminology* (3rd ed.). New York: Macmillan.

Leedy, P. D. (1993). *Practical Research: Planning and Design* (5th ed.). New York: Macmillan.

Lincoln, Y. S., & Guba, E. G. (1985). *Naturalistic Inquiry.* Beverly Hills, CA: Sage.

Merton, R. K. (1968). *Social Theory and Social Structure* (rev. and enlarged ed.). New York: Free Press.

Nachmias, C. F., & Nachmias, D. (1992). *Research Methods in the Social Sciences* (4th ed.). New York: St. Martin's Press.

Polit, D. F., & Hungler, B. P. (1993). *Essentials of Nursing Research.* Philadelphia: J. B. Lippincott.

Popper, K. R. (1968). *Conjectures and Refutations: The Growth of Scientific Knowledge.* New York: Harper and Row.

Siegel, L. J., & Senna, J. J. (1988). *Juvenile Delinquency: Theory, Practice, and Law* (3rd ed.). St. Paul: West Publishing.

Thornton, W. E., Jr., & Voigt, L. (1992). *Delinquency and Justice* (3rd ed.). New York: McGraw-Hill.

ETHICAL ISSUES

SOCIAL SCIENTISTS, PERHAPS TO a greater extent than the average citizen, have an ethical obligation to their colleagues, their study population, and the larger society. The reason for this is that social scientists delve into the social lives of other human beings. From such excursions into private social lives, various policies, practices, and even laws may result. Thus, researchers must ensure the rights, privacy, and welfare of the people and communities that form the focus of their studies.

During the past several decades, methods of data collection, organization, and analysis have become more sophisticated and penetrating. As a consequence the extent or scope of research has become greatly expanded. With this expansion has come increased awareness and concern over the ethics of research and researchers.

To a large extent concerns about research ethics revolve around various issues of harm, consent, privacy, and the confidentiality of data (Punch, 1994). This chapter considers these important ethical concerns as associated with research in general and with qualitative research in particular.

As Babbie (1983) accurately points out, "All of us consider ourselves ethical; not perfect perhaps, but more ethical than most of humanity." Unfortunately, one problem in social science is that ethical considerations are subjective. Researchers eager to gain access to some population that might otherwise be difficult to reach may really not see that their plans are unethical. Some overly zealous researchers, while realizing that certain of their practices may be unethical, nonetheless plunge forward, justifying their actions under the excuse that it isn't illegal!

Many experienced researchers could tell with regret war stories about having violated some tenet of ethics in their less experienced years. The transgression may have involved allowing some gatekeeper to manipulate subjects to take part in a study (under veiled threat of some loss of privilege), or it may have involved some covert investigation that resulted in subtle invasions of privacy. In any case, these now experienced researchers are still likely to feel somewhat embarrassed when they think about these instances—at least one hopes they do.

Often, glaring violations of ethical standards are recognized nearly as soon as the researchers have conceived them. Frequently, during planning stages, particularly when conducting research together with a colleague, ethical problems are identified and worked through. This is not to say that practices that might appear unethical to others outside the study are always eliminated. Rather, the process, like much of qualitative research, is a negotiation, a tradeoff of the amount of access to subjects the researchers are willing to accept in exchange for the amount of ethical risk they are willing to take.

It is not difficult to understand that injecting unknowing subjects with live AIDS virus is unethical. It may not be quite as easy to see that studying drug dealers and then turning over their addresses and field notes as evidence to the police is also unethical. This latter example is somewhat more difficult to see because a law-abiding attitude is probably so well ingrained in most researchers that the logical response seems obvious—namely, if citizens can assist the police, they have a moral obligation to do so. However, precisely because such tensions between logic and ethics exist, careful consideration of ethical issues is critical to the success or failure of any high-quality research involving humans.

The first portion of this chapter examines some of the historical background of research ethics, including some of the major events that influenced current ethical research practices. Ethical elements commonly considered important when researchers involve human subjects in their research are then addressed.

RESEARCH ETHICS IN HISTORICAL PERSPECTIVE

There are almost as many historical explanations for the current interest in research ethics as there are research books on college library shelves. Some authors point to the civil rights movements during the late 1950s as having raised researchers' awareness of ethical issues (Barber, 1973). Other writers suggest that current concerns result from attempts to control federally funded research as available funds grew in quantum leaps following World War II (Smith, 1967; Sykes, 1967). Still others point to particular studies with especially questionable ethics as "pivotal points" in the concern over the rights and welfare of human subjects (Babbie, 1983, pp. 457ff).

There is, however, general agreement that current concerns about research ethics grew out of biomedical research, particularly the ghoulish torture and dismemberment perpetrated under the guise of medical research by Nazi scientists during World War II. For instance, in the name of science, Nazi physicians exposed subjects to freezing temperatures, live viruses, poisons, malaria, and an assortment of untested drugs and experimental operations (Berger, 1990; Burns & Grove, 1993). This wartime medical research led in 1949 to the Nuremberg Code, which established principles for researching human subjects, most notably that subjects must *voluntarily consent* to participate in a study (Wexler, 1990, p. 81).

This ethical canon became the foundation of the Declaration of Helsinki, adopted by the World Health Organization in 1964 and revised in 1975 (Levine, 1986). It was also the basis for the "Ethical Guidelines for Clinical Investigation" adopted by the American Medical Association in 1966 (Bower & de Gasparis, 1978). Yet, as Katz (1972) indicates, years later and thousands of miles away from the bloodstained walls of Nazi operating rooms, extremely risky—sometimes fatal—research was being carried out on unknowing patients here in the United States. Consider, for example, the case of two research physicians at the Brooklyn Jewish Chronic Disease Hospital, who during the mid-1960s injected a suspension containing live cancer cells into 22 unsuspecting elderly patients (Levine, 1986). Although media and public pressure brought an end to the experiment, neither physician was ever prosecuted on any sort of criminal charge (Hershey & Miller, 1976).

Interestingly, before the 1960s, few laws regulated the research process. As Bower and de Gasparis (1978) suggest, with the exception of medical malpractice laws, virtually no federal or state statutes regulated research. Consequently, no legal redress was available to subjects, even if they believed they had been wronged by a behavioral scientist. Highly questionable practices in research throughout the late 1950s and 1960s repeatedly demonstrated the need for regulation and control of studies involving human subjects.

For instance, among the more glaring violations of ethical practices was a study conducted by the U.S. Public Health Service known as the Tuskegee Syphilis Study (Brandt, 1978). This project, which spanned more than 40 years, was a longitudinal study whose purpose was to identify a population of syphilitic black men and to observe in these subjects, over a period of time, the consequences of untreated syphilis.

Although the researchers on the study did not themselves infect the subjects, once the study had begun the investigative team actively interfered with the lives and health of the subjects without their consent (Chadwick et al., 1984). The study began during the mid-1930s, when no cure for syphilis existed, but after a cure (penicillin) was identified, the research team actively sought to keep treatment from their sample. This included offering free so-called treatment and health services to the sample of men, as well as contacting local black physicians and instructing them not to treat (for syphilis) any of the 400 men involved in the study.

In order to ensure that an autopsy could be done on each of the subjects who died during the experiment, the team offered free burial services.

Surviving family members typically were unaware that the burial was conditional on allowing an autopsy.

The study ended in 1972 after the news media exposed it and public pressure forced officials to terminate the study. Estimates of how many men died directly from advanced syphilis range from 28 to 100 subjects (Brandt, 1978). Shortly after termination of the study, the Department of Health, Education, and Welfare (the parent agency of the Public Health Service) appointed a panel that concluded that the research had been "ethically unjustified."

Many other biomedical experiments conducted during the sixties were also "ethically unjustified" (Hershey & Miller, 1976), and during this same period, many behavioral scientists were involved in potentially ethically unjustified research as well—for example, Stanley Milgram's experiment on following orders and control. Milgram (1963) was interested in learning about human tendencies to obey authority figures. In order to observe this phenomenon, he told his voluntary subjects that they were to teach another person, supposedly another volunteer subject, a simple word association task. The other volunteer, however, was actually another investigator on the study.

The subject/teacher was instructed by Milgram to administer an electric shock to the learner (the confederate in an adjacent room) whenever the learner made a mistake. The subject/teacher was told that this electric shock was intended to facilitate learning and should be increased in intensity progressively with each error. Many of the subjects obediently (in fact, gleefully) advanced the shock levels to potentially lethal levels.

In reality, the supposed learner received no shocks at all. Rather, each time the subject/teacher administered a shock, a signal indicated that the learner should react as if shocked. Nonetheless, the deception aroused considerable emotional anguish and guilt in the subjects.

Another example of research with questionable ethical tactics is Humphreys's (1970) study of casual homosexual encounters, *Tearoom Trade*. Humphreys was interested in gaining understanding not only about practicing homosexuals but also about heterosexuals who briefly engaged in homosexual encounters. In addition to observing encounters in public restrooms in parks (tearooms), Humphreys developed a way to gain access to detailed information about the subjects he covertly observed.

While serving as a watch queen (a voyeuristic lookout), Humphreys was able both to observe the encounters and to catch a glimpse of participants' car license plates. Once Humphreys had their license plate numbers, he could locate their home addresses through the local department of motor vehicles. Next, he disguised himself and deceived these men into believing that he was conducting a survey in their neighborhood. The result was that Humphreys managed to collect considerable amounts of information about each of the subjects he had observed in the tearooms.

FIGURE 3.1 The Research Risk Benefit Scale

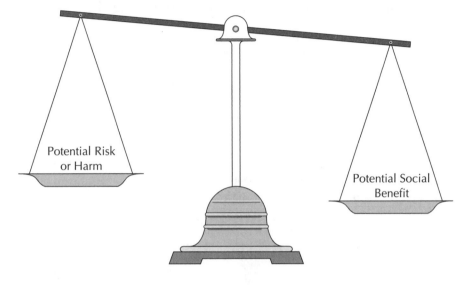

Shortly after the publication of Humphreys's work in 1970, there was a considerable outcry against the invasion of privacy, misrepresentation of researcher identities, and deception commonly being practiced during the course of research. Many of the controversies that revolve around Humphreys's research remain key ethical issues today. Paramount among these issues are the justifications that the subject matter was of critical importance to the scientific community and that it simply could not have been investigated in any other manner.

Naturally, this begs the question of considering the potential benefit of a research project weighed against the potential harm. This utilitarian argument essentially sets up a kind of scale where risk and harm are placed on one side and benefits are placed on the other side (see Figure 3.1). If the determination is that the amount of benefit outweighs the amount of potential risk or harm, then the research may be seen from an ethical point of view as permissible (Taylor, 1994). This notion, of course, assumes that there is no potential serious risk of harm, injury, or death possible for any research subject.

In the case of Humphreys's study, there are many researchers who maintain that the social, legal, and psychological policy changes that have resulted far outweigh any minor invasions of privacy. This is not to suggest that there are not other researchers who argue that the research was unethical no matter how great the benefits have been.

FROM GUIDELINES TO LAW:
REGULATIONS ON THE RESEARCH PROCESS

Early attempts to devise rigorous biomedical experimentation guidelines failed. One major reason was the inability to develop a single code of ethics that, as Bower and de Gasparis (1978, p. 5) put it, "could cover with equal adequacy and flexibility the entire range of biomedical experimentation." However, in 1966, the Surgeon General issued what may have been the first official rules concerning all Public Health Service research. This statement specified that any research financially supported by the Public Health Service was contingent on a review by an institutional committee. The committee was charged with the responsibility of ensuring that study procedures would not harm human subjects and that subjects were informed of any potential risks (and benefits) from their participation.

Several revisions of this general policy occurred during 1967–1969. Finally, in 1971, the Department of Health, Education, and Welfare (DHEW) published a booklet entitled "The Institutional Guide to DHEW Policy on Protection of Human Subjects," which extended the requirement of an institutional review committee to all DHEW grant and contract activities involving human subjects. In addition, this booklet specified the requirement to obtain *informed consent* from subjects before including them in the research.

In 1974, the National Research Act was passed by Congress, and the National Commission on Protection of Human Subjects of Biomedical and Behavioral Research was created by Title II of this law. The National Research Act directed all institutions that sponsored research to establish institutional review committees, today more commonly called *institutional review boards* (IRBs). Locally based in-house IRBs were now charged with the responsibility of carefully reviewing any proposed research that involved human subjects.

Among several other issues, IRBs were expected to ensure that research investigators had considered both potential risks and benefits to subjects, that important scientific knowledge could be derived from the project, that legally informed consent would be obtained from each subject, and that the rights and interests of subjects were protected (Liemohn, 1979).

Another important piece of research-related legislation is the education amendments of 1974. These laws, better known as the Buckley Amendments, were intended to protect the privacy of parents and students (Holden, 1975). In essence, these laws limited access to official records concerning (and identifying) an individual, and they prohibited release of such personal information (with some exceptions) to anyone else without written consent of the student (and the parent in the case of minors).

Finally, the Privacy Acts of 1974 offered additional legal assurances against invasive research on human subjects. This legislation was primarily designed to protect citizens from large private corporations and federal institutions and from the release of potentially erroneous information and records. In addition, however, it provided individuals with judicial machinery for redressing indiscriminate sharing of personal information and records without prior written consent—including when obtained by deceptive researchers. A fair number of these regulations are informally overseen by institutional review boards. Let us consider IRBs in greater detail.

INSTITUTIONAL REVIEW BOARDS

Whenever someone brings up the topic of institutional review boards, he or she runs the risk of evoking strong feelings among social science researchers. Some researchers see IRBs as handcuffs impeding their search for scientific answers to social problems. Some researchers simply believe that contemporary IRBs have grown too big for their breeches and that they tend to overstep their perceived purpose and limits. Other researchers say IRBs are staffed with clinicians unable to understand the nuances of certain social scientific styles of research. Indeed, there are many who view IRBs as villains rather than as necessary—let alone virtuous—institutions. Ideally, IRBs should be seen as a group of individuals who selflessly give their time and expertise to ensure that human subjects are neither physically nor emotionally injured by researchers. Ironically, while few researchers today really believe that IRBs are not necessary, these same individuals are likely to view IRBs in less than positive terms.

In the academic community of the 1990s, research continues to uphold its position as a critically important element. Fundamentally, and somewhat altruistically, research holds the promise of important revelations for collective thinking and changes for the better in society. At a more pragmatic level, social science research, especially federally funded studies, offers the academician opportunities for publication that, in turn, form the rungs in academic promotion and tenure ladders. In contrast to this altruistic and practical research optimism, however, are the previously mentioned research studies of the recent past that exploited human subjects in deplorable ways. The question that remains unanswered, however, is: Exactly what are the institutional review boards' duties?

IRBs and Their Duties

Among the important elements considered by IRB panels is the assurance of informed consent. Usually, this involves requirements for obtaining written informed consent from potential subjects. This requirement has drawn heavy critical fire from social scientists (Fields, 1978; Gray, 1977; Meyer,

1977). Qualitative researchers, especially those involved in ethnographic research, have been particularly vocal. Their concerns often pertain to the way formal requirements for institutional review and written informed consent damages their special fieldworker-informant relationships (Berg et al., 1992; Cassell, 1978; Wax, 1977).

The National Commission for the Protection of Human Subjects, created by the National Research Act of 1974, has reviewed its own guidelines (Department of Health, Education, and Welfare, 1978a) and offered revisions (*Federal Register*, 1978). These revisions are more specific about the role the IRB should play than were previous documents. For example, the *Federal Register* states that board members may be liable for legal action if they exceed their authority and interfere with the investigator's *right* to conduct research. These revised guidelines also recommend that the requirement for written informed consent could be waived for certain types of *low-risk styles of research*.

Because their research procedures are more formalized and require contacts with subjects, the more limited and predictable characteristics of quantitative methodologies are generally simpler to define. As a result, the specific exemptions for styles of research that can be expedited through IRBs largely are quantitative survey types, observation in public places, research involving educational tests (diagnostic, aptitude, or achievement), and archival research (Department of Health, Education, and Welfare, 1978b).

The temporary (usually single-visit) and formal nature of most quantitative data-gathering strategies makes them easier to fit into the federal regulations. In quantitative research, confidentiality is also rather easy to ensure. Written consent slips can be held separately from surveys and secured in innovative ways. It becomes a simple task to ensure that names or other identifiers will not be connected in any way with the survey response sheets.

Qualitative research, especially ethnographic strategies, offer IRBs greater challenges. To be sure, most qualitative researchers will make every effort to comply with the federal regulations for the protection of human subjects. However, compliance is not always easy. In order to ensure consistency, lists of names are sometimes maintained even when pseudonyms are used in field notes. Furthermore, the very nature of ethnographic research makes it ideal for studying secret, deviant, or difficult-to-study populations. Consider, for example, drug smugglers (Adler, 1985). It would be virtually impossible to locate sufficient numbers of drug smugglers to create a probability sampling or to administer a meaningful number of survey questionnaires. Imagine, now, that you also needed to secure written informed-consent slips. It is not likely that anyone could manage these restrictions. In fact, the researcher's personal safety might be jeopardized even by announcing his or her presence (overt observation).

It is similarly unlikely that you would gain much success trying to locate a sufficient number of patrons of pornographic bookstores to administer questionnaires. Yet observational and ethnographic techniques might work very well (see, for example, Tewksbury, 1990).

Many qualitative researchers have arrived at the same conclusion about the relationship between researcher and subjects in qualitative research; namely, that the qualitative relationship is so different from quantitative approaches that most conventional procedures for informed consent and protection of human subjects amount to little more than ritual (Bogdan & Biklen, 1992). In the kind of research for which these guidelines have been written, subjects and researchers have very circumscribed relationships. The researcher presents some survey or questionnaire to the subject who, in turn, fills it out. Or the researcher describes the requirements of participation in some experiment, and the subject participates. In these quantitative modes of research, it is a fairly easy task to predict and describe to the subject the content of the study and the possible risks from participation. As Janice Morse suggests, at some institutions, the IRB requires distribution of a "Bill of Rights," whenever a subject is included in an experiment (Morse, 1994, p. 338).

With qualitative research, on the other hand, the relationship between researcher and subject is frequently an ongoing and evolving one. Doing qualitative research with subjects is more like being permitted to observe or take part in the lives of these subjects. At best, it may be seen as a social contract. But as in all contracts, both parties have some say about the contents of the agreement, and in regulating the relationship. While it is not difficult to predict possible risks in quantitative survey studies, this task can be quite a problem in some qualitative research projects.

Consider, for example, a study where a researcher seeks to observe the gambling behavior of people during their active participation in drinking alcohol while in taverns (McSkimming, 1996). Can the researcher actually determine whether people who are drinking alcohol and gambling as part of their social worlds will be at risk *because* he or she is present in the same tavern watching them? Certainly, any time people consume alcohol and engage in something as volatile as gambling there is the potential for violence. From the standpoint of the IRB, a declaration from the researcher that there is no greater risk to subjects because the researcher is present observing their behaviors is likely to be sufficient; in short, the research project itself does not increase or cause risk. Of course this does nothing to diminish the usual risk of these behaviors.

Some researchers may have thrown in the towel and, in order to avoid confrontations with IRBs, simply never research certain controversial topics. That is, these researchers may have taken the moral position that not all topics are appropriate for academic study. This, however, could lead to a serious problem for the scientific community. Such a stance promotes the development of sterile, boring, and largely insignificant research. Clearly, the kinds of social research that rally passion among researchers and IRB board members also are likely to offer paths for social change. Innocuous, unimpassioned research is less likely to inspire or motivate people or changes in structure.

The other problem, of course, is that one man's meat is another man's poison. In other words, topics or populations repulsive to one researcher may be fascinating to another. For example, many researchers study the police. Yet for some people (academics and lay persons alike), the police represent a reprehensible group of mindless, brutal stooges for the local government. For these people, the police (perhaps even other elements of the criminal justice system) are corrupt, repulsive, and certainly not areas worthy of academic research. While certain research populations or topics may be unacceptable to some researchers, agreement on which populations and topics these are may be difficult to obtain.

The claim that *some* police officers are racist, sexist, corrupt, and brutal is indisputable. To say that others are enthusiastic, altruistic, humane, caring, and good is likewise indisputable. To discontinue researching all police officers because some are despicable might even prevent us from learning this truth. Yet there appears to persist a dichotomy of opinions about police officers.

Clarifying the Role of IRBs

Initially, IRBs were charged with the responsibility to review the adequacy of consent procedures for the protection of human subjects in research funded by the U.S. Department of Health, Education, and Welfare. This mandate was soon broadened to include a review of all research conducted in an institution receiving any funds from DHEW—even when the study itself did not (Burstein, 1987; Department of Health, Education, and Welfare, 1989).

As part of the institutional review boards' duties, they were to ensure that subjects in research studies were advised of both the potential risks from participation and the possible benefits. This task seems to have evolved among some IRBs to become an assessment of risk-to-benefit ratios of proposed studies. In some cases, this is based upon the IRB's impression of the *worth* of the study. In other cases, this may be based upon the IRB's presumed greater knowledge of the subject and methodological strategies than potential subjects are likely to possess (Burstein, 1987). Thus, in many cases, IRBs and not subjects determine whether the subject will even have the option of participating or declining to participate in a study.

Today, many IRBs have further extended their reach to include evaluation of methodological strategies, not, as one might expect, as these methods pertain to human subject risks but in terms of the project's methodological adequacy. The justification for this, apparently, is that even where minimum risks exist, if a study is designed poorly, it will not yield any scientific benefit (Berg et al., 1992).

During the past several years IRBs seem to have begun to *moralize* rather than assess the potential harm to subjects. As an example, consider the following situation that arose recently during an IRB review of a proposal at a mid-sized university on the East Coast. The project was designed to ethnographically examine the initiation of cigarette smoking and alcohol consumption among middle- and high-school-age youths. The design called for identified field researchers to spend time in public places observing youths. The idea was to observe how smoking and alcohol fit into the social worlds of these youths.

Several of the IRB committee members were extremely concerned that ethnographers would be watching *children* smoking and drinking without notifying their parents of these behaviors. During a review of this proposal with the investigator, these committee members argued that it was unthinkable that no intervention would be taken on the part of the field workers. They recommended that the researchers tell the youths' parents that they were engaging in these serious behaviors. The investigator explained that this would actually be a breach of confidentiality, and potentially expose the subjects to serious risk of corporal punishment.

One committee member asked, "What if the youth was observed smoking crack? Wouldn't the field worker tell his or her parents then?" The investigator reminded the committee that these observations were to be in public places. The field workers did not have a responsibility to report to the parents what their children were doing—no matter how potentially unhealthy it may be. The investigator further explained that there was no legal requirement to inform on these subjects, and in fact, to do so would make the research virtually undoable. The committee member agreed that there may be no legal requirement, but went on to argue that there certainly was a moral one!

Eventually, a compromise was struck. The researcher agreed to include in the proposal a statement indicating that if the field workers observed what they believed were children engaging in behavior that would likely result in immediate and serious personal injury or imminent death, they would intervene. Of course, such a statement seemed unnecessary for the researcher, since it was already agreed upon by the research team. It did, however, appease the committee members who continued to grumble that the parents should be informed about their children's behavior.

Active versus Passive Consent

Another type of moralizing has recently arisen over the controversy surrounding active versus passive informed consent by parents of children involved in research. Active consent may be defined as the "formal written permission by an informed parent or legal guardian that allows a child to participate in a research project" (Deschenes & Vogel, 1995). Passive consent is usually based on the assumption that parental permission is granted if parents do not return a refusal form after being informed about the study's purpose (Ellickson & Hawes, 1989; Deschenes & Vogel, 1995).

Even the federal government has gotten into the picture. In 1995, they began considering a bill that would require active consent for research involving children. If this legislation passes, it could put a considerable damper on the research undertaken by many educational researchers. By 1996, legislation still had not been passed.

In the past, researchers who have employed an active consent style have reported that it yields unacceptably low response rates. This translates into the underrepresentation of relevant study subjects, often the very ones involved in or at risk from the study behaviors (Thompson, 1984; Kearney et al., 1983; Severson & Ary, 1983).

To avoid excluding relevant study subjects, many researchers have turned to the passive consent method (Ellickson & Hawes, 1989). The moral questions here rests on the argument that passive procedures do not fully inform parents about the research or give them sufficient opportunities to refuse participation. Some researchers question whether parents have actually intentionally decided to allow their child to participate and consciously not sent in the refusal notice. In this case, one might interpret non-response as more of an indicator of sloppy or lackadaisical parental attitudes—but not necessarily consent.

Active consent requires informed consent rigor that may be too stringent for many qualitative research endeavors. This is especially true since most qualitative projects implement a series of diligent data safeguards such as removal of identifiers to ensure confidentiality. Carefully designed passive consent procedures can avoid various negative consequences of active consent, while still ensuring parents are being informed.

The use of active consent begs the question of how extensive it must be, and how it should be implemented in qualitative research. For example, if an investigator is interested in observing the interactions between children at play and during their studies, how extensive would the active consent need to be. Certainly, if observations are being made in a classroom, all of the parents would need to be notified, but would all have to actively agree before the researcher could enter the room. If one parent said no, would that mean that the child could not be included in the researcher's notes, or that the research could not be undertaken? If the researcher wanted to observe this class of children on the playground, would he or she need the active consent of the parents of every child in the school?

Again, these concerns seem to direct themselves more to quantitative than qualitative studies. In most quantitative projects, a researcher can easily avoid giving a survey to any child or exclude the child from inclusion in some experiment, if he or she has not obtained a parental consent. Similarly, a researcher could exclude youths from an interview study if they fail to provide written permission from their parents. It is not as easy, however, to exclude youths from school-based observational studies. Thus, if a researcher desires to undertake this type of research, under the guidelines of active consent, he or she might not be able to. Naturally, this suggests, once more, the push toward what could be called "research of the sterile and mundane."

IRBs in today's research community are quite complicated groups of people dealing with a myriad of difficult technological, ethical, and recently moralistic problems. A reasonable question to ask is who in his or her right mind would want to serve on such a panel. This, however, brings us to the question of exactly who does serve on these review boards.

Membership Criteria for IRBs

The federal regulations specify that "each IRB shall have at least five members, with varying backgrounds to promote complete and adequate review of research activities commonly conducted by the institution" (Code of Federal Regulations, 1989, p. 7). There are also the provisions that IRBs should not be composed entirely of women, men, single racial groups, or one profession. Furthermore, each IRB should contain at least one member whose primary work does not include the sciences or social sciences (e.g., lawyers, ethicists, or members of the clergy). However, federal guidelines do not articulate how to select or locate IRB members, what research qualifications members should have, what lengths members' terms should be, or how to establish an IRB chairperson. The federal regulations do require that "assurances" be submitted to the Office for Protection from Research Risks, National Institutes of Health.

Among these assurances must be a list of IRB members' names, their "earned degrees; representative capacity; indications of experience such as board certifications, licenses, etc." (Code of Federal Regulations, 1989, p. 6). While no suggestion is given about what types of degrees people should have in order to sit on the IRB, the allusion to board certification and licenses does convey the notion of clinicians rather than social scientists. While many social scientists may believe that their institution's IRB is composed of clinicians, it is likely that it is not. The possibility may exist, however, that members of IRBs have never themselves conducted research on human subjects or, for that matter, conducted any research. The federal regulations do not require that IRB members themselves have a research history; hence, the situation that some do not is quite conceivable.

Institutional review boards are really still in their infancy. They are certainly a necessary element in maintaining safe and ethical research in the social sciences. Exactly what their role should be, who should hold board positions, and what scientific role they should play in the research community remain to be worked out.

There are no quick fixes for establishing IRBs that are able to ensure both safety to human subjects and unhampered research opportunities for investigators. As the serious ethical infractions that occurred before the advance of IRBs demonstrate, social scientists left to their own designs sometimes go astray. On the other hand, researchers may be correct in their stance that IRBs left to their own devices may grow too restrictive. Nonetheless, IRBs should be able to operate in concert with researchers rather than in opposition to them. Social scientists need to become more involved in the IRB process and seek ways to implement board goals and membership policies that are responsive to changing times, social values, and research technologies.

ETHICAL CODES

During the past several decades, changing social attitudes about research as well as changing legislation have led professional associations to create codes of ethical conduct. For example, the American Nurses' Association developed *Human Rights Guidelines for Nurses in Clinical and Other Research* (1975). The American Sociological Association produced its code of ethics during the early 1980s (American Sociological Association, 1984, 1992). Ethical guidelines for psychologists emerged in the American Psychological Association (American Psychological Association, 1981) in a document entitled "Ethical Principles of Psychologists" and again in 1984 in a document entitled "Ethical Principles in the Conduct of Research with Human Participants" (American Psychological Association, 1984). The American Society of Criminology has not formally adopted a code of ethics. Hagan (1993), however, suggests that most criminologists and criminal justice researchers tend to borrow from connate disciplines. Certainly, paramount among these borrowed elements is the avoidance of harm to human subjects.

SOME COMMON ETHICAL CONCERNS
IN BEHAVIORAL RESEARCH

Among the most serious ethical concerns that have received attention during the past two decades is the assurance that subjects are voluntarily involved and informed of all potential risks. Yet even here there is some controversy.

In general, the concept of voluntary participation in social science research is an important ideal, but ideals are not always attainable. In some instances—such as the one illustrated by Humphreys's (1970) study—violating the tenet of voluntary participation may appear justified to certain researchers. Typically, such justifications are made on the basis of an imaginary scale described as tipped toward the ultimate social good as measured against the possible harm to subjects.

Another argument against arbitrary application of this notion of voluntary participation concerns the nature of volunteering in general. First, if all social research included only those persons who eagerly volunteered to participate, little meaningful understanding would result. There would be no way of determining if these types of persons were similar to others who lacked this eagerness to volunteer. In other words, both qualitative and aggregated statistical data would become questionable.

Second, in many cases, volunteer subjects may in reality be coerced or manipulated into volunteering. For instance, one popular style of sample identification is the college classroom. If the teacher asks the entire class to voluntarily take part in a research project, there may be penalties for not submitting even if the teacher suggests otherwise. Even if no punishments are intentionally planned, if students believe that not taking part will be noticed and might somehow be held against them, they have been manipulated. Under such circumstances, as in the case of the over-eager volunteers, confidence in the data is undermined.

Babbie (1992) similarly notes that offering reduced sentences to inmates in exchange for their participation in research—or other types of incentives to potential subjects—represents yet another kind of manipulated voluntary consent. As Martin et al. (1968) suggest, voluntary participation in studies among prisoners results from a strange mix of altruism, monetary gain, and hope for a potential way of enhancing their personal prestige and/or status.

A third justification for not gaining the voluntary consent of subjects is suggested by Rainwater and Pittman (1967). They believe that social science research enhances accountability in public officials. Consequently, research in many public institutions must be conducted covertly (thus, without voluntary participation on the part of subjects) if it is to be meaningful—and in some instances if it is to be conducted at all.

In contrast to these justifications for not obtaining voluntary participation, Kelman (1972) outlines how various invasions of privacy and manipulations of research subjects occur in fairly powerless segments of society and organizations. On the one hand, researchers might justify this invasion as the conduct of do-gooders who focus on such disadvantaged groups as drug abusers, the unemployed, and the poor because social service agencies are interested in helping people with social problems. On the other hand, researchers can create as strong a case for social agencies' desires to get a firmer grip on these disadvantaged groups, and certainly government agencies use social science research to formulate their policies (Lakoff, 1971).

Regardless of the justification, because of their lack of political, social, and financial power, these disadvantaged groups are more accessible to researchers than many more powerful groups are. In consequence, researchers must be responsive to these conditions and clearly explain to subjects the rights and responsibilities of both the researchers and the participants.

No hard and fast answers exist for resolving the dilemma of voluntary participation. Researchers must balance how voluntary subjects' participation will be against their perceptions of personal integrity; their responsibilities to themselves, their profession, and their discipline; and the ultimate effects for their subjects. In other words, in the end, researchers must define for themselves what is ethical in research.

PHYSICAL AND ETHICAL DANGERS IN COVERT RESEARCH

A similar ethical concern centers on the decision about whether to enter the field as an overt (announced) or covert (secret) investigator (discussed briefly in Chapter 3). The highly illegal nature of certain deviant careers and activities—the very thing that may make them sociologically interesting—may preclude overtly investigating them. The adoption of a covert research role, however, must be carefully considered, for in addition to potentially violating the rights of the subjects, there is a very real possibility that the researchers themselves might come to some harm or legal complication. The Adlers, for example, explain their attempt to strike a balance between overt and covert researcher roles (Adler, 1985, pp. 17, 27):

> *In discussing this issue [whether to overtly or covertly investigate drug trafficking] with our key informants, they all agreed that we should be extremely discreet (for both our sakes and theirs). We carefully approached new individuals before we admitted that we were studying them. With many of these people, then, we took a covert posture in the research setting. . . . Confronted with secrecy, danger, hidden alliances, misrepresentations and unpredictable changes of intent, I had to use a delicate combination of overt and covert roles.*

There is also the problem, particularly when conducting covert field research on deviants, that one will necessarily break the law (Adler, 1985; Becker, 1963; Carey, 1972; Polsky, 1969). Again, the Adlers (Adler, 1985, p. 23) provide an excellent illustration of the various levels of illegality one might become guilty of:

This [law violation] occurs in its most innocuous form from having "guilty knowledge": information about crimes that are committed. Being aware of major dealing and smuggling operations made us an accessory to their commission, since we failed to notify the police. We broke the law, secondly, through our "guilty observations," by being present at the scene of a crime and witnessing its occurrence. . . . Lastly, we broke the law through our "guilty actions," by taking part in illegal behavior ourselves. Although we never dealt drugs (we were too scared to be seriously tempted) we consumed drugs and possessed them in small quantities.

Although deception may be seen as a minor ethical violation by some investigators, it remains a serious breach of ethical conduct for others (Kelman, 1967). The decision about whether to assume an overt or a covert researcher role, then, involves a negotiated and, I will hope, a balanced weighing of the potential gains against the potential losses.

Of course, other concerns related to decisions about ethical research practices can more easily be detailed and considered. Elaboration of each of these elements may assist researchers (particularly the inexperienced) in determining how to deal with ethical concerns in research. These elements include informed consent, implied consent, confidentiality and anonymity, securing the data, and objectivity and careful research design.

INFORMED CONSENT AND IMPLIED CONSENT

Issues surrounding informed consent grow out of the concern to avoid—or at least identify and articulate—potential risk to human subjects. Risks associated with participation in social scientific research include exposure to physical, psychological, or social injury.

Informed consent means the knowing consent of individuals to participate as an exercise of their choice, free from any element of fraud, deceit, duress, or similar unfair inducement or manipulation. In the case of minors or mentally impaired persons, whose exercise of choice is legally governed, consent must be obtained from the person or agency legally authorized to represent the interests of the individual.

In most institutionally sponsored research, consent must be ensured in writing. Typically, *informed consent slips* contain a written statement of potential risk and benefit and some phrase to the effect that these risks and benefits have been explained. As a rule, these slips are dated and signed by both the potential subject and the researchers or their designated representative.

There are chiefly two rationales behind the requirement to obtain signed informed consent slips. First, they systematically ensure that potential subjects are *knowingly* participating in a study and are doing so of their own choice. Second, signed consent slips provide IRBs a means by which to monitor (by examining signed slips) the voluntary participation of subjects.

Obtaining a signed informed consent slip, as may be obvious, presents in itself a slight ethical dilemma. A written record of the subjects' names (and frequently their addresses as well) means that a formal record of participants exists. In order to preserve privacy, these slips are usually kept under very careful guard by the principal investigator(s) and are revealed to IRBs only if questions arise concerning ethical practices in a given study.

Sometimes in large-scale survey questionnaire studies, separate signed informed consent slips are eliminated and replaced with implied consent. *Implied consent* is indicated by the subject taking the time to complete the lengthy questionnaire. In these circumstances, explanations of the study's purpose and potential risks and benefits are explained at the beginning of the survey.

A similar kind of implied consent can replace a signed consent slip when researchers conduct tape-recorded in-depth interviews. In this instance, the interviewers fully explain the nature of the project and the potential risks and benefits at the beginning of each interview. Next, the interviewers ask the subjects if they understand the information and are still willing to take part in the interview. Affirmative responses and completed interviews serve the purpose of implying consent in the absence of a signed consent slip. The benefit of this particular style of informed consent is the elimination of any record of the subjects' names. This procedure is particularly helpful when interviewing people who might otherwise refuse to take part in a study. To a large measure, this type of implied consent is related to the next topic—namely, confidentiality and anonymity.

CONFIDENTIALITY AND ANONYMITY

Although *confidentiality* and *anonymity* are sometimes mistakenly used as synonyms, they have quite distinct meanings. *Confidentiality* is an active attempt to remove from the research records any elements that might indicate the subjects' identities. In a literal sense, *anonymity* means that the subjects remain nameless. In some instances, such as self-administered survey questionnaires, it may be possible to provide anonymity. Although investigators may know to whom surveys were distributed, if no identifying marks have been placed on the returned questionnaires, the respondents remain anonymous.

In most qualitative research, however, because subjects are known to the investigators (even if only by sight and a street name), anonymity is virtually nonexistent. Thus, it is important to provide subjects with a high degree of confidentiality.

Researchers commonly assure subjects that anything discussed between them will be kept in strict confidence, but what exactly does this mean?

Naturally, this requires that the researchers systematically change each subject's real name to a pseudonym or case number when reporting data. But what about the names of locations? Place names, in association with a description of certain characteristics about an individual, may make it possible to discover a subject's identity (Gibbons, 1975). Even if people are incorrect about their determination of who is being identified, the results may nonetheless make people wary of cooperating in future research. Researchers, therefore, must always be extremely careful about how they discuss their subjects and the settings as well (Hagan 1993; Hessler, 1992).

Keeping Identifying Records

It is not unusual for researchers, particularly ethnographers, to maintain systematically developed listings of real names and pseudonyms for people and places. As discussed in Chapter 6, the use of such systematic lists ensures consistency during later analysis stages of the data. However, the existence of such lists creates a potential risk to subjects. Although court battles may eventually alter the situation, social scientists are presently unable to invoke professional privilege as a defense against being forced to reveal names of informants and sources during criminal proceedings. In other words, under normal conditions, lists of names and places can be subpoenaed along with other relevant research notes and data.

Strategies for Safeguarding Confidentiality

In effect, researchers may be placed in an ethical catch twenty-two. On one hand, they have a professional obligation to honor assurances of confidentiality made to subjects. On the other hand, researchers, in most cases, can be held in contempt of court if they fail to produce the subpoenaed materials. Still, investigators can take several possible steps to safeguard their reputations for being reliable concerning confidentiality.

First, as mentioned in Chapter 6, researchers may obtain a *Federal Certificate of Confidentiality.* Under provisions set forth as conditions of award, investigators cannot be forced to reveal notes, names, or pertinent information in court. Unfortunately, few of the many thousands of researchers who apply are awarded a Federal Certificate of Confidentiality.

A second tack, which is more effective, is to avoid keeping identifying records and lists any longer than is absolutely necessary. Although this may not prevent the courts from issuing a subpoena and verbally questioning investigators, the likelihood of this occurring is reduced in the absence of written records. In the mid-1980s, a court case resulted in a federal judge ruling in favor of a sociologist's right to protect subjects by refusing to release his field notes to a grand jury investigating a suspicious fire at a restaurant where he worked and conducted covert research (Fried, 1984; see discussion of the Brajuha case in Chapter 6). This case, however, has yet to result in significant changes in judicial attitudes about the nature of research and field notes. Certainly, the potential for legal problems is likely to persist for some time.

Because of the various precedents and differing state statutes, speculating or generalizing about how a particular case may be resolved is impossible (see Boruch & Cecil, 1979; Carroll & Knerr, 1977). Even if researchers choose to risk imprisonment for contempt, the fact that there exists a moral obligation to maintain their promise of confidentiality to the best of their ability should be apparent.

SECURING THE DATA

Although court-related disclosures provide particularly difficult problems, they are rare cases. A more likely—as well as more controllable—form of disclosure comes from careless or clumsy handling of records and data. In other words, researchers must take intentional precautions to ensure that information does not accidentally fall into the wrong hands or become public.

Researchers frequently invent what they believe are unique strategies to secure pieces of research information. More often than not, though, these innovations simply represent attempts to separate names or other identifiers from the data. Regardless of whether you store data in multiple locations or place them in metal boxes inside locked closets or a locked desk drawer, precautions against accidental disclosure must be taken.

Precautions should also be taken to ensure that research-related information is not carelessly discussed. Toward this end, signing a *statement of confidentiality* is common for each member of a research team. This is sometimes referred to as a *personnel agreement for maintaining confidentiality* (see Figure 3.2). These statements typically indicate the sensitive nature of the research and offer a promise not to talk to anybody about information obtained during the study.

Although a signed statement of confidentiality may not stand up in court if an investigator is subpoenaed, it does provide at least some assurance that personnel on the research team will not indiscriminately discuss the study.

OBJECTIVITY AND CAREFUL RESEARCH DESIGN

Although you may take an assortment of complicated measures to ensure confidentiality, perhaps the most effective strategy is to think through the project carefully during the design stage. Slovak (1983, pp. 458–459), for

FIGURE 3.2 Personnel Agreement for Maintaining Confidentiality

---

This form is intended to further ensure confidentiality of data obtained during the course of the study entitled "Drinking by American College Students During Social Gatherings." All parties employed in this research will be asked to read the following statement and sign their names indicating they agree to comply.

> I hereby affirm that I will not reveal or in any manner disclose information obtained during the course of this study. I agree to discuss material directly related to this study only with other members of the research team. In any reports, papers, or published materials I write, I agree to remove obvious identifiers.

Name: _____

Signature: _____

Project Director's Signature: _____

---

example, details how a student once approached him about conducting a study of the effects of television violence on children. As Slovak reports, this is an interesting and potentially important research topic. The student was encouraged to develop a research design, which she did. Her plan was to select a sample of children and then randomly assign them to either an experimental or control group. Next, the experimental group was to be given the treatment of watching a selection of violent cartoons, while the control group would watch nonviolent cartoons. Following this treatment, the children were to be observed during play and assessed on the basis of whether they played aggressively or passively. The hypothetical premise was that the experimental group would play more aggressively than the control group.

Slovak (1983, p. 459) points out that although the student's design was essentially feasible technically, it was ethically unacceptable. His explanation follows:

> *Let's presume, for the sake of argument, that my student's hypothesis was correct—that watching violence did lead to aggressive behavior among children. Were that the case generally, it should also hold among the particular children she planned to study. In that event, the latent function of her project would*

have been nothing less than to "cause" an experimental group of children to be aggressive.

One might speculate that even if aggression were aroused in the experimental group of children, its effects might be short lived. However, even the short-lived aggressive behavior might have some lasting harmful effects on some of these children. As previously discussed, although researchers certainly do have a professional responsibility to search for knowledge, they also have an ethical responsibility to avoid exposing subjects to potential harm. Assessing long-range consequences of social research participation, although highly problematic, is nonetheless necessary.

Nurse researchers may have additional ethical problems because some of their research overlaps into the biomedical realm. Polit and Hungler (1993, pp. 354–345), for example, outline a number of research problems and potential ethical dilemmas that each may involve. Two of these sample problems are shown below (Polit & Hungler, 1993, p. 354):

Research Problem: *How empathic are nurses in their treatment of patients in intensive care units?*

Ethical Dilemma: *Ethical research generally involves having subjects be fully cognizant of their participation in a study. Yet if the researcher informs the nurses serving as subjects that their treatment of patients will be observed, will their behavior be "normal"? If the nurses' behavior is distorted because of the known presence of observers, the value of the study would be undermined.*

Research Problem: *Does a new medication prolong life in cancer patients?*

Ethical Dilemma: *The best way to test the effectiveness of interventions is to administer the intervention to some subjects but withhold it from others to see if differences between groups emerge. If the intervention is untested (e.g., a new drug), however, the group receiving the intervention may be exposed to potentially hazardous side effects. On the other hand, the group not receiving the drug may be denied a beneficial treatment.*

As these examples suggest, some research situations place the researcher in an ethical bind. On the one hand, researchers want to advance scientific knowledge and understanding in the most rigorous manner possible. On the other hand, they must be careful not to violate the rights of subjects or to place them in harm's way.

Even if researchers can protect subjects from harm during the course of research, they must also consider what happens thereafter as a direct result of the research. Particularly when conducting policy-laden research on various drug or crime-involved subjects, what investigators learn from these subjects may change the subjects' lives—and not necessarily for the better.

Disseminating results that provide law enforcement agencies with improved techniques for interception could be construed as causing harm to the subjects (Lakoff, 1971).

In addition to deciding against a given project during the design stage, researchers may consider possible ways of protecting the interests of subjects both during and following the actual study. By carefully considering possible harm to subjects in advance, researchers can sometimes avoid personal embarrassment and breaches of confidentiality.

The practice of researchers ensuring confidentiality in order to obtain the cooperation of subjects is likely to continue. It is quite important, therefore, that novice researchers recognize the potential tension between what might be called *academic freedom* and enforcement of the laws of the land. As Hofmann (1972) points out, social scientists must be responsible—and accountable—for their actions. With this firmly in mind, researchers ultimately may continue to question whether their ethical practices are justified by their ends. The ethical justification of research must be considered situationally, case by case.

TRYING IT OUT

You have been asked to sit on an institutional review board to consider a professor's planned research project. The summary for this project follows:

> *My proposed research will involve an ethnographic study of interactions among workers and inhabitants in a shelter for the homeless. I propose to enter the setting under the cover of being a homeless person myself. I will covertly take notes and systematically alter all names and identifying titles. I plan to examine interactions among the shelter workers as well as among the residents of the shelter. Naturally, I will augment my observations with numerous informal interviews with subjects.*

After reading the preceding summary proposal, answer the following questions:

1. What are some of the important ethical concerns to consider regarding this proposed research project?
2. If you were the researcher, how might you justify conducting a covert project of this sort?
3. How might a project be proposed that would likely provide similar information but would not require covert entry?
4. What safeguards should the researcher take to protect the subjects in the proposed project?

REFERENCES

Adler, P. A. (1985). *Wheeling and Dealing.* New York: Columbia University Press.

American Nurses' Association. (1975). *Human Rights Guidelines for Nurses in Clinical and Other Research.* Kansas City, MO: Author.

American Psychological Association. (1981). Ethical principles of psychologists. *American Psychologist 36,* 633–638.

American Psychological Association. (1984). *Ethical Principles in the Conduct of Research with Human Participants.* Washington, DC: American Psychological Association.

American Sociological Association. (1984). *Code of Ethics.* Washington, DC: American Sociological Association.

American Sociological Association. (1992, March). Code of ethics. *Footnotes 10,* 9–10.

Babbie, E. (1983). *The Practice of Social Research* (3rd ed.). Belmont, CA: Wadsworth Publishing.

Babbie, E. (1992). *The Practice of Social Research* (5th ed.). Belmont, CA: Wadsworth Publishing.

Barber, B. (1973). Prepared Statement to the House Subcommittee on Health Hearing, Protection of Human Subjects Acts. Congress, Washington, DC.

Becker, H. S. (1963). *Outsiders: Studies in the Sociology of Deviance.* New York: Free Press.

Berg, B. L., Austin, W. T., & Zuern, G. A. (1992, March). *Institutional review boards: Who, what, where, and why?* Paper presented at the annual meeting of the Academy of Criminal Justice Sciences, Pittsburgh.

Berger, R. L. (1990). Nazi science: The Dachau hypothermia experiments. *New England Journal of Medicine 322*(20), 1435–1440.

Bogdan, R., & Biklen, S. K. (1992). *Qualitative Research for Education* (2nd ed.). Boston: Allyn and Bacon.

Boruch, R. F., & Cecil, J. (1979). *Assuring the Confidentiality of Social Research Data.* Philadelphia: University of Pennsylvania Press.

Bower, R. T., & Gasparis, P. (1978). *Ethics in Social Research.* New York: Praeger.

Brajuha, M., & Hallowell, L. (1986). Legal intrusion and the politics of fieldwork. *Urban Life 14*(4), 454–478.

Brandt, A. M. (1978, December). Racism and research: The case of the Tuskegee syphilis study. *Hasting Center Report,* 21–29.

Burns, N., & Grove, S. (1993). *The Practice of Nursing Research* (2nd ed.). Philadelphia: W. B. Saunders.

Burstein, A. G. (1987, February). The virtue machine. *American Psychologist,* 199–202.

Carey, J. T. (1972). Problems of access and risk in observing drug scenes. In J. D. Douglas (Ed.), *Research on Deviance.* New York: Random House.

Carroll, J. D., & Knerr, C. (1977, January 6). *The confidentiality of research sources and data.* Testimony presented to the Privacy Protection Study Commission. Washington, DC.

Cassell, J. (1978). Risk and benefit to subjects of fieldwork. *American Sociologist 13,* 134–143.

Chadwick, B. A., Bahr, H. M., & Albrecht, S. L. (1984). *Social Science Research Methods.* Englewood Cliffs, NJ: Prentice Hall.

Department of Health and Human Services. (1989). Code of Federal Regulations (45 CFR 46). *Protection of Human Subjects*. Washington, DC: National Institutes of Health, Office for Protection from Research Risks.

Department of Health, Education, and Welfare. (1978a). *Report and Recommendations on Institutional Review Boards* (Pub. no. [05] 78-008). Washington, DC: Author.

Department of Health, Education, and Welfare. (1978b). *Belmont Report* (Pub. no. [05] 78-0012). Washington, DC: Author.

Deschenes, L. P., & Vogel, R. E. (1995). *Ethical and practical issues in school-based research: A case study of active consent.* Paper presented at the annual meeting of the American Society of Criminology, Boston.

Ellickson, P. L., & Hawes, J. A. (1989). An assessment of active versus passive methods for obtaining parental consent. *Evaluation Review 13*(1), 45–55.

Federal Register. (1978, November 30). Protection of human subjects: Institutional review boards, 943 FR56174.

Federal Register. (1991, June 18). Federal policy for the protection of human subjects: Notices and rules (part II), FR Doc. 91-14257.

Fields, C. M. (1978, March 12). Universities fear impact of rules to protect research subjects. *Chronicle of Higher Education*, 5–6.

Fried, J. P. (1984, April 8). Judge protects waiter's notes on fire inquiry. *New York Times*, p. A47.

Gibbons, D. C. (1975). Unidentified research sites and fictitious names. *American Sociologist 10*, 32–36.

Gray, B. G. (1977). The functions of human subjects review committees. *American Journal of Psychiatry 134*, 907–909.

Hagan, F. E. (1993). *Research Methods in Criminal Justice and Criminology*. New York: Macmillan.

Hershey, N., & Miller, R. (1976). *Human Experimentation and the Law*. Germantown, MD: Aspen Systems.

Hessler, R. M. (1992). *Social Research Methods*. New York: West Publishing.

Hofmann, G. (1972). The quest for relevance: Some implications for social research. *ET AL. 3*, 50–57.

Holden, C. (1975). Privacy: Congressional efforts are coming to fruition. *Science 188*, 713–715.

Humphreys, L. (1970). *Tearoom Trade: Impersonal Sex in Public Places*. Chicago: Aldine.

Katz, J. (1972). *Experimentation with Human Beings*. New York: Russell Sage.

Kearney, K., et al. (1983). Sample bias resulting from a requirement for written parental consent. *Public Opinion Quarterly 47*, 96–102.

Kelman, H. C. (1967). The human use of human subjects: The problem of deception in social psychological experiments. *Psychological Bulletin 67*, 1–11.

Kelman, H. C. (1972). The rights of the subjects in social research: An analysis in terms of relative power and legitimacy. *American Psychologist 27*, 989–1015.

Lakoff, S. A. (1971). Knowledge, power, and democratic theory. *Annals 394*, 5–12.

Levine, R. J. (1986). Declaration of Helsinki. *Ethics and Regulations of Clinical Research* (2nd ed.). Baltimore: Urban and Schwarzenberg.

Liemohn, W. (1979). Research involving human subjects. *Research Quarterly 50*(2), 157–163.

Martin, D. C., Arnold, J. D., Zimmerman, T. F., & Richard, R. H. (1968). Human subjects in clinical research—A report on three studies. *New England Journal of Medicine 279*, 1426–1431.

McSkimming, M. J. (1996). *Gaming and gambling in tavern life*. Doctoral dissertation. Department of Criminology, Indiana University of Pennsylvania, Indiana, PA.

Meyer, R. E. (1977, August). Subjects' rights, freedom of inquiry, and the future of research in the addictions. *American Journal of Psychiatry 134*(8), 899–903.

Milgram, S. (1963). Behavioral study of obedience. *Journal of Abnormal and Social Psychology 67*, 371–378.

Morse, J. M. (1994). *Critical Issues in Qualitative Research Methods*. Thousand Oaks, CA: Sage.

Polit, D. F., & Hungler, B. P. (1993). *Essentials of Nursing Research* (3rd ed.). Philadelphia: J.B. Lippincott.

Polsky, N. (1969). *Hustlers, Beats, and Others*. New York: Doubleday.

Punch, M. (1994). Politics and ethics in qualitative research. In N. K. Denzin and Y. S. Lincoln (Eds.), *Handbook of Qualitative Research*. Beverly Hills, CA: Sage.

Rainwater, L., & Pittman, D. J. (1967). Ethical problems in studying a politically sensitive and deviant community. *Social Problems 14*, 357–365.

Severson, H., & D. Ary (1983). Sampling bias due to consent procedures with adolescents. *Addictive Behaviors 8*, 433–437.

Slovak, J. S. (1983). Ethical issues in studying TV violence. In E. Babbie (Ed.), *The Practice of Social Research* (3rd ed.). Belmont, CA: Wadsworth Publishing.

Smith, M. B. (1967). Conflicting values affecting behavioral research with children. *Children 14*, 53–58.

Sykes, G. M. (1967). Feeling our way: A report on a conference on ethical issues in the social sciences. *American Behavioral Scientist 10*, 8–11.

Taylor, R. B. (1994). *Research Methods in Criminal Justice*. New York: McGraw-Hill.

Tewksbury, R. (1990). Patrons of porn: Research notes on the clientele of adult bookstores. *Deviant Behavior 11*(3), 259–272.

Thompson, T. (1984). A comparison of methods of increasing parental consent rates in social research. *Public Opinion Quarterly 48*, 779–787.

Wax, M. L. (1977). On fieldworkers and those exposed to fieldwork: Federal regulations and moral issues. *Human Organizations 36*(3), 321–327.

Wexler, S. (1990). Ethical obligations and social research. In K. L. Kempf (Ed.), *Measurement Issues in Criminology* (pp. 78–107). New York: Springer-Verlag.

A DRAMATURGICAL LOOK
AT INTERVIEWING

USUALLY *INTERVIEW* IS DEFINED simply as conversation with a purpose. Specifically, the purpose is to gather information. This standard definition of interviewing has been discussed in this manner by Denzin (1978), Spradley (1979), Patton (1980), De Santis (1980), Lincoln and Guba (1985), Salkind (1991), Frankfort-Nachmias and Nachmias (1996), Babbie (1992), and Leedy (1993).

Unfortunately, the consensus on how to conduct an interview is not nearly as high. Interviewing and training manuals vary from long lists of specific *do's* and *don'ts* to lengthy, abstract, pseudotheoretical discussions on empathy, intuition, and motivation. The extensive literature on interviewing contains numerous descriptions of the interviewing process. In some cases, being a good interviewer is described as an innate ability or quality possessed by only some people (and not by others). Interviewing, from this perspective, has been described as an art rather than a skill or a science. In other cases, interviewing has been described as a game in which the respondents receive intrinsic rewards (Holmstrom, cited in Manning, 1967). In still other instances, interviewing has been described as a technical skill you can learn in the same way you might learn to change a flat tire. In this case, the interviewer is like a laborer or a hired hand (Roth, 1966). In many sources, interviewing is described as some sort of face-to-face interaction, although exactly what distinguishes this type of interaction from others is often left to the imagination (Leedy, 1993; Salkind, 1991).

To be sure, there is some element of truth to each of the preceding characterizations. Certainly, anybody can be instructed in the basic orientations, strategies, procedures, and repertoire (to be discussed later in this chapter) of interviewing. Gorden (1992), for example, offers a clear, step-by-step description of how to go about the process of interviewing. To a large extent, Gorden (1992) and others offer the basic rules of the game. Furthermore, there is assuredly something extraordinary (if not unnatural) about a conversation in which one participant has an explicitly or implicitly scripted set of lines and the other participant does not. To judge any of these characterizations exclusively, however, seems somewhat inadequate. Just as some artists and actors are perceived by their peers to be exceptional while others in the field are viewed as mediocre, so can this assessment be made about interviewers. The previous characterizations have served little more than to circumscribe what might be termed the possible range of an interviewer's ability; they have not added appreciably to the depth of understanding about the process of interviewing or how you might go about mastering this process.

This chapter is devoted to the latter effort and draws upon the symbolic interactionist paradigm, the stream of symbolic interaction more commonly referred to as *dramaturgy*.

DRAMATURGY AND INTERVIEWING

This chapter attempts to illustrate dramaturgy's beneficial effects on interviewing beyond the interviewer training stage. Discussions will include types of interview structures, survey construction, the interviewer role, the roles of the interviewer (social roles played by the investigator), rapport, reactivity, and accessing difficult or sensitive material.[1]

Research, particularly field research, is sometimes divided into two separate phases—namely, getting in and analysis (Shaffir et al., 1980). *Getting in* is typically defined as various techniques and procedures intended to secure access to a setting, its participants, and knowledge about phenomena and activities being observed. *Analysis* makes sense of the information accessed during the getting-in phase. In consequence, any literal boundaries between these two phases may well be blurred—if they really exist—during the actual process of research.

Nonetheless, for the purposes of clarity, this chapter will reify the two phases and consider each in regard to interviewing as distinct. In the case of the former, this chapter addresses getting in as learning the ropes of various skills and techniques necessary for effective interviewing (Geer et al., 1968; Gorden, 1987; Lofland, 1976; Shaffir et al., 1980). Regarding the latter, as this chapter will show, there are a number of ways you may go about making sense out of accessed information.

This chapter explores the process of interviewing, specifically the notion of interviewing as an "encounter" (Goffman, 1967) or as a "face-to-face interactionary performance" (Babbie, 1983). All discussions of interviewing are guided by some model or image of the interview situation, and here interviewing is perceived as a "social performance" (Goffman, 1959) organized around the premise that interviewing is best accomplished if guided by a dramaturgical model (Burke, 1957, 1966).

Dramaturgy, as a theoretical perspective, involves the elements and language of theater, stagecraft, and stage management. This theoretical perspective derived in part from the symbolic interactionists' general assumption that humans perceive and interact in reality through the use of symbols. Drama, then, is a mode of symbolic action in which some individuals act symbolically for others who watch symbolically. In the case of the former, the term used to describe acting individuals is usually simply *actor*. In the case of the latter, the reference typically is *social audience* or simply *audience*.

The symbolic action that passes between actor and audience is called a *social performance* or a *performance*. In this chapter, the language of dramaturgy is applied metaphorically to a concrete situation—namely, the interview. More theoretical and detailed discussions of dramaturgy may be found in Burke, 1957, 1966; Goffman, 1959; Messenger et al., 1962; and more recently, Douglas, 1985; and Peshkin, 1988.

The dramaturgical orientation offered in this chapter is similar in some ways to what Douglas (1985) terms creative interviewing. Creative interviewing involves using a set of techniques to move past the mere words and sentences exchanged during the interview process. It includes creating an appropriate climate for informational exchanges and for mutual disclosures. This means that the interviewer will display his or her own feelings during the interview, as well as elicit those of the subject. However, the dramaturgical orientation presented here is also similar in many ways to what Holstein and Gubrium (1995) call active interviewing. From their perspective, the interview is not arbitrary or one-sided. Instead, the interview is viewed as a dynamic, meaning-making occasion where the actual circumstance of the meaning construction is important (Holstein & Gubrium, 1995). Where the proposed dramaturgical model differs most from the active interview is its emphasis on the interviewer *using* the constructed relationship of the interviewer and subject to draw out information from the subject. The various devices used by the dramaturgical interviewer, therefore, moves this orientation slightly closer to the creative interviewing model.

TYPES OF INTERVIEWS

No consideration of interviewing would be complete without at least some acknowledgment of the major interview structures. These are sometimes referred to as "the family of qualitative interviews" (Rubin & Rubin, 1995). Some sources mention only two—namely, formal and informal (Fitzgerald & Cox, 1987, pp. 101–102). Other sources refer to this research process as either structured or unstructured (Leedy, 1993; Fontana & Frey, 1994). However, at least three major categories may be identified (Babbie, 1995; Denzin, 1978; Gorden, 1987; Frankfort-Nachmias & Nachmias, 1996; Nieswiadomy, 1993):

the standardized (formal or structured) interview, the unstandardized (informal or non-directive) interview, and the semistandardized (guided-semistructured or focused) interview.

The Standardized Interview

The *standardized interview* uses a formally structured schedule of interview questions. The interviewers are required to ask subjects to respond to each question. The rationale here, of course, is to offer each subject approximately the same stimulus so that responses to the questions, ideally, will be comparable (Babbie, 1995). Researchers using this technique have fairly solid ideas about the things they want to uncover during the interview (Schwartz & Jacobs, 1979). In other words, researchers assume that the questions scheduled in their interview instruments are sufficiently comprehensive to elicit from subjects all (or nearly all) information relevant to the study's topic(s). They further assume that all the questions have been worded in a manner that allows subjects to understand clearly what they are being asked. Stated in slightly different terms, the wording of each question is equally meaningful to every subject. Finally, they assume that the meaning of each question is identical for every subject. These assumptions, however, remain chiefly "untested articles of faith" (Denzin, 1978, p. 114).

In sum, standardized interviews are designed to elicit information using a set of predetermined questions that are expected to elicit the subjects' thoughts, opinions, and attitudes about study-related issues. Standardized interviews thus operate from the perspective that one's thoughts are intricately related to one's actions. A typical standardized interview might look like this diet history (J. Berg, 1986):

1. When is the first time you eat or drink on a typical day?
2. What is the first thing you eat?
3. When is the next time you eat or drink?
4. What do you eat or drink?
5. When is the next time you eat or drink?
6. What do you eat or drink?
7. What else do you eat or drink on a typical day?
8. How many times a week do you eat eggs? Cheese? Milk? Fish? Beef? Pork? Beans? Corn? Grits? Bread? Cereal? Ice Cream? Fruits? Vegetables?
9. Which protein foods do you like best?
10. Which protein do you not eat?
11. What foods do you like to eat between meals?

The Unstandardized Interview

In contrast to the rigidity of standardized interviews, *unstandardized interviews* do not utilize schedules of questions. Naturally, unstandardized interviews operate from a different set of assumptions. First, interviewers begin with the assumption that they do not know in advance what all the necessary questions are. Consequently, they cannot predetermine fully a list of questions to ask. They also assume that not all subjects will necessarily find equal meaning in like-worded questions—in short, that subjects may possess different vocabularies.

In an unstandardized interview, interviewers must develop, adapt, and generate questions and follow-up probes appropriate to the given situation and the central purpose of the investigation. Schwartz and Jacobs (1979, p. 40) note that this results in appropriate and relevant questions arising from interactions during the interview itself.

Unstandardized interviews are sometimes used during the course of field research to augment field observations. Such unstructured interviews allow researchers to gain additional information about various phenomena they observe by asking questions of participants. This type of interview may also be useful for establishing rapport, what Douglas (1985) calls "chit chat." In some other instances, unstandardized interviews are useful when researchers are unfamiliar with respondents' life styles, religious or ethnic cultures or customs, and similar attributes.

The Semistandardized Interview

Located somewhere between the extremes of completely standardized and completely unstandardized interviewing structures is the *semistandardized interview*. This type of interview involves the implementation of a number of predetermined questions and/or special topics. These questions are typically asked of each interviewee in a systematic and consistent order, but the interviewers are allowed freedom to digress; that is, the interviewers are permitted (in fact expected) to probe far beyond the answers to their prepared and standardized questions.

Again, certain assumptions underlie this strategy. First, if questions are to be standardized, they must be formulated in words familiar to the people being interviewed (in the vocabularies of the subjects). Police officers, for example, do not speak about all categories of persons in a like manner. Special terms they use include "scrots" (derived from the word *scrotum*), used as a derogatory slur when describing an assortment of bad guys; "skinners," used to describe rapists; and "clouters," used to describe persons who break into automobiles to steal things. Questions used in a semistandardized interview can reflect an awareness that individuals understand the world in varying ways. Researchers thus approach the world from the subject's perspective. Researchers can accomplish this through unscheduled probes (described in greater detail in the following interview excerpt) that arise from the interview process itself.

One study of adolescents' involvement in alcohol, drugs, and crime (Carpenter et al., 1988) used, in part, a semistandardized interview schedule. Although many of the primary questions asked each of 100 subjects derived from the predetermined schedule, the youths' perceptions were often more fully elaborated after being asked an unscheduled probe. For example, while the schedule asked a number of questions about various drugs the subjects might have tried, following the subjects' lead in order to uncover fully their substance-use patterns, their beliefs about drugs, and the value they placed on using certain drugs was frequently necessary. An example of scheduled and unscheduled questions and probes from interview transcript number 116 illustrates this (Berg, 1982).[2]

Scheduled Questions
Interviewer: Have you ever tried angel dust?
Subject: Yes. Once.

Scheduled Probe
Interviewer: Tell me about that.
Subject: Oh, I was working at the Adam's Field Days [a local fair]. And, um, the way it was set up was, like we'd go in at 9 in the morning, and work till 5 p.m. And we would take an hour break. And then, set up again for the night. And when we took an hour break, two of the guys that I was working with, one's name was Bill and the other one's name was Tom, asked me if I wanted to go get high. And I said "yeh, sure." So we walked back to Tom's trailer and we rolled a couple of joints, and we smoked. And nothing happened. I didn't feel anything at all for a long time. And then we went back to work, and I was working in the booth, um, and all of the sudden, like, everything was going in and out of focus. And I thought, okay, this is creepy. I'm just, you know, super buzzed. But then people's faces started, started turning into prisms, um, and stuffed animals that we were giving away were like huge lions and tigers and 20-foot stuffed snakes, and they started coming real. They'd come toward me, and like the snake was slithering down on the walls and comin' toward me. And, um, ... [Response continues for another half page] [The next morning] I found out I had smoked Arizona weed laced with angel dust. So I never smoked with them [Bill and Tom] again. That was a really bad experience for me. . . .

Unscheduled Probe

Interviewer: Did you ever try angel dust intentionally?

Subject: No.

Unscheduled Probe

Interviewer: Would you have smoked the pot, if you had known it was laced?

Subject: No.

Unscheduled Probe

Interviewer: How come?

Subject: Too scared to. I'd be afraid, you know, like, something that happened would happen. And, you know, I've heard about people who've had bad trips off it. And I just, I was not up for a bad trip. So, you know, that's why I never done acid, any acid or anything. I don't think I'm ready to. I would like to, you know, do a hallucinogenic drug. I would like to do acid at least once, just to see what it's like, but, I'm too scared for it, right now. And I think with my mental state, that it would affect the high. And, you know, I could freak myself out really bad. So until I get myself into a state [of mind] where I'm sure that I want to do it, and I'm with somebody that I trust, you know at the time, 'cause I won't do it alone. . . . [response continues half page further].

Unscheduled Probe

Interviewer: How about if someone was to offer you some say, acid, free acid right now? Would you try it?

Subject: It has happened to me, and no, I did not try it.

THE INTERVIEW SCHEDULE

Traditionally, the term *survey* refers to both interviews and pencil-and-paper questionnaires. In this text, the term *survey*, unless otherwise indicated, is exclusively used in the context of interviewing. Typically, the choice to use an interviewing technique rather than a survey questionnaire technique is based on the selected procedure's ability to provide maximum opportunity for complete and accurate communication of ideas between the researcher and the respondent (Cannell & Kahn, 1968, p. 554). Among other things, this notion of accurate communication of ideas implies that researchers have clear ideas about the type of information they want to access and about the purpose and aims of their research.

The interview is an especially effective method of collecting information for certain types of research questions and, as noted earlier in this chapter, for addressing certain types of assumptions. Particularly when investigators are interested in understanding the perceptions of participants or learning how participants come to attach certain meanings to phenomena or events, interviewing provides a useful means of access. However, interviewing is only one of several ways researchers can obtain answers to research questions. The determination of which data-gathering technique to use is necessarily linked to the type of research question being asked.

For instance, Becker (1963) suggests that if you are interested in knowing how frequently a subject smokes marijuana (how many times daily, weekly, monthly, and so on), then you may effectively use a questionnaire survey, but if you are interested in the sensation of marijuana smoking (the emotion-laden sensory experience as perceived by the subject), a more effective means of obtaining this information might be an open-ended interview question.

A similar consideration is necessary when you determine what sort of structure an interview should have. For example, Rossman (1992) used semi-structured interviews in his examination of the development of Superfund community relations plans. (Superfunds are federal funds offered to assist communities in environmental clean-up activities.) Rossman (1992, p. 107) explains:

> *Because of the nature of the information collected, applied researchers who develop community relations plans are best advised to use interviews and interviewers. Questionnaires lack the flexibility that is required to capture the subtle character of risk definition, especially a risk that is often defined ambiguously within a community. Risks such as those associated with Superfund sites are a major part of the community's social structure, but are less crystallized than risk associated with crime, or even natural environmental risk.*

Conversely, Miller (1986) found that in her study of female street hustlers, an unstructured interview served her purposes best. Miller (1986, p. 26) writes:

> *Seventy women agreed to taped interviews with me during which they shared with me the details of their lives. Special attention was paid to the initiation of these women into street hustling and the development of a career as a street hustler. Although the same broad topics were introduced during each interview, many of my questions changed over time.*

Thus, when determining what type of interview format to use, you must consider the kinds of questions you want to ask and the sorts of answers you expect to be offered. This line of thought naturally leads to consideration of how to create questions and an interview schedule.

SCHEDULE DEVELOPMENT

The first step to interview schedule construction has already been implied: Specifically, researchers must determine the nature of their investigation and the objectives of their research. This determination provides the researchers with a starting point from which to begin developing a schedule of questions.

Selltiz et al. (1959), Spradley (1979), Patton (1980), and Polit and Hungler (1993) suggest that researchers begin with a kind of *outline*, listing all the broad categories they feel may be relevant to their study. This preliminary listing allows them to visualize the general format of the schedule. Next, researchers should develop sets of questions relevant to each of the outlined categories. For instance, the interview schedule for a study of volunteer police officers (Berg & Doerner, 1987) was developed by first listing general relevant areas gleaned from a reading of the literature. (See Chapter 2 on the spiraling nature of the research process.) These included:

1. Demographics
2. Police-related questions
3. Organizational memberships
4. Friends and family involved in police work
5. Personality style (passive, aggressive, authoritative, and so on)
6. Leisure activities

Following this, we generated separate lists of questions for each of the six major thematic categories. For instance, under demographics, we listed questions about birth date, level of education, marital status, and so forth. Under police-related questions we asked, "What would you say are the reasons you joined the reserve officers unit?" "How long have you been a reserve officer?" "Have you ever served as a regular police officer anywhere?" and so on. The purpose of these questions was to elicit information about how the subjects' relationships corresponded to various attitudes and behaviors described elsewhere in the interviews.

Question Order, Content, and Style

The specific ordering (sequencing), phrasing, level of language, limit to subject matter, and general style of questions depend on the educational and social level of the subjects as well as their ethnic or cultural traits, age, and so forth. Additionally, researchers must take into consideration the central aims and focuses of their studies.

In order to draw out the most complete story about various subjects or situations under investigation, four types or styles of questions must be included in the survey instrument: essential questions, extra questions, throw-away questions, and probing questions.

Essential Questions

Essential questions exclusively concern the central focus of the study. They may be placed together or scattered throughout the survey, but they are geared toward eliciting specific desired information. For example, Glassner and Berg (1980, 1984) sought to study drinking patterns in the Jewish community. Consequently, essential questions addressing this specific theme were sprinkled throughout our 144-structured-question survey instrument. For instance, among a series of questions about friends and people the family feels proud of, the following question was introduced: "Has anyone in the family ever thought anyone else drank too much?" Later during the interview, among general questions about ceremonial participation in the Jewish holiday of Passover, the interviewer systematically asked:

> *There is a question that we are a little curious about, because there seems to be some confusion on it. During the Passover story, there are seven or eight places it speaks about lifting a glass of wine. And there are three or four places which speak directly of drinking the wine. In some people's homes they drink a cup each time, and in some people's homes they count a sip as a cup. How is it done in your home?*

Another regularly scheduled question during this segment of the interview asked: "Another question that interests us is, what becomes of the cup of wine for Elijah [ceremonially poured for the Angel Elijah]?" Later, during a series of questions centering on Chanukkah observance styles, the interviewer asked: "What drinks are usually served during this time?"

Separating these essential questions, however, were numerous other essential questions addressing such other research concerns as ritual knowledge and involvement, religious organization membership, leisure activities, and so on. In addition, there were three other types of questions intended for other purposes.

Extra Questions

Extra questions are those questions roughly equivalent to certain essential ones but worded slightly differently. These are included in order to check on the reliability of responses (through examination of consistency in response sets) or to measure the possible influence a change of wording might have.

Throw-Away Questions

Frequently, you find throw-away questions toward the beginning of an interview schedule. *Throw-away questions* may be essential demographic questions or general questions used to develop rapport between interviewers and subjects. You may also find certain throw-aways sprinkled throughout a survey to set the interviewing pace or to allow a change in focus in the interview. Throw-away questions, as the term implies, are incidental or unnecessary for gathering the important information being examined in the study. Nonetheless, these throw-away questions may be invaluable for drawing out a complete story from a respondent.

On occasion, throw-away questions may serve the additional purpose of cooling out the subject (Becker, 1963; Goffman, 1967). On these occasions, a throw-away question (or a series of them) may be tossed into an interview whenever subjects indicate to the interviewers that a sensitive area has been entered. The interviewer offhandedly says something to the effect of, "Oh, by the way, before we go any further, I forgot to ask you . . ." By changing the line of questions, even for only a few moments, the interviewer moves away from the sensitive area and gives the interviewee a moment to cool out.

Probing Questions

Probing questions, or simply *probes,* provide interviewers with a way to draw out more complete stories from subjects. Probes frequently ask subjects to elaborate on what they have already answered in response to a given question—for example, "Could you tell me more about that?" "How long did you have that?" "What happened next?" "Who else has ever said that about you?" or simply, "How come?" Along similar lines, Lofland and Lofland (1984, p. 56) write:

> *In interview[s] . . . the emphasis is on obtaining narratives or accounts in the person's own terms. You want the character and contour of such accounts to be set by the interviewees or informants. You might have a general idea of the kinds of things that will compose the account but still be interested in what the interviewees provide on their own and the terms in which they do it. As the informants speak, you should be attentive to what is mentioned and also to what is not mentioned but which you feel might be important. If something has been mentioned about which you want to know more, you can ask, "You mentioned _____; could you tell me more about that?" For things not mentioned, you might ask, "Did _____?" or "Was _____ a consequence?"*

Often, interviewers incorporate a structured series of probes triggered by one or another type of response to some essential question. Probes, then, are intended to be largely neutral. Their central purpose is to elicit more information about whatever the respondent has already said in response to a question.

Question Wording

In order to acquire information while interviewing, researchers must word questions so that they will provide the necessary data. Thus, you must ask questions in such a manner as to motivate respondents to answer as completely and honestly as possible. As in the saying about computers, "garbage in, garbage out," so it is in interviewing. If the wrong questions are asked or if questions are asked in a manner that inhibits or prevents a respondent from answering fully, the interview will not be fruitful—garbage will come out. Denzin offers the following guidelines for formulating interview questions (Denzin, 1970, p. 129):

Questions should accurately convey meaning to the respondent; they should motivate him to become involved and to communicate clearly his attitudes and opinions; they should be clear enough so that the interviewer can easily convey meaning to the respondent; they should be precise enough to exactly convey what is expected of the respondent . . . ; any specific question should have as a goal the discerning of a response pattern that clearly fits the broad contents of the investigation . . . ; if questions raise the possibility of the respondent's lying or fabricating (which is always a possibility), care should be taken to include questions that catch him up, or reveal to him and the interviewer that his previous answers have been incorrect.

COMMUNICATING EFFECTIVELY

Perhaps the most serious problem with asking questions is how to be certain the intentions of the questions have been adequately communicated. Researchers must always be sure they have clearly communicated to the subjects what they want to know. The interviewers' language must be understandable to the subject; ideally, interviews must be conducted at the level or language of the respondents.

Becker and Geer (1957, pp. 28–29) note the seriousness of knowing the language of the interviewee both in order to ask understandable questions and to interpret correctly what the interviewee says in response. They state:

Although we speak one language and share in many ways in one culture, we cannot assume that we understand precisely what another person, speaking as a member of such a group, means by any particular word. In interviewing members of groups other than our own, then, we are in somewhat the same position as the anthropologist who must learn a primitive language, with the important difference that, as Icheiser has put it, we often do not understand that we do not understand and are thus likely to make errors in interpreting what is said to us.

When developing surveys that will be applied to a large and diverse general population, many researchers choose what may be termed the *zero order level of communications*. In such instances, the words and ideas conveyed by survey questions are simplified to the level of the least sophisticated of all potential respondents. Although this should tend to minimize potential communication problems with a range of respondents, it may also create some problems: The more sophisticated respondents may react negatively to questions asked in too simplistic a manner.

When you are investigating a homogeneous subculture, this problem becomes somewhat less critical. However, when interviewing a cross section of subjects on the same topic, you may need to consider varying levels of language.

Similarly, you must allow for special languages (both real and symbolic) that certain groups may use. For example, in the Glassner and Berg (1980, 1984) study, the interviewer needed to be moderately versed in Yiddish idioms in order both to conduct many of the interviews and to assist transcribers in accurately reproducing interview transcripts. In another instance, when Berg and Doerner (1987) conducted a study of volunteer police officers, the interviewer needed a general understanding of "cop speak," the jargonized symbolic language frequently used by police officers, illustrated earlier in this chapter.

More recently, Murray (1991) points out that serious problems may arise if researchers ignore dialect differences, sometimes termed *language codes* in linguistics. For example, the phrases used in Black English or Chicano Spanish are genuine modes of communication that may be lost on interviewers not versed in these dialects.

A FEW COMMON PROBLEMS
IN QUESTION FORMULATION

Several other problems arise when constructing interview questions. Among the more serious ones are affectively worded questions, double-barreled questions, and overly complex questions.

Affectively Worded Questions

Affective words arouse in most people some emotional response, usually negative. Although these questions may not be intended as antagonistic, they nonetheless can close down or inhibit interview subjects. For instance, the word *why*, in American culture, tends to produce in most people a negative response. One possible explanation has to do with the punitive connotation of this question, as in "Why did you do that wrong thing?" Consequently, when subjects mention some form of conduct or an attitude and are then asked by the interviewers, "Why?" they may not respond accurately or completely. On the other hand, if asked in response to these same statements, "How come?" they may offer complete responses in a relaxed manner.

Kinsey, Pomeroy, and Martin (1948) similarly found that when affective topics were considered, neutralizing the sense of the questions (reducing their affects) improved the likelihood of a full answer. They cite as an example asking subjects in a study of human sexuality, "Do you masturbate?" Virtually all the initial respondents answered immediately, "I never masturbate." Yet, when the question was reworded—"About how many times a week would you say you masturbate?"—suddenly many respondents were willing to offer responses. The second version of the question tends to neutralize or normalize the affect (sensitivity) of the question. Asking how often one masturbates implies that others do so as well, thereby reducing the affect of the word and concept *masturbate*.

The Double-Barreled Question

Among the more common problems that arise in constructing survey items is the double-barreled question. This type of question asks a subject to respond simultaneously to two issues in a single question. For instance, one might ask, "How many times have you smoked marijuana, or have you only tried cocaine?" It should be noticed that the two issues in this single question are slightly unrelated. In the first clause, the question asks the frequency of marijuana usage. The second clause confuses the issue and asks whether marijuana or cocaine have ever been used by the subject.

The logical solution to the double-barreled question, of course, is to separate the two issues and ask separate questions. Failure to separate the two issues may yield some answers, because people tend to be obliging during interviews and may answer almost anything they are asked, but analysis of a response to a double-barreled question is virtually impossible.

Complex Questions

The pattern of exchange that constitutes verbal communication in Western society involves more than listening. When one person is speaking, the other is listening, anticipating, and planning how to respond. Consequently, when researchers ask a long, involved question, the subjects may not really hear the question in its entirety. Their response, then, may be only to some small portion of a greater concern woven into the complex question. Thus, keeping questions brief and concise allows clear responses and more effective analysis of the answers.

Question Sequencing

The arrangement or ordering of questions in an interview may significantly affect the results. Interviews typically begin with mild, nonthreatening questions concerning demographic matters. These questions tend to be easy for the subjects to answer and allow interviewers to develop rapport through eye contact and general demeanor. As the interview conversation proceeds, more complex and sensitive questions may be introduced.

PRETESTING THE SCHEDULE

Once researchers have developed the instrument and are satisfied with the general wording and sequencing of questions, they must pretest the schedule. Ideally, this involves at least two steps. First, the schedule should be critically examined by other people familiar with the study's subject matter—technical experts, other researchers, or persons among the type to be studied. This first step facilitates the identification of poorly worded questions, questions with offensive or emotion-laden wording, or questions revealing the researchers' own biases, personal values, or blind spots.

The second step in pretesting before the instrument can be used in a real study involves several practice interviews to assess how effectively the interview will work and whether the type of information being sought will actually be obtained. Chadwick et al. (1984, p. 120) suggest five questions for assessing an instrument:

1. Has the researcher included all of the questions necessary to test the research hypothesis?
2. Do the questions elicit the types of response that were anticipated?
3. Is the language of the research instrument meaningful to the respondents?
4. Are there other problems with the questions, such as double meaning or multiple issues embedded in a single question?
5. Finally, does the interview guide, as developed, help to motivate respondents to participate in the study?

A careful pretest of the instrument, although time consuming in itself, usually saves enormous time and cost in the long run.

LONG VERSUS SHORT INTERVIEWS

Interviewing can be a very time-consuming, albeit valuable, data-gathering technique. It is also one that many uninitiated researchers do not fully understand. This is particularly true when considering the length of an interview. Many quantitative researchers who dabble at interviewing are convinced that interviews must be short, direct, and businesslike. Some who use interviews over the telephone even recommend keeping them to no more than about five minutes (Hagan, 1995). As a result, one issue surrounding interviews is exactly how long or short they should be.

There are several ways to answer this question, but all will immediately direct your attention back to the basic research question(s). If potential answers to research questions can be obtained by asking only a few questions, then the interview may be quite brief. If, on the other hand, the research question(s) are involved, or multi-layered, it may require a hundred or more questions. Length also depends upon the type of answers constructed between the interviewer and the subject. In some cases, where the conversation is flowing, a subject may provide rich, detailed, and lengthy answers to the question. In another situation, the subject may respond to the same question with a rather matter-of-fact, short, cryptic answer.

Obviously, the number of questions on the interview schedule is at least partially related to how long an interview is likely to take. On the average, an interview schedule with 165 questions is likely to take longer than one with only 50 questions. Yet, there are several misconceptions about long interviews that sometimes creep into research methods class lectures. For instance, some researchers believe that most subjects will refuse to engage in an interview once they know it may last for two or more hours. Others maintain that subjects may not remain interested during a long interview, and it will end in a withdrawal. Or, conversely, some researchers believe that short interviews do not provide any useful information. In fact, I am certain that such conditions do occasionally occur. However, they do not represent binding rules or even terribly viable guidelines.

Interviews, unlike written surveys, can be extremely rewarding and interesting situations for both the interviewer and the subject. Believing that subjects would quickly weary with a written survey containing 175 questions may be true. I for one believe such a situation is boring. However, talking with an interviewer about things that matter to the interviewee and doing so in a way that provides him or her with appropriate feedback often provides subjects with a kind of intangible yet intrinsic reward. For subjects to comment after a long interview that they did not actually realize so much time had already passed is common. I will liken this to reading a good book. At some time or another, most of us have begun reading some exciting or engaging novel, and not realized that hours had actually past. So it is with a well run long interview. Even after several hours, there is often a feeling that only minutes have passed.

Certain types of research lend themselves to longer interviews than others. For example, when one conducts a *life history*, the researcher is interested in the life events of those being interviewed (Rubin & Rubin, 1995). In this case, the interview may go on for a very long time, perhaps carrying over to several separate sessions on different days. On the other hand, the interview may involve some single topic, and require only a brief interview situation.

To suggest that all interviews must be lengthy if they are to yield useful information is not accurate. In 1989, Cal Larson and I conducted interviews in a maximum security prison among an assortment of inmates (Berg & Larson, 1989). Our research question involved an interest in the ways inmates perceived predetermined or fixed sentences—a flat length of time such as 5 years or 10 years—compared to their view of indeterminate sentences—a time range such as 5 to 10 years or 10 to 20 years. We were not interested in the family backgrounds or social experiences of inmates who committed particular categories of crime. We were not interested in determining explanations for why or how inmates committed their particular crimes, nor whether inmates received deals or plea bargains, or any of an assortment of other interesting but unconnected issues. We simply wanted to know about their views of determinant and indeterminant sentences and a number of related questions. As a result, we focused directly on these issues, and the interviews lasted an average of about 45 minutes.

What we learned, however, was very interesting and important information. First, that inmates seldom think about getting caught when they commit a crime. As a result, the idea of a particular crime carrying a long fixed sentence did not offer any deterrence to their committing the crime (Berg & Larson, 1989). Second, several armed robbers indicated that if they did become concerned about lengthy fixed sentences, they would likely leave no witnesses, whereas their previous criminal style was to avoid harming bystanders. In short, we learned that fixed sentences might have the unintended effect of increasing the level of violence associated with some crimes.

You should understand that length is a relative concept when conducting interviews. Some topics and subjects will produce long interviews while others will create short ones. What is important to remember is that simply because an interview contains many questions or only a few, this does not in itself immediately translate into a long or short interview.

CONDUCTING AN INTERVIEW: A NATURAL OR AN UNNATURAL COMMUNICATION?

Everyone actually receives some training and has experience in interviewing. Children, for example, commonly ask mom or dad questions whenever they see or experience something different, unusual, or unknown. In school, students ask questions of their teachers and respond to questions put to them by teachers. People regularly observe exchanges of questions and answers between teachers and other students, siblings and parents, employers and employees, and among friends. Thus, one might assume that since everyone has received tacit training in both asking questions (sending messages) and answering questions (receiving messages), the research interview is just another natural communication situation. But the research interview is *not* a natural communication exchange.

Beyond acquiring the ability to send and receive messages while growing up in society, people also learn how to avoid certain types of messages. Goffman (1967) has termed this sort of avoidance *evasion tactics*. Such tactics may involve a word, phrase, or gesture that expresses to another participant that no further discussion of a specific issue (or in a particular area) is desired. Conversely, people also usually acquire the ability to recognize these evasion tactics and, in a natural conversational exchange, to respect them. This sort of *deference ceremony* (Goffman, 1967, p. 77) expresses a kind of intrinsic respect for the other's avoidance rituals. In return, there is the unspoken expectation that this respect will be reciprocated in some later exchange.

As anyone who has ever conducted an interview already knows, this sort of deference ceremony simply cannot be permitted during the course of a research interview. In fact, the emergence of evasion tactics during the course of an interview is among the most serious obstacles to overcome—but overcome them you must! At the same time, you do not want to jeopardize the evolving definition of the situation, the potential rapport with the subject, or the amount of falsification and gloss a subject may feel compelled to use during the interview. As Gorden (1987, p. 70) suggests:

> *If all respondents said nothing, responded with truth, or said "I won't tell you!" the task of the interviewer would be much simpler. Unfortunately the respondent can avoid appearing uncooperative by responding voluminously with irrelevancies or misinformation, and this presents a challenge to the interviewer.*

In other words, the interviewer must maneuver around a subject's avoidance rituals in a manner that neither overtly violates social norms associated with communication exchanges nor causes the subject to lie. This can be accomplished through the dramaturgical interview.

THE DRAMATURGICAL INTERVIEW

There are a number of necessary terms and elements connected with understanding the dramaturgical interview and learning how to maneuver around communication-avoidance rituals. Central to these is the differentiation between the *interviewer's role* and the *roles an interviewer may perform*. As De Santis (1980, p. 77) suggests, the interviewer may be seen as "playing an occupational role," and "society can be expected to have some knowledge, accurate or inaccurate, about the norms which govern the role performance of various occupations." For instance, in our society, one might expect a farmer to wear jeans, not a fine three-piece suit, while working in the field. Similarly, one can expect certain things about appearance, manner, style, and language connected with other occupational roles, including that of an interviewer. For example, Maccoby and Maccoby (1968, p. 462) state:

> *What are some of the roles in which respondents may perceive an interviewer? Much depends, of course, on the auspices of the study and the setting of the interview. If the study has been sponsored by a prestigeful institution and covers topics on which the interviewer might be assumed to have expert knowledge, the interviewer may find himself placed in a role similar to that of the family doctor; he is consulted for advice on the respondent's problems.*

The implication of the preceding description of the role of an interviewer is that preconceived notions do exist among interviewees, but these notions are malleable. Since a subject's preconceptions about interviewers may be based on both correct and incorrect information, the actual conception of the interviewer role rests on the definition of the situation established during the course of the interview itself.

In a number of sources on interviewing, the interviewer's role is discussed in terms of *biasing effects*, or *reactivity* (Babbie, 1995; Chadwick et al., 1984). But the role of the interviewer is not necessarily established in granite, nor do the interviewer and interviewees operate within a vacuum! As Kahn and Cannell (1957, p. 62) suggest, "The role of the interviewer . . . is determined in part by the expectations of others." It is, therefore, within the capacity of an interviewer to affect (without biasing results) the notions, even preconceived ones, subjects may have about the interviewer's role.

Many roles are available to an interviewer. Regardless of any preconceived notion and expectation about the interviewer's role as perceived by the interviewee, it is possible (within certain limits) for the interviewer to shape, alter, and even create desired role images. Gorden (1987, p. 213) describes this as *role-taking*. He explains that "role-taking is a conscious selection, from among one's actual role repertory, of the role thought most appropriate to display to a particular respondent at the moment."

As explained in the next section, by changing roles, the interviewer can also effectively circumvent many of the avoidance tactics an interviewee might otherwise effectively use.

Interviewer Roles and Rapport

One dominant theme in the literature on interviewing centers on the interviewer's ability to develop *rapport* with an interview subject. Connected to the notion of rapport is the interviewee's expectations of the interviewer's role (in an occupational sense of the term *role*). It is often assumed that if the interviewer measures up to the interviewee's role expectations, the interviewer is awarded the prize of good rapport with the subject. If, on the other hand, the interviewer fails to measure up to these role expectations, the interviewer is turned away from the door (either literally or figuratively).

However, this simplistic assumption does not explain situations in which an interviewer did not entirely correspond to a subject's interviewer-role expectations but was nonetheless permitted to conduct an interview—for instance, when an interviewee says something to the effect of, "Oh, you're the interviewer; you're nothing like I thought you'd be!"

Much of the literature of interviewing, especially in relation to the concepts of reactivity and rapport, suggests that the interviewee's conception of the interviewer centers around aspects of appearance and demeanor. Overt, observable characteristics such as race, gender, ethnicity, style of dress, age, hairstyle, manner of speech, and general demeanor provide information used by an interviewee to confirm or deny expectations about what an interviewer ought to be like. The negative, reactive effects of an interviewer's observable social characteristics and personal attributes are extensively discussed in the literature on interviewing (see Burns & Grove, 1993; De Santis, 1980; Gorden 1975, 1980, 1987; Nieswiadomy, 1993; Patton, 1980). In each source, however, the emphasis is on the effect an interviewer's characteristics have on obtaining the interviewee's consent to participate in an interview. Another theme emphasized in the literature is the potential bias arising from the effects of the interviewer's attributes.

There is little question that, as Stone (1962, p. 88) states, "Basic to the communication of the interview meaning is the problem of appearance and mood. Clothes often tell more about the person than his conversation." Is it really sufficient merely to look the part? If a man dons an ermine cape and robe, places a gold crown on his head, attaches a perfectly sculpted crepe beard to his face, and regally struts about, is this a guarantee that he will perform *King Lear* in an adequate, let alone a convincing fashion? To be sure, the interviewer's appearance, accreditation, sponsorship, and characteristics are important to interviewing (see, for example, Benny et al., 1956). All of these, of course, are within the absolute control of the interviewer. Attributes of appearance are in many ways analogous to the old door-to-door vacuum-cleaner salesman's trick of placing a foot between the open door and its jamb—a trick that neither ensured a sale nor prevented the injury of the salesman's foot as the door was slammed shut.

Similarly, there are no guarantees that the interviewer will, simply by looking the part, be granted or afforded good and relaxed rapport. Furthermore, if an interviewer relies passively on appearance, credentials, and general social characteristics, there is still the very real danger that the interviewer will be unable to deal adequately with the role expectations perceived by the interviewee.

Even if an interviewer is attentive to differences in class, gender, society, and race, it is impossible to know in advance whether all these differences have been accounted for. Nor, for that matter, is it possible to know in advance whether various strategies undertaken by the interviewer will be interpreted correctly (as intended) by the interviewee. Rapport, like interviewer role development, must be actively sought and worked out.

For example, in the course of conducting a door-to-door canvass of a variety of neighborhoods, an interviewer found an interesting response to his presence.[3] The neighborhood he had entered had recently been subjected to a rash of daytime burglaries. As a result, neighborhood watch groups had formed, and all strangers in the neighborhood were immediately considered suspect. The interviewer knew this neighborhood was chiefly composed of middle-class Italian and Irish Catholic families. Knowing this, and following all the good literature on reactivity to differences, he had dressed accordingly in a dark suit with his hair trimmed and combed. He was carrying a dark briefcase containing a letter of introduction written on a local university's stationery and a photo identification card issued by the school. Nonetheless, because of the way the community had defined the presence of strangers, this interviewer met with an unusual reception. In spite of all of his credentials and appearance, he could not, merely by looking the part, break through the preconceived notions that had emerged in this community. He was treated as a criminal suspect.

Throughout the entire day, the interviewer failed to arrange even a single interview. At the sixteen homes he approached, only three times had people even acknowledged his presence by answering the doorbell. However, in at least six other homes, people were at home: He saw eyes peering out from behind curtained windows and he heard hushed voices and barking dogs being quieted by whispering owners.

From the three persons who did answer their doorbells (but who were careful to stay behind the safety of their locked doors), the interviewer learned what the problem was. Several evenings earlier, the neighborhood watch group had shown a film wherein criminals took on a variety of occupational roles in order to gain access to homes: The film included criminals impersonating door-to-door interviewers! Now things began to make sense, even if people recognized the interviewer's intended appearance as their expected image of a criminal impostor.

The interviewer realized he needed to assure the neighborhood that he was, in fact, who he claimed to be and posed no criminal threat. He sought a more acceptable stage than their front steps and recruited a convincing supporting cast to assist him.

Among the three people who were willing to speak with the interviewer was a man in his late fifties who the interviewer later learned was a family court judge. The judge suggested that the interviewer consider attending one of the neighborhood watch meetings "if you really are on the level." The interviewer took this cue as both a test of his legitimacy as a researcher/ interviewer and an opportunity to present himself in a more acceptable setting. The judge informed the interviewer that a watch meeting was planned for that evening. He offered the name and telephone number of the watch committee's chairperson. The judge also indicated that the interviewer could mention to the chairperson that he (the judge) had actually seen the letter of introduction in the interviewer's briefcase.

After calling and explaining the situation—and also carefully mentioning the judge by name several times as someone who had seen his credentials—the interviewer convinced the chairperson to mention the study that night. He told the interviewer, "I might mention that a study is going on in the area provided that you are in attendance this evening, and only if I can check out the story with your department at the university." The interviewer had certainly gotten his foot in the door but still had to make the sale. It remained to convince the neighborhood residents that he was who he claimed and, moreover, that they should take part in the study.

At the meeting that evening, the interviewer used every conversation with other attendees to explain the project he was working on. He was also careful to speak very loudly when talking with people who appeared to be important to the meeting (in order to be seen speaking with these individuals). These central characters included the three police officers attending and lecturing at the evening's meeting, a local city councilman credited with having spearheaded this watch group, the watch chairperson, his co-chairperson, and several people who were simply seated near the interviewer in the audience. Additionally, the interviewer persuaded the chairperson to call on him during the evening so that he could explain the project and offer his department's telephone number so that people could call and confirm his story for themselves.

All the interviewer's actions were intentional, had been carefully planned earlier that day, and were, in effect, fully scripted. Dramaturgically, however, the actual script used when speaking with central characters was less important than the image of the interviewer speaking with these reputable people. Although they didn't know it, these central characters became the interviewer's supporting cast. Merely by patiently listening to the interviewer, these characters supplied him with sufficient moral legitimacy for the audience to accept the interviewer for what he was—a real research interviewer.

The next day, the interviewer went to ten homes and was received by eight occupants, all of whom were willing to participate in the study (although only three matched the necessary demographics for the sample). Several individuals mentioned that they had seen the interviewer at the neighborhood watch meeting the previous night. Some specifically mentioned having seen the interviewer speaking with one of the central characters; they said that since these people felt it was all right to speak with him, the interviewer must be for real. The interviewer's performance at the watch meeting had indeed been successful—he had sold his vacuum cleaner.

It should be clear from the preceding illustration that while looking the part of an interviewer (in the occupational sense) is certainly necessary, playing the part (in the dramaturgical sense) is as, or perhaps more, important. This illustration also demonstrates how, as Douglas (1985) implies, the interviewer can serve as a determinant of what goes on.

Peshkin (1988, p. 51), reflecting on his research on school and community in the midwestern town of "Mansfield" (Peshkin, 1978) elaborates a similar use of a supporting cast:

Mr. Tate, Mansfield's beloved and charismatic superintendent of schools, arranged our transition from the high school to the community. He would introduce me to the mayor, for example, or to Mansfield High School's oldest living graduate and venerable ex-newspaper editor. Such people couldn't refuse Tate's request that they meet me; moreover, they were very curious to learn who I was and what I was doing.

Interviewers clearly can make effective use of elements and actors in the natural environment in order to develop working relationships with their subjects.

The Interviewer as a Self-Conscious Performer

The performance of the interviewer, as illustrated in the preceding anecdotes, is not at all haphazard. Actions, lines, roles, and routines must be carefully prepared and rehearsed in advance and thus constitute a *self-conscious performance.*

The literature on interviewing techniques often describes interviewers who react spontaneously to responses offered by interviewees in areas not scheduled on the interview instrument. Interviewers are described as using their insight and/or intuition to formulate the next question or probe almost instinctively. However, even though following up subject areas initiated by interviewees is important (even when the areas may not have been seen as relevant during the interview's design stage), the notion that interviewers respond spontaneously is faulty. The use of terms such as *intuition* likewise seems loose and inaccurate.

Goode and Hatt (1952, p. 186) voiced a similar concern more than 30 years ago. They stated: "This is an unfortunate term [intuition] since for many it possesses overtones of vagueness, subjectivity and even mysticism."

Perhaps a more accurate understanding of the meaning of interviewer's intuition is what Archer (1980) calls *social interpretations.* The process of social interpretation, although not fully understood, is nonetheless evidenced by convincing empirical research (see Archer & Akert, 1977, 1980). Even when interviewers are presented with a unique response by an interviewee, it is highly unlikely that a similar (spontaneously created) action or statement is required from the interviewers. In the majority of interview situations, even novice interviewers will use some version of social interpretation and draw on a response taken from their repertoire of tactics (discussed in detail in a following section). Lincoln and Guba (1985) have similarly mentioned the effects of tacit knowledge with regard to nonverbal cues relevant to communications between senders and receivers—in other words, subtly and often implicitly learned pieces of knowledge that trigger associations between actions and meanings.

More recently, Holstein and Gubrium (1995, p. 7) indicate that interviewers often have some preconceived notion about their subjects:

If only tacitly, there is always a model of the research subject *lurking behind persons placed in the role of interview respondent. Considering the epistemo-*

logical activity of the interview requires us to ask how inter-viewers relate to respondents, as imagined subjects, and to the conversations they have with those subjects.

Social Interpretations and the Interviewer

Social interpretations are defined as the affected messages transferred from one acting individual to another through nonverbal channels. These nonverbal channels include body gestures, facial grimaces, signs, symbols, and even some phonemic sounds such as tongue clicks, grunts, sighs, and similar visible indicators of communication (e.g., physical proximity between participant actors, their blocking, and so forth). As Gorden (1987, p. 75) suggests, interviewers must hear not only *what* the subjects say, but also *how* they say it.

Nonverbal channels include a variety of diverse elements. Each of these elements, taken individually, provides only a fragment of the information necessary for an accurate social interpretation. When rendered in combination, or as Archer and Akert (1980, p. 396) describe it, "in symphony," they provide sufficient cues and clues to convey clear messages and social meanings.

These nonverbal channels of communication, together with more obvious verbal channels, make up the conversational interaction situation or what has been called *full channel communication.*

Social interpretations are learned, not instinctive, and can be accurately made in a matter of seconds (Archer & Akert, 1977, 1980; Rosenfeld & Civikly, 1976; Rosenthal et al., 1979). Social interpretations are formed by observing the complex presentation of clues in real-life situations, from filmed versions of these interactions, or from still photographs in which even the nonverbal channels have been frozen in motionlessness as well as silence.

Throughout the interview process, the interviewer and the interviewee simultaneously send and receive messages on both nonverbal and verbal channels of communication. This exchange is in part a conscious social performance. Each participant is aware of the other's presence and intentionally says something and/or acts in certain ways for the other's benefit. However, to some extent, the interactions in an interview are also *unconscious*, which does not necessarily mean *unintended*. Unconscious behaviors should be understood as second-nature behaviors. An illustration of this sort of second-nature (automatic) interaction can often be observed when someone answers the telephone. The telephone voice is frequently almost melodic, even when only moments before the same voice may have been raised in angry shrieks directed toward a spouse or child. The social performance, of course, is for the benefit of whoever has just telephoned. Following the call, this individual's voice may again be raised in tones of anger—just as quickly and unconsciously.

Whenever interviewers realize they have trespassed on some unpleasant area of a respondent's life, or one the respondent does not want to talk about, it is not due to intuition or insight. This realization is derived from a social interpretation of the messages sent by the interviewee. The ways interviewers respond to these messages, however, will have a profound effect on the quality of the interview as a whole. For example, if interviewers ignore what they have interpreted as a very sensitive area and plunge ahead, they may force the respondent to lie, change the subject, not respond, or withdraw from the interview. If, on the other hand, interviewers do defer to the avoidance rituals used by the respondent, they may lose valuable information necessary to the study.

However, if an interviewer, in response to the clues, offers some demonstration that he or she has received the message and will at least to some extent respect the interviewee's desires, the interview will probably continue. It is also likely that the interviewer will be able to redirect the respondent back to this unpleasant area at a later point in the interview.

The use of social interpretations as described above certainly resembles Goffman's (1967) *deference ceremony*. There are, however, several critical distinctions, perhaps the most significant being that the deference is only temporary.

It has been suggested previously that throughout the performance, you as an interviewer must be conscious and reflective. You must carefully watch and interpret the performance of the subject. Your interpretations must be based on the cues, clues, and encoded messages offered by the interviewee. Included in the information these interactions supply may be the communication of a variety of moods, sentiments, role portrayals, and stylized routines, which represent the interviewee's script, line cues, blocking, and stage directions. You, the interviewer, then must play several other roles simultaneously with that of interviewer. You must participate as an actor but must serve as director and choreographer as well.

Interviewer as Actor

As an actor, you must perform your lines, routines, and movements appropriately. This means that in addition to reciting scripted lines (the interview questions), you must be aware of what the other actor (the interviewee) is doing throughout the interview. You must listen carefully to line cues in order to avoid stepping on the lines of the interviewee (interrupting before the subject has completely answered a question).

Interviewer as Director

At the same time as you are performing as an actor, you must also serve as director. In this capacity, you must be conscious of how you perform lines and move, as well as of the interviewee's performance. As an interviewer, you must reflect on each segment of the interview as if you were outside the performance as an observer. From this vantage point, you must assess the adequacy of your performance (for example, whether you are responding correctly to line cues from the interviewee and whether you are handling avoidance messages appropriately).

Interviewer as Choreographer

The various assessments made in the role of director involve a process similar to what Reik (1949) described as "listening with the third ear." By using what you have heard (in the broadest sense of this term) in a self-aware and reflective manner, you as interviewer manage to control the interview process. As a result, as choreographer, you can effectively block your own movements and gestures and script your own response lines.

From this dramaturgical perspective, you as interviewer do not respond to any communication, verbal or nonverbal, scheduled (on the interview) or initiated by the subject, by means of spontaneous intuition or innate insight. Instead, the entire interview performance is a self-conscious social performance. You and the interviewee are constantly in the process of performing and evaluating your own and each other's performance. Using these assessments, both participants are able to adjust scripts and movements in response to messages sent and received throughout the interview.

THE INTERVIEWER'S REPERTOIRE

Interviewers make adjustments throughout the interview consisting largely of switching from one role to another or altering their style of speech, manner, or set of lines. These devices comprise the interviewer's *repertoire*. Interviewers seldom genuinely improvise a spontaneous technique or strategy during the course of an actual interview. Certainly, a new technique would hardly be tried unless the repertoire of standard strategies had already been exhausted.

Preparation is a major guideline in interviewing. This is not to say that you should not actively pursue a topic initiated by the interviewee. However, even when interviewers pursue unplanned leads, they still can do it in a consistently scripted, rather than novel, fashion. At the very least, interviewers should be prepared with a series of scripted questions that may be triggered by virtually any possible topic area. These questions, very simply, include "Who with?" "Where?" "How come?" "How often?" "How many?" and a variety of similar questions relevant to the specifics of the study. In other words, during the design stages of the research, one must think about the possibility that unanticipated subject areas might arise. Consequently, even the unanticipated can be planned for!

For example, although one of the major foci in the Jewish drinking study conducted by Glassner and Berg (1980, 1984) was alcohol use, we were also interested in our subjects' possible involvement in other drugs. However, this interest was incidental, and we were thus only interested in drug use if the subjects raised the issue. For example, whenever a subject initiated a discussion connected with marijuana use, regardless of where in the structured interview it occurred, the interviewer pursued the topic through use of a series of systematically scripted questions. Following the completion of the question series, the interviewer returned to the place in the interview schedule from which he had digressed. The use of a consistent and systematic line of questions for even unanticipated areas is particularly important for reliability and for possible replication of a study. This is especially true when interviewing from a dramaturgical perspective. Since interviewers as actors, directors, and choreographers may not be able to provide future researchers with detailed descriptions of the various character portrayals, routines, and devices they used during individual interview performances, it is crucial that, at least, a comparable script exist.

The idea of interviewers possessing a repertoire of prepared lines, routines, and communication devices sometimes conjures up the image of a little black bag of dirty tricks. It should not. As suggested earlier in this chapter, the research interview is not a natural communication interaction. It is necessary when interviewing to remain in control of the interaction. Similarly, the interviewers' ability to move gracefully into and out of a variety of characterizations should not be seen as phony behavior. The characterizations are also components of the interviewers' repertoire, and they provide interviewers with the means of effectively conducting research interviews without violating social norms or injuring subjects.

An interviewer's ability to accurately read lines and cues offered by an interviewee and to play effectively to them is not some insincere ploy intended only to obtain desired information. Quite the contrary—if these were the only objectives, there would be no reason to vary roles and/or characters to adjust to the subject's responses. The various tactics and characterized roles used by dramaturgical interviewers allow interviewees to feel more comfortable. The performance is thus not a phony one. Zurcher (1983, p. 230) writes:

> *Why do we select a particular role for enactment? Why do we conform to some roles and modify or create others? What influences our choices or strategy for resolving role conflict or marginality? Why do we accept some identities and reject others? The circumstances of the social setting and the socialization process in which we find ourselves instrumentally affect the character of our role selections and enactments.*

Extending Zurcher's (1983) notions on role enactments, one can see that in many situations, character projections present effective opportunities to develop or increase rapport. For example, one rapport-building tool that can be used before beginning an interview is *chatting* (Berg & Glassner, 1979; Douglas, 1985). By briefly speaking with the subject on non-study-related issues, such as the weather, sports, family, cars, television, the movies, and so forth, the interviewer develops rapport with the interviewee even before the interview has begun.

As Goffman (1967) aptly states, the initial self-projection of the interviewers commits them to being what and who they purport to be. Thus, when interviewers identify themselves as such, namely, as research interviewers, they are committed to portraying a convincing characterization of this role. How they develop the character is variable and dependent on the other participant(s) in the interview performance.

As the interview unfolds from the initial encounter, various modifications, alterations, and adaptations used by the interviewer may be added to the initial projection of the interviewer's character. It is essential, of course, that these additions neither contradict nor ignore earlier character developments or the initial projection of self. Instead, these additions should be built on previous expressions of the interviewer's projected image.

For example, during the Glassner and Berg (1980, 1984) study, while arranging for initial interview appointments by telephone, I found it was important to amend my initial projection as simply an interviewer: I needed to express the fact that I was a *married* interviewer. I came to add this element intentionally to my character projection as a result of a number of line cues expressed to me by female potential interviewees. They usually asked what sex the interviewer was and then paused silently after learning that I was the interviewer. Many of these women then amended their character projections. Each explained that she would consent to the interview provided that her husband could be present. Picking up this line cue, I originally went into a well-rehearsed series of lines on the confidential nature of the interview and my concern that she be comfortable to speak freely throughout the interview. I carefully added that her husband could certainly be present but would have to refrain from answering any questions I put to her, at least until she had completed her own answers. Although this tended to work effectively (these women did conditionally consent to the interview), it was a long and somewhat involved script.[4]

Almost by accident, I discovered I could easily indicate that I was married. I accomplished this by simply pausing in my conversation with female interviewee prospects and asking my wife a question (usually having to do with booking an interview date). In most cases, I would carefully attempt to have the telephone pick up my wife's voice when she answered. In some cases, however, I put the questions to my wife when she was not even at home, and the performance was nonetheless effective in altering my character projection. Suddenly, I no longer posed any further threat to these female subjects (at least not on the basis of my possibly being an unmarried male).

My character amendment had not contradicted or ignored my original and initial role projection. I was still the interviewer, but I was now additionally known to be married. My performance did not trick the subjects into doing something they fundamentally did not want to do. Rather, the performance was a sincere attempt to reduce the potential interviewees' fears and anxieties—in short, to make them feel more comfortable with the idea of being interviewed.

Interviewer's Attitudes and Persuading a Subject

Attitudes toward the interview process strongly affect the quality of the resulting research. One interesting and fairly common assumption novice interviewers make is that subjects will not discuss certain topics with them. Interestingly, however, once subjects have been persuaded to participate in an interview, they often tell far more intimate details than the interviewers would ever want to know.

The problem actually involves getting novice interviewers over the first few nervous moments when they attempt to persuade potential subjects to take part in the research. Naturally, if everybody always happily participated in research projects, there would be no problem for novice interviewers. Unfortunately, people often resist or are skeptical and need to be convinced.

When they meet this sort of resistance, novice interviewers are often panic stricken. Nervousness is to be expected, especially if you are unprepared. On the other hand, countless interviewers have already encountered this situation and have developed a number of effective responses. Knowledge of these responses should both reassure novice interviewers and provide a means of persuading the majority of resistant individuals to take part in a research project.

Some individuals will not cooperate regardless of how persuasive one is or how they are approached. Backstrom and Hursh (1981) offer a variety of typical statements by skeptical potential subjects, along with sample responses. As they suggest, subjects tend to ask, "Why me and not someone else?" and insist, "I simply don't have the time." For example, a potential subject might ask, "Why [or how] was I picked?" The best answer is a simple and direct one: "You were chosen by chance according to a random selection procedure."

It is also sometimes necessary to convince subjects that what they have to say is important. For instance, a common response from a potential subject is, "Gee, I don't know too much about [whatever the subject is]; maybe you should interview someone else." Again, simplicity is the key: "It isn't what you know about [whatever the subject is], just what you think about it. I'm interested in your opinions."

If potential respondents insist that they simply have no time, researchers may be faced with a somewhat more difficult problem. Several strategies may be necessary. First, depending on the actual length of time required for the interview, they may volunteer to conduct it during late evening hours (if that is convenient for the subject). Or they may suggest conducting the interview in several segments, even during lunch breaks at the work site, if that is possible. Frequently, if interviewers simply indicate that they realize time is an important commodity and they really appreciate the sacrifice the potential subject will be making, some accommodation will be made. In the Glassner and Berg (1980, 1984) study, for example, interviews were conducted at the homes of individuals or in their offices, and periodically began as late as 11:30 at night or as early as 5:30 in the morning. In other words, it is important to be flexible.

Developing an Interviewer Repertoire

One final question that naturally arises is how neophyte interviewers develop their repertoires. People do not usually wake up one morning and suddenly decide, I'm going to run out and conduct research using interviews to collect my data! People also do not become expert interviewers immediately after reading books on interviewing. Interviewing requires practice. Whether first attempts at conducting interviews are called pilots, role-playing, pretests, practice interviews, mock interviews, or any other euphemism, they all reduce simply to doing interviews. Certainly, reading about how to interview, particularly ethnographic accounts, offers neophyte interviewers some necessary strategies and tactics. However, without actually conducting interviews, students cannot manage to develop appropriate repertoires.

Perhaps the most effective way to learn how to interview is by role-playing with more experienced interviewers. Although many sources on interviewing recommend role-play, few specify that at least one participant should be experienced. To have two inexperienced interviewers role-play with each other seems analogous to having two plumbers teach each other neurosurgery. It is particularly fruitless, furthermore, to have neophyte interviewers assume the role of interviewees. Although it would be impossible for even the most experienced interviewer to characterize all the different kinds of individuals and sorts of responses neophytes will encounter in the field, it is far less likely that other neophytes could perform the role of interviewee adequately. It is, however, possible for experienced interviewers to draw upon their actual past performances and to develop composite characterizations of different interviewee types. By working with these projected characterizations in the process of a mock interview, neophytes are afforded an opportunity to acquire various lines and routines necessary for maintaining control over the entire interview performance.

Taking the Show on the Road

After neophyte interviewers have become novices and have developed their repertoire, they are ready to play their role before an audience. Just as a musical show seldom opens on Broadway until it has played smaller cities such as Boston or New Haven, novice interviewers should also not run immediately into the field. Broadway productions take to the road in order to obtain feedback from critics and audiences. In a similar manner, novice interviewers must try out their performances in front of an audience of competent critics, who may include experienced interviewers and/or the kinds of people they may be interviewing for a given study.

This sort of taking to the road should allow interviewers to polish their performances. The most effective way to accomplish this is a dress rehearsal—that is, conducting an interview as if it were the real thing. Following this dress-rehearsal period, novice interviewers should be ready to enter the field.

The Ten Commandments of Interviewing

Borrowing an idea from Salkind (1991, p. 135), I have constructed the following ten points, or *ten commandments of interviewing*. I believe they nicely summarize the basic rules for conducting a decent interview. Better interviews will result only from practice and interviewer self-development.

1. *Never begin an interview cold.* Remember to spend several minutes chatting and making small talk with the subject. If you are in the subject's home, use what's there for this chatting. Look around the room and ask about such things as photographs, banners, books, and so forth. The idea here is to set the subject at ease and establish a warm and comfortable rapport.
2. *Remember your purpose.* You are conducting an interview in order to obtain information. Try to keep the subject on track, and if you are working with an interview schedule, always have a copy of it in front of you—even though you should have your questions memorized.
3. *Present a natural front.* Because your questions are memorized, you should be able to ask each one as if it had just popped into your head. Be relaxed, affirmative, and as natural as you can.
4. *Demonstrate aware hearing.* Be sure to offer the subjects appropriate nonverbal responses. If they describe something funny, smile. If they tell you something sad, look sad. If they say that something upset them, try to console them. Do not present yourself as uninterested or unaware.
5. *Think about appearance.* Be sure you have dressed appropriately for both the setting and the kind of subject you are working with. Generally, business attire is most appropriate. If you are interviewing children, a more casual appearance may be more effective. Remember to think about how you look to other people.

6. *Interview in a comfortable place.* Be sure that the location of the interview is somewhere the subject feels comfortable. If the subject is fearful about being overheard or being seen, your interview may be over before it ever starts.

7. *Don't be satisfied with monosyllabic answers.* Be aware when subjects begin giving yes-and-no answers. Answers like these will not offer much information during analysis. When this does occur, be sure to probe with questions such as, "Can you tell me a little bit more about that?" or "What else happened?" Even a simple pause and an *uncomfortable silence* might yield additional information.

8. *Be respectful.* Be sure the subject feels that he or she is an integral part of your research and that any answer he or she offers is absolutely wonderful. Often subjects will say things like, "You don't really want to know how I feel about that." Assure them that you really do!

9. *Practice, practice, and practice some more.* The only way to actually become proficient at interviewing is to interview. Although this book and other manuals can offer guidelines, it is up to you as a researcher to develop your own repertoire of actions. The best way to accomplish this task is to go out and do interviews.

10. *Be cordial and appreciative.* Remember to thank the subject when you finish, and answer any questions he or she might have about the research. Remember, you are always a research emissary. Other researchers may someday want to interview this subject or gain access to the setting you were in. If you mess things up through inappropriate actions, you may close the door for future researchers.

KNOW YOUR AUDIENCE

If you have ever attended the live performance of a pretty good comedian, you may have noticed that he or she seemed to know their audience. The comedian seemed to know how much *blue material* the audience wanted and would tolerate. He or she even may have used local names of people or places in the routine. In fact, in the case of really good comedians, he or she may even have incorporated certain local *insider* jokes during the course of the routine. All of these things were because the comedian had taken the time to prepare and get to know his or her audience.

When interviewing, it is likewise advisable to *know your audience*. In this case, however, it means understanding the group or groups from which you draw your subjects. During the past several years, I have worked with a number of Asian and Middle-Eastern graduate students. They are a constant reminder to me that it is very important to understand the culture of your research subjects. Often, the kinds of questions that we in the West take for granted create significant cultural dilemmas for certain groups.

For instance, one of my graduate students was developing a dissertation project to examine delinquency in Taiwan. The student, himself Chinese, began developing questions using information he found in the literature.

Among the original questions we discussed was what seemed to be a fairly innocuous one: "About how often do you date?" The student explained that he could not ask Chinese adolescents this question. I was a bit surprised, being somewhat ignorant about Chinese culture. He went on to explain that proper Chinese adolescents do not date as we Westerners think about dating. In other words, an adolescent boy and girl would never go off on their own to the movies, or roller skating, or any other traditional *date*. In fact, such an activity would be viewed by most proper adults as indecent since dating tends to have sexual connotations in Taiwan. Furthermore, it would be impolite to ask adolescents such a question. He also explained that this did not mean that Chinese adolescents did not have their own form of dating. This variation in dating might be called *group dating*. In this form, five or six male friends will meet five or six girls at a skating rink—not so much by chance as by design. Once there, the groups tend to pair off, but they would never describe this as *a date*.

The solution to this problem was to craft a question that asked whether the youths ever intentionally went to certain locations with friends of the same gender to meet with groups of friends of the opposite gender.

In another situation, one of my students from Jordan was interested in examining issues of delinquency among a population of incarcerated Jordanian youths. His study population included both male and female delinquents. Among the questions commonly asked, according to the literature he reviewed, pertained to sexual activity. He came to me quite upset. He explained that under Islamic law he simply could not discuss sexual activity with young girls. Not only would it be improper for him, and embarrassing to the girls, it might actually force these girls to lie if they were, in fact, sexually active. Ironically, we circumvented this problem by asking these girls about dating practices.

These examples suggest a very important issue that must not be underplayed. This issue is understanding the culture of the subjects you work with. It is of critical importance that when you develop interview schedules, the language as well as the nature of the questions remain inoffensive. In the ever-shrinking electronic world we currently live in, it is becoming more and more possible to conduct comparative research projects. As a result, many researchers are dealing with a wide variety of different and literally foreign cultures. It is critical, then, that you carefully plan out the types of questions you want to ask, and the types of individuals you use to conduct interviews in these situations. In short, know your audience before your performance!

Curtain Calls

In concluding this section on learning the ropes of dramaturgical interviewing, it is important to note that some individuals may never achieve the status of highly skilled interviewer. However, just as there are B-movie actors who make their entire careers by acting in dozens of low-budget films and never achieve stardom, so too can there be effective B-movie interviewers. Put simply, some individuals will be able to obtain sufficient information from an interview to conduct viable research, yet will always remain awkward or clumsy in their performance.

Other individuals will completely fail to conduct interviews successfully. These individuals fail to become even B-level interviewers not because of interpersonal limitations but because of their failure to achieve a self-aware performance. These individuals are unable to adapt their scripts and blocking in order to accommodate the interviewee while continuing to maintain effective control over the interview process.

ANALYZING DATA OBTAINED FROM THE DRAMATURGICAL INTERVIEW

When novice interviewers have mastered to some extent interviewing strategies and practices and have conducted a number of interviews, the next problem is how to organize all the data accumulated in the interviews. How should the interviewers proceed with the task of taking many hours of tape-recorded interviews, for example, and analyzing them? Janice Morse (1994, p. 23) observes that despite the proliferation of qualitative research methodology texts, the process of data analysis remains fairly poorly described.

Although analysis is without question the most difficult aspect of any qualitative research project, it is also the most creative. Because of the creative component, it is impossible to establish a complete step-by-step operational procedure that will consistently result in qualitative analysis. Unlike quantitative research, qualitative analysis does not lend itself to this sort of certainty. One cannot pull out numbers (operationally reduce responses) from the interviews and expect to plug them into a qualitative analysis computer program—none exists! For these reasons, the following points are intended more as recommendations, tips, and hints on how to organize interview data rather than as a specific, rigid guide. Although some of the suggestions may suit certain projects nicely, the analysis of data is primarily determined by the nature of the project and the various contingencies built in during the design stages.

It is important to note that while qualitative analysis is sometimes thought to lack the precision assumed to be present in quantitative research, this is not necessarily the case. Good qualitative research, like good quantitative research, is based on calculated strategies and methodological rigor. Insights obtained from qualitative research cannot only add texture to an analysis but also demonstrate meanings and understandings about problems and phenomena that would otherwise be unidentified. Qualitative analysis cannot be undertaken quickly, neatly, or lightly, but this should never be viewed as a liability or limitation. Instead, this characteristic of qualitative analysis is perhaps its greatest strength. When qualitative analysis is undertaken, certain priorities must be established, assumptions made during the design and data-collection phases must be clarified, and a particular research course must be set. Quantitative data are sometimes incorrectly leaf raked (particularly by computer programs) in order to find results, but qualitative analysis cannot be conducted in this manner.

From an interactionist position, interviews are essentially symbolic interactions. From the dramaturgical interview's perspective, these interactions can be described along the lines of performances. The social context of the interview, therefore, is intrinsic to understanding the data that were collected (Silverman, 1993).

Beginning an Analysis

Analysis of interview data cannot be completely straightforward or cut and dry, but it is still necessary to understand what to do when you reach this phase in the research. The most obvious way to analyze interview data is *content analysis.* Although you may certainly abstract reducible items from interview data in order to quantify them, your analysis immediately ceases to be qualitative. A comprehensive consideration of content analysis is the subject of Chapter 11. This section outlines how to organize and prepare for analyzing the data collected from depth interviews. In order to analyze data, you must first arrange them in some ordered fashion. In the next section, some suggestions about ordering data are offered.

Systematic Filing Systems

As Lofland and Lofland (1984) suggest, "First, and perhaps foremost is the establishment of some kind of filing system." By *filing,* Lofland and Lofland literally mean a physical (mechanical) means of maintaining and indexing coded data and sorting data into coded classifications. Files may involve placing material into boxes, file cabinets, or envelopes, or even on floppy disks. The obvious purpose of a filing system is to develop a means by which to access various aspects of the data easily, flexibly, and efficiently. Of course, the central issue is what should be filed. In Chapter 11, a related and comprehensive examination of what Strauss (1987) calls *open coding* is offered. In this chapter, however, it is assumed that each interview was recorded on tape and transcribed verbatim and is ready for a thorough reading and annotating of codable topics, themes, and issues.

To begin, you simply seek naturally occurring classes of things, persons, and events, and important characteristics of these items. In other words, you look for similarities and dissimilarities—patterns—in the data. But you must look for these patterns systematically!

Typically, a systematic indexing process begins as researchers set up several sheets of paper with major topics of interest listed separately. Below these major interest topics are usually several other subtopics or themes. For example, Glassner and Berg (1980) began analysis with 16 separate major thematic topic sheets, each containing from 2 to 13 minor topics or subthemes (Berg, 1983, p. 24). A total of 80 specific subthemes were consistently sought, coded, and annotated on interview transcripts.

Ideally, this process should be accomplished by two or more researchers/coders, independently reading and coding each of several transcripts. This process is intended to establish the various topics to be indexed in the filing system. Using two or more independent coders ensures that naturally arising categories are used rather than those a particular researcher might hope to locate—regardless of whether the categories really exist. The consequence of this process, if correctly executed, is a precise, reliable, and reproducible coding system.

These *index sheets* should contain some type of code identifying the transcript in which it has been located, the page number of the specific transcript, and a brief verbatim excerpt (no more than a sentence). Traditionally, codes used to identify transcripts are pseudonyms or case numbers (randomly assigned). A typical index sheet might look something like the one in Table 4.1.

As implied in the preceding example, every subtheme is annotated from each transcript. When more than one subtheme is mentioned in the same passage, it is nonetheless shown under each subtheme (see the entries for #6 under the headings *Beer* and *Wine*). Cross referencing in this fashion, although extremely time consuming during the coding stage, permits much easier location of particular items during the later stages of analysis.

When every interview transcript has been read and index sheets have been appropriately annotated, researchers should have a comprehensive means for accessing information. Additionally, the index sheets provide a means for counting certain types of responses in order to suggest magnitudes in response sets or for beginning content analysis of various specific themes.

TABLE 4.1 Alcohol Use [Major Topic/Theme]

SUBTHEMES		
Beer	**Wine**	**Hard Liquors**
#12, pp. 3–6: I only drink beer when I am with my . . .	#6, pp. 2–4: I love the taste of wine, but I hate beer.	#7, pp. 22–25: When I'm feeling real up, I'll have a drink.
#6, pp. 2–4: (see wine) #9, pp. 3–4: Whenever I am really warm, like in the summer, I'll have a beer.	#5, p. 8: I only drink wine during the ceremonies, you know, the religious ceremonies.	#5, p. 23: I almost never drink liquor, just that one I told you about.

Short-Answer Sheets

In addition to developing a comprehensive filing and indexing system, researchers may want to create a *quick response* or short-answer sheet to include in their files. Particularly when conducting standardized interviews, it is possible to complete brief responses for each of the questions asked as you read through and code each transcript. In essence, the questions become the interview schedule, and coders simply write short responses for each. Frequently this can be accomplished by reducing many of the responses to either affirmative (yes), negative (no), no clear response (unclear), or a very brief excerpt (no more than one sentence) including page reference.

Short-answer sheets are included primarily for convenience. They can be stored in separate files and/or with each interview transcript. They summarize many of the issues and topics contained in each transcript (for example, a respondent's income, age, gender, occupation, and so forth). Since answers for which more detail was provided have been captured and coded in the indexing sheet procedure, these short-answer sheets offer another type of cross-reference summary.

Analysis Procedures: A Concluding Remark

Stacy (1969) suggests that the collection of qualitative data is often so extensive that researchers can feel that their jobs must be complete when they have gathered it all in. This conclusion, of course, is far from accurate. As they listen to the interviewees, researchers frequently develop many interesting (and sometimes unreliable) impressions about possible patterns. After the interviews are completed, however, researchers must closely examine potential patterns to see what findings actually emerge directly from the data (Glaser & Strauss, 1967; Schatzman & Strauss, 1973). Such grounded findings, emerging from the data themselves, are frequently among the most interesting and important results obtained during research, even though they may have gone unnoticed during the data-collecting phase. Procedures used to identify these grounded concepts and patterns are discussed in greater detail in Chapter 6.

TRYING IT OUT

Naturally a certain amount of mental effort is required to learn the skills necessary for conducting effective interviews. These mental juices have been flowing as you read this chapter on interviewing. But, as previously mentioned, there is no substitute for practice. You will have to go out and conduct several interviews. There are many public places where you can practice interviewing. Consider, for example, conducting several unstructured interviews with people at your local public library, on a busy downtown street corner, or even while feeding pigeons in a public park.

You might also consider creating a brief semistructured instrument (either individually or as a class) on some timely issue. These instruments can then be used as practice schedules during interviews either among classmates or in public places. Some possible topics include how the threat of AIDS may have affected dating practices, whether all workers should be subject to urine analysis as a condition of employment, or whether elementary and secondary school teachers should be required to pass competency examinations as conditions of their retention in schools. Or simply select a topic from the headlines of the local newspaper. Remember, your purpose is to practice interviewing skills, not to derive actual scientific empirical research.

Good interviewers work on improving their listening skills. The better an interviewer hears what is being said by the subject, the more effectively he or she can play the interviewer role. Classrooms are excellent places to practice *aware hearing* techniques. In our culture, we have a tendency to interrupt speakers in order to interject our own views or comments. It is, in fact, quite difficult for novice interviewers to learn that they cannot say such things as, "Oh yeah, I did that once," or "Gee, that's really something, but have you ever tried . . . ," or similar interruptions. Remember, when interviewing, the ideal is to have the subject speaking 80 to 90 percent of the time. When interviewers take up too much of the conversation, little research information is gained.

It is likewise important to demonstrate to the subject that you are really listening—*aware listening*, as it may be called. This means you are not thinking about your next question or about how smart you can make yourself look with some comment—the usual style of natural conversational exchange.

Try the following in order to practice aware listening skills: The instructor pairs off all the students in the class. Each pair is positioned so that their seats are facing each other, but not too close together. The teacher arbitrarily assigns a listener and a speaker in each pair. Now the teacher asks each speaker to talk for 30 seconds on some mundane topic—for example, "my favorite color," "my favorite food," or "the best day in my life." The instructor times this exercise and, after 30 seconds have elapsed, calls out "Stop!" At this point, the *listener* repeats verbatim everything he or she heard. This includes using first person singular ("I" statements) if the original speaker used them.

Following this, the participants reverse roles. The original speaker becomes the listener and vice versa. The teacher again times a 30-second mundane-topic exchange. After this is complete, the time is increased to 60 seconds, and the teacher suggests a slightly more personal topic, such as "the most embarrassing thing that ever happened to me," "something I really like about myself," "something I would change about myself if I could," or "something I dislike about myself."

It is important to be sure you do not make any verbal statements, responses, or comments when in the role of the listener. You may make nonverbal gestures, such as a nod or use of eyes or eyebrows, to show appropriate response to statements.

When you have completed the exchanges, consider the following questions:

1. Did your body language change during the exchanges? For example, did you move closer or further apart? Did you cross or uncross your legs or arms?
2. Did the level of sound change at all when you went from the mundane question to the more revealing personal one?
3. Was there less (if any) giggling and movement during the more self-revealing questions as compared with the mundane questions?
4. Was it difficult to sit silently and concentrate on listening?

NOTES

1. Few accounts of the interviewing process directly make use of a dramaturgical mode. One notable exception is Douglas (1985), who uses dramaturgy to describe creative interviewing. Another exception is Denzin (1973, 1978), who applies several dramaturgical elements to his description of the interview situation. However, traditional descriptions of the interviewing process ignore, or at most make rudimentary use of, the notion of role-playing. The description of role-playing itself is usually isolated from the actual interviewing process and appears under such headings as "training interviewers" or "piloting surveys" (Benny & Hughes, 1956; Bingham & Moore, 1959; Denzin, 1970, 1973, 1978; Kahn & Cannell, 1957; Smith, 1975). Occasionally, more knowledgeable authors correctly identify Moreno (1977) as a major contributor to the development of role-playing as a means of training researchers and therapists. Yet these same sources

fail to recognize the benefit of role-playing and other dramaturgical elements beyond the interviewer-training stage.

2. This excerpt came from a series of scheduled questions asking respondents whether they had ever tried marijuana, hash, cocaine, angel dust, acid, and so forth. After identifying substances the subject had experienced, the interviewer reviewed each with several scheduled probes, such as "When was the first time you tried _____?" "When was the last time you tried _____?" "Who else was with you?" and several others.

3. The interviewer was attempting to develop a matched sample for a study of mania and depression being conducted by Dr. Barry Glassner of the department of sociology at Syracuse University.

4. Very few of the women actually had their husbands sit through any portion of the interview. In most cases, it seemed sufficient for their husbands to look over the interviewer and be present in the house.

REFERENCES

Archer, D. (1980). *Social Intelligence*. New York: Evans.

Archer, D., & Akert, R. M. (1977). Words and everything else: Verbal and nonverbal cues in social interpretation. *Journal of Personality and Social Psychiatry 35,* 443–449.

Archer, D., & Akert, R. M. (1980). The encoding of meaning: A test of three theories of social interaction. *Sociological Inquiry 50*(3-4), 393–419.

Babbie, E. (1992). *The Practice of Social Research* (6th ed). Belmont, CA: Wadsworth Publishing.

Babbie, E. (1995). *The Practice of Social Research* (7th ed.). Belmont, CA: Wadsworth Publishing.

Backstrom, C. H., & Hursh, G. D. (1981). *Survey Research*. New York: Wiley.

Becker, H. S. (1963). *Outsiders: Studies in the Sociology of Deviance*. New York: Free Press.

Becker, H. S., & Geer, B. (1957). Participant observation and interviewing: A comparison. *Human Organization 16,* 28–32.

Benny, M., & Hughes, E. C. (1956). Of sociology and the interview: Editorial preface. *American Journal of Sociology 62,* 137–142.

Benny, M., Riesman, D., & Star, S. (1956). Age and sex in the interview. *American Journal of Sociology 62,* 143–152.

Berg, B. L. (1982). *Adolescents involved in alcohol, drugs, and crime study*. Interview no. 65. Unpublished interview.

Berg, B. L. (1983). *Jewish identity: Subjective declarations or objective life styles*. Doctoral dissertation, Syracuse University.

Berg, B. L. (1986). Arbitrary arbitration: Diverting juveniles into the justice system. *Juvenile and Family Court Journal 37*(5), 31–41.

Berg, B. L., & Doerner, W. G. (1987, November). *Volunteer police officers: An unexamined aspect of police personnel*. Paper presented at the annual meeting of the American Society of Criminology, Montreal, PQ.

Berg, B. L., & Glassner, B. (1979). *Methodological strategies for a study of Jews and drinking.* Paper presented at the annual meeting of the American Sociological Association, Boston, MA.

Berg, B. L., & Larson, C. (1989). Inmates' perspectives on determinate and indeterminate sentencing. *Journal of Behavioral Science and the Law* 7(1), 127–137.

Berg, J. P. (1986). *Dietary protein intake: Compliance and knowledge in hemodialysis patients.* Master's thesis, University of Florida, Gainesville.

Bingham, W., & Moore, B. V. (1959). *How to Interview* (4th ed.). New York: Harper and Bros.

Burke, K. (1957). *The Philosophy of Literary Form: Studies in Symbolic Action.* New York: Vintage.

Burke, K. (1966). *Language as Symbolic Action: Essays on Life, Literature, and Method.* Berkeley: University of California Press.

Burns, N., & Grove, S. K. (1993). *The Practice of Nursing Research* (2nd ed.). Philadelphia: W. B. Saunders.

Cannell, C. F., & Kahn, R. L. (1968). Interviewing. In G. Lindzey & E. Aaronson (Eds.), *Handbook of Social Psychology* (Vol. 2, pp. 526–595). Reading, MA: Addison-Wesley.

Carpenter, C., Glassner, B., Johnson, B., & Loughlin, J. (1988). *Kids, Drugs, and Crime.* Lexington, MA: Lexington Books.

Chadwick, B. A., Bahr, H. M., & Albrecht, S. L. (1984). *Social Science Research Methods.* Englewood Cliffs, NJ: Prentice Hall.

De Santis, G. (1980). Interviewing as social interaction. *Qualitative Sociology* 2(3), 72–98.

Denzin, N. K. (1970). *Sociological Methods: A Sourcebook.* Chicago: Aldine.

Denzin, N. K. (1973). *The Research Act.* Chicago: Aldine.

Denzin, N. K. (1978). *The Research Act* (5th ed.). New York: McGraw-Hill.

Douglas, J. D. (1985). *Creative Interviewing.* Beverly Hills, CA: Sage.

Fitzgerald, J. D., & Cox, S. M. (1987). *Research Methods in Criminal Justice.* Chicago: Nelson-Hall.

Fontana, A., & Frey, J. H. (1994). Interviewing: The art of science. In N. K. Denzin & Y. S. Lincoln (Eds.), *Handbook of Qualitative Research.* Thousand Oaks, CA: Sage.

Frankfort-Nachmias, C., & Nachmias, D. (1996). *Research Methods in the Social Sciences* (5th ed.). New York: St. Martin's Press.

Geer, B., Haas, J., ViVona, C., Miller, S. J., Wood, C., & Becker, H. S. (1968). Learning the ropes: Situational learning in four occupational training programs. In I. Deutscher & E. Thompson (Eds.), *Among the People: Encounters with the Poor* (pp. 209–233). New York: Basic Books.

Glaser, B., & Strauss, A. (1967). *The Discovery of Grounded Theory: Strategies for Qualitative Research.* Chicago: Aldine.

Glassner, B., & Berg, B. L. (1980). How Jews avoid alcohol problems. *American Sociological Review* 45(1), 647–664.

Glassner, B., & Berg, B. L. (1984). Social locations and interpretations: How Jews define alcoholism. *Journal of Studies on Alcohol* 45(1), 16–25.

Goffman, E. (1959). *The Presentation of Self in Everyday Life.* Garden City, NY: Doubleday.

Goffman, E. (1967). *Interaction Ritual*. New York: Anchor Books.

Goode, W. J., & Hatt, P. K. (1952). *Methods in Social Research*. New York: McGraw-Hill.

Gorden, R. L. (1975). *Interviewing* (2nd ed.). Chicago: Dorsey Press.

Gorden, R. L. (1980). *Interviewing* (3rd ed.). Chicago: Dorsey Press.

Gorden, R. L. (1987). *Interviewing* (4th ed.). Chicago: Dorsey Press.

Gorden, R. L. (1992). *Basic Interviewing Skills*. Itasca, IL: F. E. Peacock Publishers.

Hagan, F. (1995). *Research Methods in Criminal Justice and Criminology* (4th ed.). New York: Macmillan.

Holstein, J. A., & Gubrium, J. F. (1995). *The Active Interview*. Thousand Oaks, CA: Sage.

Holstrom, E. I. (1967). *A talk on talk: Conversations and the interview.* Paper presented at the annual meeting of the Southern Sociological Meetings. Cited in Peter K. Manning, Problems of interpreting interview data, *Sociology and Social Research* 15 (1967), 302–316.

Kahn, R. L., & Cannell, C. F. (1957). *The Dynamics of Interviewing*. New York: Wiley.

Kinsey, A. C., Pomeroy, W. B., & Martin, C. E. (1948). *Sexual Behavior in the Human*. Philadelphia: W. B. Saunders.

Leedy, P. (1993). *Practical Research: Planning and Design* (5th ed.). New York: Macmillan.

Lincoln, Y. S., & Guba, E. G. (1985). *Naturalistic Inquiry*. Beverly Hills, CA: Sage.

Lofland, J. A. (1976). *Doing Social Life: The Qualitative Study of Human Interaction in Natural Settings*. New York: Wiley.

Lofland, J. A., & Lofland, L. H. (1984). *Analyzing Social Settings: A Guide to Qualitative Observation and Analysis*. Belmont, CA: Wadsworth Publishing.

Maccoby, E., & Maccoby, N. (1968). The interview: A tool of social science. In G. Lindzey & E. Aaronson, *Handbook of Social Psychology* (Vol. 2, pp. 459–470). Reading, MA: Addison-Wesley.

Manning, P. K. (1967). Problems of interpreting interview data. *Sociology and Social Research 15*, 302–316.

Messenger, S. L., Sampson, H., & Towne, R. D. (1962). Life as theater: Some notes on the dramaturgical approach to social reality. *Sociometry 25*(1), 988–110.

Miller, E. M. (1986). *Street Woman*. Philadelphia: Temple University Press.

Moreno, J. L. (1977). *Psychodrama* (Vol. 1). Beacon, NY: Beacon House.

Morse, J. M. (1994). *Critical Issues in Qualitative Research Methods*. Thousand Oaks, CA: Sage.

Murray, S. O. (1991). Ethnic differences in interpretive conventions and the reproduction of inequality in everyday life. *Symbolic Interaction 14*(2), 165–186.

Nachmias, C. F., & Nachmias, D. (1992). *Research Methods in the Social Sciences* (4th ed.). New York: St. Martin's Press.

Nieswiadomy, R. M. (1993). *Foundations of Nursing Research* (2nd ed.). Norwalk, CT: Appleton and Lange.

Patton, M. Q. (1980). *Qualitative Evaluation Methods*. Beverly Hills, CA: Sage.

Peshkin, A. (1978). *Growing Up American: Schooling and Survival of Communities*. Chicago: University of Chicago Press.

Peshkin, A. (1988). The researcher and subjectivity: Reflections on an ethnography of school and community. In G. Spindler (Ed.), *Doing the Ethnography of Schooling* (pp. 48–67). Prospect Heights, IL: Waveland Press.

Polit, D. F., & Hungler, B. P. (1993). *Essentials of Nursing Research*. Philadelphia: J. B. Lippincott.

Reik, T. (1949). *Listening with the Third Ear*. New York: Farrar, Straus.

Rosenfeld, L. B., & Civikly, J. M. (1976). *With Words Unspoken: The Nonverbal Experience*. New York: Holt, Rinehart, & Winston.

Rosenthal, R., Hall, J., Dimatteo, M. R., Rogers, P. L., & Archer, D. (1979). *Sensitivity to Nonverbal Communication: The PONS Test*. Baltimore, MD: Johns Hopkins University Press.

Rossman, E. J. (1992). The use of semistructured interviews in developing superfund community relations plans. *Sociological Practice Review 3*(2), 102–108.

Roth, J. (1966). Hired hand research. *The American Sociologist 1*, 190–196.

Rubin, H. J., & Rubin, I. S. (1995). *Qualitative Interviewing: The Art of Hearing Data*. Thousand Oaks, CA: Sage

Salkind, N. J. (1991). *Exploring Research*. New York: Macmillan.

Schatzman, L., & Strauss, A. (1973). *Field Research: Strategies for a Natural Sociology*. Englewood Cliffs, NJ: Prentice Hall.

Schwartz, H., & Jacobs, J. (1979). *Qualitative Sociology: A Method to the Madness*. New York: Free Press.

Selltiz, C., Jahoda, M., Deutsch, M., & Cook, S. W. (1959). *Research Methods in Social Relations*. New York: Holt, Rinehart & Winston.

Shaffir, W. B., Stebbins, R. A., & Turowetz, A. (1980). *Fieldwork Experience: Qualitative Approaches to Social Research*. New York: St. Martin's Press.

Silverman, D. (1993). *Interpreting Qualitative Data*. Thousand Oaks, CA: Sage.

Smith, H. W. (1975). *Strategies of Social Research*. Englewood Cliffs, NJ: Prentice Hall.

Spradley, J. P. (1979). *The Ethnographic Interview*. New York: Holt, Rinehart & Winston.

Stacy, M. (1969). *Methods of Social Research*. New York: Pergamon.

Stone, G. P. (1962). Appearance and the self. In A. Rose (Ed.), *Human Behavior and Social Processes*. Boston: Houghton Mifflin.

Strauss, A. L. (1987). *Qualitative Analysis for Social Scientists*. New York: Cambridge University Press.

Zurcher, L. A. (1983). *Social Roles*. Beverly Hills, CA: Sage.

FOCUS GROUP INTERVIEWING

WHAT ARE FOCUS GROUP INTERVIEWS?

The *focus group* may be defined as an interview style designed for small groups. Using this approach, researchers strive to learn through discussion about conscious, semiconscious, and unconscious psychological and socio-cultural characteristics and processes among various groups (Basch, 1987; Lengua et al., 1992). It is an attempt to learn about the biographies and life structures of group participants. To be more specific, focus group interviews are either guided or unguided discussions addressing a particular topic of interest or relevance to the group and the researcher.

A typical focus group session consists of a small number of participants under the guidance of a facilitator, usually called the *moderator*. Krueger (1994) suggests that for complex problems focus group size should be kept to no more than about seven participants.[1] Thus, larger groups of subjects may be divided into a series of smaller focus groups. The moderator's job, like the standard interviewer's, is to draw out information from the partici-pants regarding topics of importance to a given research investigation. The informal group discussion atmosphere of the focus group interview struc-ture is intended to encourage subjects to speak freely and completely about behaviors, attitudes, and opinions they possess.

Focus group interviews also provide a means for collecting qualitative data in some settings and situations where a one-shot collection is necessary. Although one-shot data collections usually are associated with survey ques-tionnaires, in some cases, focus group interviews may serve a similar pur-pose. Certain groups of interest to social scientists may remain available for study only for limited amounts of time. For example, say you are interested in studying battered women. You might decide that access to a sample of such women can be best obtained through a battered women's shelter. However, women typically remain in such shelters only for short periods of time, perhaps as little as a month. Now imagine there are 40 or 50 women residing in the shelter at any given time. While individual interviews might not be a practical strategy for data collection, considering the time that would be required to conduct that many interviews, focus group interviews might work well. You could easily hold four or five sessions during the course of a single week and collect necessary research information.

Along with more traditional populations, then, semitransient ones such as prisoners, hospital patients, students in special courses, migrant workers, parents at PTA meetings, and even conventioneers may be suitable for focus group interviews. Even the settings where these semitransient groups are found lend themselves to data-collection plans that are faster than traditional face-to-face interviews.

When focus groups are administered properly, they are extremely dynamic. Interactions among and between group members stimulate discussions in which one group member reacts to comments made by another. This group dynamism has been described as a "synergistic group effect" (Stewart & Shamdasani, 1990; Sussman et al., 1991). The resulting synergy allows one participant to draw from another or to *brainstorm* collectively with other members of the group. A far larger number of ideas, issues, topics, and even solutions to a problem can be generated through group discussion than through individual conversations. Indeed, it is this group energy that distinguishes focus group interviews from more conventional styles of one-on-one, face-to-face interviewing approaches.

By this time, some readers are asking themselves one central question about focus group interviews: If focus group interviews are so compelling, why haven't they been more widely used in the social sciences? The answer to this question requires a little background on how focus group interviews have evolved over the past 50 or so years.

THE EVOLUTION OF FOCUS GROUP INTERVIEWS

As a research technique, focus group interviews or discussions have existed since the beginning of World War II (Libresco, 1983; Merton, 1987; Morgan, 1989).[2] At that time, military psychologists and civilian consultants used group interviews to determine the effectiveness of radio programs designed to boost army morale. While social scientists did originally make active use of this technique, until recently it was more extensively used and developed by marketing researchers.

At the 1986 meeting of the American Association of Public Opinion Research (AAPOR), Robert K. Merton described his introduction to focus group interviewing (Merton, 1987). Merton explained that in November 1941, he was invited to dinner at the home of a colleague, Paul Lazarsfeld, who had just been asked by the Office of Facts and Figures—predecessor to the Office of War Information and later the Voice of America—to test responses to several radio morale programs.

Lazarsfeld invited Merton to attend a session and witness how audience responses were tested. Merton (1987, p. 552) explains his first reactions:

> *Do try to see it through my then naïve eyes and remember that your present sophistication is the legacy of almost half a century of evolving inquiry. I entered a radio studio for the first time, and there I see a smallish group—a dozen, or were there twenty?—seated in two or three rows. Paul and I take our places as observers at the side of the room as unobtrusively as we can; there is no one-way mirror or anything of that sort. These people are being asked to press a red button on their chairs when anything they hear on the recorded radio program evokes a negative response—irritation, anger, disbelief, boredom—and to press a green button when they have a positive response. . . . Thereafter, we observe one of Paul's assistants questioning the test-group—the audience—about their "reasons" for their recorded likes and dislikes.*

Merton was intrigued by this strategy for gathering information about people's attitudes. Lazarsfeld persuaded Merton to work with him on the radio response project (Merton, 1987). Later, Merton, with Patricia Kendall (1946), published an article in the *American Journal of Sociology* entitled "The Focused Interview." In 1956, Merton published a book by the same title (Merton, Fiske, & Kendall, 1956). He explained in his 1986 presentation that the book sold only a few thousand copies and quickly went out of print (Merton, 1987). And, in many ways, so did the technique of focused group interviews go out of print for many of the social sciences.

Focus group interviews found a home within the confines of marketing research. In fact, focus groups remain the predominant form of qualitative research for marketing researchers (e.g., Bartos, 1986; Hayes & Tathum, 1989; Moran, 1986; Morgan, 1989). Among most social scientists, however, little attention was paid to focus group interviewing as a technique until its reemergence during the 1980s. During the 1980s and early 1990s, focus group interviewing conducted in social scientific research was sometimes labeled *group interviewing*. Yet the basic elements, even of these group interviews, closely resemble the purpose and procedures of focus group interviews.

For example, Hochschild (1983) conducted group interviews among a sample of flight attendants in *The Managed Heart*, and Gubrium (1987) observes and questions members of an Alzheimer's support group in his *Old Timers and Alzheimer's*. Focus groups have been used to assess health beliefs among heart attack patients (Morgan & Spanish, 1983), to consider beliefs about causes and treatments of AIDS among Latina women (Flaskerund & Calvillo, 1991), and even notions about what constitutes an appropriate age for marriage in Thailand (Pramualratana et al., 1985). In 1990, Hanrahan reported on a multiple methods research study examining fear of crime among elderly women.

In the Hanrahan study, the strategy of focus group interviews is combined with the use of intensive interviews. The focus groups were conducted at three different senior citizens' centers in New Jersey. Hanrahan's (1990, pp. 164–167) focus group guide or schedule consisted of 10 central questions. These questions guided the women toward their possible concerns about personal safety and crime. They resulted in discussion of things like changes in their daily lives and activities they restricted or avoided because of perceived threats of crime.

Also in the 1980s, we find that the group interviewing strategy entered the feminist methods literature. For example, Callahan (1983) used group interviews to study attitudes concerning mobility among working-class women who became psychologists. Her nine-person group interviews are essentially the same as a standard focus group interview session.

Reinharz (1992, p. 223) reports that one of Callahan's (1983, p. 38) reasons for using focus group interviews was the influence of Oakley's (1981) notions about interviewing women and her

> belief that the women's participation and the flow of ideas and information would be enhanced by being able to listen to each other's experience and to interact with each other. . . . A group interview format facilitates women building on each other's ideas and augments the identification of patterns through their shared experience. (as quoted in Callahan)

During the 1990s, one begins to see what may be a reversal in the elitist attitude that focus group interviewing belongs to the somehow vulgar realm of marketing research. Instead, social scientists have begun regarding the approach with greater respect. Sussman and his associates (1991, p. 773) have gone so far as to state that "Focus group methodology is one of the most widely used qualitative research tools in the applied social sciences." Similar arguments have been offered by Basch (1987, 1989) and by Stewart and Shamdasani (1990). Clearly, there are some advantages to the use of this data-collecting orientation in certain situations. Likewise, and as is true with all data-collection technologies, there are some disadvantages. Let's consider both.

ADVANTAGES AND DISADVANTAGES
OF FOCUS GROUP INTERVIEWING

As a qualitative technique that has only recently reemerged in the social sciences, what does focus group interviewing offer that other, more traditional strategies may not? Like participant observations, focus group interviews allow the researcher to observe a process that is often of profound importance to qualitative investigations—namely, interaction. However, like traditional face-to-face interviews, focus group interviews also allow researchers to access the substantive content of verbally expressed views, opinions, experiences, and attitudes. Similar to certain aspects of unobtrusive data-collection strategies, such as solicited documents, focus groups provide a means for assessing intentionally created conversations about research topics or problems. Focus groups, like letters or diaries, also access fragments of a person's biography and life structure.

In effect, to assess benefits and limitations of focus group interviewing, we must actually compare it with several conventional qualitative data-collection approaches. The following sections illustrate such comparisons.

Focus Group Interviewing and Face-to-Face Interviewing

One important distinction between focus group and face-to-face interviewing is the ability to observe interactions about a discussion topic during the focus group session. Researchers can observe session participants interacting and sharing specific attitudes and experiences, and they can explore these issues. In truth, traditional interviewing styles permit a more detailed pursuit of content information than is possible in a focus group session. Traditional interviewing approaches, however, sacrifice the ability to observe interaction for greater amounts of detail on various attitudes, opinions, and experiences. As a consequence, researchers may never learn how subjects might have discussed these issues among themselves.

In many ways, it is the very give-and-take interactions characteristic of focus group interviews that lead to spontaneous responses from session participants. Hearing how one group member responds to another provides insights without disrupting underlying normative group assumptions. Meanings and answers arising during focus group interviews are socially constructed rather than individually created. Situations such as focus group interviews provide access to both actual and existentially meaningful or relevant interactional experiences. Such naturally arising glimpses into people's biographies are necessary for *interpretive interactionism* (Denzin, 1989).

Because interaction between group members largely replaces the usual interaction between interviewer and subject, greater emphasis is given to subjects' viewpoints. As with informal interviewing, focus groups can sometimes be undertaken without preconceived questions, focus questions, or guidelines (Morgan, 1989; Morgan & Spanish, 1984). This can effectively eliminate the researcher's perspective from the resultant data. Conversely, should we desire more guided responses, focus interviews, like individual ones, can be made more formal and structured.

Focus group sessions can even be phenomenological and provide a means for a sort of *bracketing* (Husserl, 1913; 1962, p. 86) of discussion topics. In bracketing, you hold some phenomenon up for close and careful inspection. It is removed from the natural world where it occurs and is then examined. This unmasks, defines, and determines the phenomenon's basic elements and essential structure. For example, you might examine a criminal episode such as a store robbery. In this case, you would consider all the activities of the robbery per se and bracket, or hold in exclusion, the social history of the robber, the victim, and other precursors that may have led to the episode. The phenomenon of the robbery itself becomes central.

Information from the focus group is treated as text or a document representing an instance of the phenomenon being studied. The phenomenon is not interpreted in terms of the standard meanings given to it by the scientific community. Those preconceived notions are isolated and held in abeyance by bracketing. Instead, multiple comments, stories, and descriptions that converge in shared experience during the focus group allow the phenomenon to be confronted, as much as possible, on its own terms. While individual interviews can also be phenomenological, this usually involves emergent informal interviews, not convergent experiences.

Another perceived benefit of focus group interviews is the belief by some that they are less expensive to conduct than individual interviews. This may be the case in some study situations, but is not an accurate blanket rule. Much will depend upon the way the investigator designed his or her study. (Design is discussed extensively in Chapter 2.) Certainly, if a researcher plans to pay subjects, hire a professional moderator, employ transcribers and coders, and purchase specialized equipment, costs could soar. On the other hand, costs could be low if the investigator conducted his or her own focus group interviews and did the data organization and analysis himself or herself.

Similarly, in face-to-face interviewing, costs largely depend upon how much of the works is done by "hired hands" (Roth, 1966) and how much by the researcher. Likewise, costs will be affected by whether or not subjects are paid for their involvement in the study.

A more relevant comparison between focus group interviewing and individual interviewing is time costs. As suggested above, focus group interviews can be undertaken among temporary or transient populations. This is because they require far less time than individual interviews do to involve the same number of participants. At the same time, of course, these focus group interviews will produce substantially less data than individual interviews. Fern (1982), in a controlled experiment, showed that group interviews did not produce significantly more or better ideas than an equivalent number of one-on-one interviews. In fact, Fern (1982) found that the group interviews produced only about 70 percent as many original ideas as the individual interviews (those not duplicated in either the real group or the one-on-one interviews).

More recently, Sussman et al. (1991) found that focus group data tended to make subjects' responses more extreme when compared to responses offered in survey questionnaires. Taken together with Fern's (1982) earlier work, this suggests that an interviewer must be willing to give up some degree of data precision in exchange for time savings.

Focus Group Interviewing and Participant Observation

When you are involved with participant observation, you are able to observe the naturally unfolding worlds of the population under study. This includes those times when several parties in the field come together to spontaneously hold a conversation, discussion, or argument. This natural evolution, of course, is not present in the artificially created situation of the focus group. Focus groups frequently contain members who might never have come together were it not for the creation of the group. Furthermore, the facilitator or moderator can control the assembly, alter the pace of discussions, change the direction of comments, interrupt or stop conversations, and so forth. Focus groups, then, like other forms of interviewing, are not truly natural conversations.

If you are interested in observing behaviors and meanings as they emerge in their natural setting, you may find that the simulated conversations of focus groups are insufficient. More traditional forms of participant observations and various sorts of field ethnography might prove more fruitful. However, if you are interested in collecting data on a large range of behaviors, a wide variety of interactions, and comprehensive and open discussions about certain topics or issues, focus group interviews work well.

For the most part, focus group interviews are further limited by the fact that the bulk of the behavior is verbal. During the group sessions, you should take notes on various behaviors and physical expressions of participants. However, these notes will represent only a small portion of the basic verbal data typically collected during a focus group interview.

Morgan (1989) suggests that focus groups are also useful when one investigates research areas that do not have dense sets of observations readily available. In effect, researchers tend to conduct participant observation studies in settings where there is something available to observe. Organizations and organizational structures, social roles among group members, normative values among deviants, and similar topics become typical fodder for participant observers. Topics like these seem especially well suited for the structure of participant observation. Yet topics of a more psychological, cognitive, or deep attitudinal nature seem less effectively studied through participant observation. Such topics could, however, be examined during focus group interviews.

Since both participant observation and focus groups seek to examine group interaction of some sort, there are many times and many topics in which either might be used. The decision you make when selecting one over the other, of course, is based on what you are willing to give up or trade off. You must be willing to trade off emergent observations in a natural setting for concentrated interactions in a short time frame. This is likely not the sort of decision that you will make strictly on the basis of financial and time costs. Largely, such decisions are made on the basis of the value placed on the advantages or disadvantages of each technique. Also, decisions will be affected by the research topic itself and the specific interests, values, background, and training of the investigator. Certainly, among many social scientists, focus group interviews remain tainted by their long-standing relationship with marketing research. This association may also have an impact on decisions about whether to use one technique over another.

Focus Group Interviewing and Unobtrusive Measures

One main advantage to unobtrusive measures is that, by definition, they do not require intrusion into the lives of participants by investigators. This is because most unobtrusive data have been created by people and left as either residue or erosion—but without the intention of leaving research data. Other data-collection strategies, including focus group interviews, are quite intentional and invasive.

In order to conduct focus group interviews, you must first locate some population from which to select participants. Next, you must contact potential participants and convince them that their participation is important and necessary. Finally, you must actually hold the focus group session. With most unobtrusive data strategies, no subjects need be involved during the actual course of the research. There are some types of unobtrusive data collection, however, in which subjects may be more actively involved than in others. For example, if researchers ask a group of individuals to intentionally create daily diaries, the lives of subjects have been intruded upon.

Unobtrusive data may include limited elements that provide insight into the cognitive or psychological lives of individuals. However, there is no interaction between subjects or between subject and investigator. Unlike focus groups, participant observation, or other forms of interviewing, unobtrusive strategies are passive rather than dynamic. If you are interested in examining how people have lived under certain circumstances or in specific settings, there may be a number of viable unobtrusive strategies available. Even if you wanted to know how people acted and their attitudes during some event or time, unobtrusive tactics could be used. But, by their very nature, unobtrusive data usually are historical. That is, information is created at one time but identified as data at some later time.

Recently, Reinharz (1992) described a computer group diary, a strategy that in some ways resembles an unobtrusive data strategy but is also akin to focus group interviewing. Reinharz (1992) tells how women graduate students in the department of sociology at Boston College established a computer-based group diary. The original intention of this activity was to allow students, anonymously and without fear of reprisal, to communicate incidents of sexism.

The diary text was open only to the contributors and provided a means for women both to express their own thoughts and to read the thoughts of others. Reinharz (1992, p. 222) provides a glimpse of the introduction to a document produced in the department as a result of this group diary:

Who is writing this?: The Graduate Women's Forum agreed last fall to develop a document which described incidents of sexism within the department. Women participating in its writing include virtually all the graduate women currently doing course work.

Working anonymously and individually, women began the report by entering on the computer our descriptions and comments about being women students in the department. In some cases, a woman would write about an experience of another woman who found it impossible to write about it herself; sometimes passages were written together by two women. The process of writing, reading, responding, and rewriting was simultaneously an individual and a collective task, both a spontaneous and a reflective effort. The report grew quickly away from its original circumscribed goal of citing individual sexist incidents. It became a collaborative work generated by the unexpressed breadth of our experience and analysis of sexism in the department, and by the unexpected synergy of writing with each other.

Kramer (1983, pp. 3–4) has specifically called for the combined use of group sessions and diary research. In this case, Kramer refers to consciousness-raising groups: "Numerous studies have utilized the small group and consciousness-raising group . . . for information gathering, yet few have utilized the methodology as a complement to diary research."

What the unobtrusive tactic of solicited diaries lacks in interaction can be adjusted through use of focus-group-like activities of a group diary. By sharing information, thoughts, and common problems and suggesting solutions one to the other, group diaries effectively become unguided focus groups. Their discourse, then, amounts to a similar synergistically created convergence of ideas and experiences. Such biographical information provides researchers with the structure of the writers' lives. Biographical experiences are culturally influenced and created. Every culture affects its members' self-perceptions and understanding about social roles, social institutions, and social structures.

Denzin (1989, p. 39) suggests that biographical experiences have effects at two levels in a person's life: the surface level and the deep level. On the surface level, effects may be barely felt or noticed. They are often taken for granted and are nondisruptive. Picking up a container of milk on the way home from work might be an example. Effects at the deep level, however, strike at the core of an individual's life. They have a strong hold over the individual and affect how we behave, think, and understand things. Acceptance of our sexuality, self-hate, grief, and other deep-rooted epiphanies serve to illustrate deep-level life structures. While unobtrusive strategies are quite good at identifying surface-level structures of life, most are not adequate for uncovering deep-level life structures.

Focus groups, on the other hand, provide avenues to understand a variety of deep structural elements. For instance, Twiggs (1994) and Grant (1993) suggest that focus groups can be used to evaluate the strengths and weaknesses of court cases, and even to determine important issues in particular cases. Grant further suggests that information culled from focus groups may assist attorneys in selecting juries during *voir dire*.

Unobtrusive strategies and focus group interviews share an overlapping interest in the biographical experiences of group members. For the most part, unobtrusive measures remain in the realm of the surface level. On the other hand, focus group interviews possess the ability to effectively alternate between surface and deep levels. Decisions about whether to use unobtrusive measures or focus groups will be made for several reasons. Most obvious is what level of life structure you wish to examine. Another, again, may be financial. Here, however, you are likely to find that unobtrusive measures, like focus group interviews, can be created at fairly low cost. You might also consider innovatively combining the two, as in the group diary. Such a strategy allows both a variation on triangulation and a means for assessing both surface and deep levels of participants' lives.

The preceding comparisons between focus group interviews and certain more traditional strategies point out an important issue: that focus groups may be used either alone as a data-collection strategy or in combination with other techniques. In their simplest form, focus group interviews can be used as a sort of stand-alone data, what Morgan and Spanish (1984, p. 263) call *self-contained data*. This type of research is analogous to the kind of nontriangulated research you might accomplish using any single qualitative strategy.

FACILITATING FOCUS GROUP DYNAMICS: HOW FOCUS GROUPS WORK

Focus group procedures generally include having a trained and practiced facilitator ask a small group of individuals a series of open-ended questions.

The moderator may use a single standard set of questions, asking each in turn, to stimulate discussion and conversation during a given session. He or she may use this same set of questions during successive sessions. The questions may be more or less standardized depending upon the needs of the research and the inclination of the investigator.

Focus groups procedures also can be described as containing a number of necessary ingredients for effective production of research information. Similar *checklists* have been suggested by Axelrod (1975), Morgan (1993) and Byers and Byers (1996). These elements include:

1. *A Clearly Defined Objective and/or Research Problem:* Is the focus group part of several other means for collecting data or is it being used as a stand–alone data collection technique? Does the researcher have a clear understanding of the research problem, and the questions to be used during the focus group session(s)?

2. *The Nature of the Group:* What are group's characteristics? Is the group largely homogeneous or is it heterogeneous? Is it an appropriate group for the research question(s)? If you want to know about Sioux Indian culture, you simply cannot ask a group of Quakers!

3. *Atmosphere/Environment and Rapport:* As in any research project, the facilitator must assure confidentiality of information discussed during the focus group. In this case, however, the facilitator must also create rapport between him- or herself and the group, as well as between group members. In other words, the researcher must make all of the group members feel comfortable talking openly in the group.

4. *An Aware Listening Facilitator:* Facilitators, as with any interviewer, must listen to what the subjects are saying (see Chapter 4). It is important to have a schedule or agenda during the focus group; however, it should never be so inflexible that interesting topics that spontaneously arise during the group discussion are shortchanged or unnecessarily truncated. Because of the nature of group dynamics, it is possible that topics and issues not originally considered by the researcher as important surface as very important to the study groups.

5. *A Well-Organized and Prepared Facilitator:* Whether the facilitator intends to work with several specific questions, or with several general topical areas, the facilitator should have a clear idea about how things will proceed. One sure way to kill a focus group discussion is to begin it without any direction, or indication of what the flow of questions or topics will be. Often, texts recommend that facilitators be highly trained and skilled leaders of focus groups (see, for example, Krueger, 1994). Unfortunately, this is not always practical or possible. It, therefore, becomes even more important for an inexperienced researcher serving as facilitator to demonstrate clear organization and preparedness.

6. *Structure and Direction, but Restrained Contribution to the Discussion:* While the facilitator should guide the group's discussion, he or she should avoid offering opinions and substantive comments. As with any interview, the ideal product is 90 percent subjects and 10 percent researcher.

7. *Research Assistance:* Many investigators use only a single researcher/ facilitator during the course of a focus group. This procedure sometimes occurs because of costs or time necessities. A more idyllic situation is to have someone serve as facilitator, while someone else sits and observes the group. This second researcher is able to create field notes about the group dynamics, as well as assist in identifying voices when it comes time to transcribe the focus group interview recording. An even more effective record might be to videotape the focus group. Videotaping, however, is not always permissible or possible.

8. *Systematic Analysis:* Whether the data is a transcribed audiotape, or a videotape of group sessions, they must be analyzed using some systematic means. One style of analysis may be to analyze the content of the statements made by subjects during the focus group (see Chapter 11). Whatever you do with the data, they should be clearly stated to ensure their verifiability. By verifiable I mean that the analysis process should permit another researcher to arrive at similar conclusions using the same or similar documents and raw data (Krueger, 1994).

Often, researchers employ a tactic called the *extended focus group*. This procedure includes a questionnaire administered to participants before the group session. The questionnaire generally includes material that will be discussed during the focus group session. Information from this questionnaire may assist both group members and the moderator. The questionnaires allow the participants to develop a commitment to a position before any group discussion begins (Sussman et al., 1991).

Information from these pregroup questionnaires may help to ensure that the moderator draws out minority opinions as well as more dominant majority ones (Wimmer & Dominick, 1987). In some ways, this is similar to the pre-jury selection questionnaire people commonly receive when called to serve on jury duty. These questionnaires elicit information that will allow the prosecuting and defense attorneys an opportunity to get to know potential jurors. When they ask questions of the jurors in a process called *voir dire*, they are guided by comments these people made in their questionnaires. Answers to their questions help the attorneys decide whom they do and do not want on the jury.

One of the most difficult tasks of a moderator is controlling dominating respondents while simultaneously encouraging passive group members. This must be accomplished without embarrassing or completely shutting down the dominating participants. Often, like a traditional interviewer, the moderator must rely upon his or her ability to develop rapport with group members. If the moderator has been successful in this rapport development, it may be useful in efforts to encourage the quiet members to participate.

Most researchers who use focus group techniques acknowledge that group influences can distort individual opinion. Some opinions may be more extreme and some may be less verbalized than others because of the group effects (Morgan, 1989; Sussman et al., 1991). Having some idea about how individuals thought about certain topics before the group sessions allows the investigator to gauge this group effect. This is not to say that material obtained during the group session is false. Quite the contrary. The opinions voiced during the session, even those that contradict pregroup questionnaires, merely demonstrate the impact of group dynamics. Additional information, confirmation or refutation of beliefs, arguments, discussion, and solutions heard during the group session shape participants' thinking. What results is a collective understanding about issues discussed during the group session.

It is important, in fact, to bear in mind that data obtained from focus group interviews are not identical to individual interview data. Focus group data are *group data*. They reflect the collective notions shared and negotiated by the group. Individual interview data reflect only the views and opinions of the individual, shaped by the social process of living in a culture.

When you design a focus group interview study, your plans for participant selection must be undertaken very carefully. It should not be assumed that focus group samples necessarily are accidental or purposive. Even among marketing researchers, care is required to create samples that include subjects with necessary product user characteristics (Tynan & Dryton, 1989). For the more traditional social sciences, one should begin using standard strategies for sampling to create a sample pool. From this pool, the smaller focus groups may be formed.

For example, say you are interested in studying some aspect of the lives of incarcerated women. Perhaps you are interested in how these women perceive their family role as mother, even though they are separated from their children (Moloney, 1994). In most states, women's correctional facilities are not numerous. Often there may be only one or two for the entire state. Thus, you easily can begin with a *census sample*[3] of women in prison to form the initial pool. Next, you might stratify this group into those who have children currently of juvenile status (under the age of juvenile jurisdiction) and those who do not. Using the group with children, you might now have a sample of 50 or 60 women. Assuming no rejections, you could randomly assign women in this group to five or six focus groups and conduct sessions in a fairly brief amount of time.

You can develop focus groups using other strategies to create the initial sample pool. This is particularly true if you are using focus group interviews as an additional line of action in a triangulated project. For example, Berg

FIGURE 5.1 Berg Sampling Strategy

	Males		Females	
	Younger Patients (Under 45)	Older Patients (Over 45)	Younger Patients (Under 45)	Older Patients (Over 45)
Serious Asthma Condition				
Moderate Asthma Condition				

(1995) was interested in examining self-management programs and patient compliance among adult asthmatics. Her sampling strategy called for systematically selecting and stratifying adult asthma patients into the cells shown in Figure 5.1, each containing eight people for a total of 62 subjects.

Berg's (1995) design called for an experimental and a control group, so she randomly assigned the subjects in each cell to one or the other. The experimental group was presented with a structured educational program regarding the use of their asthma inhaler medication. The control group was not. Using devices designed to indicate when the inhalers were used, Berg planned to determine whether the program improved patients' self-management and compliance. To this point, Berg's research amounts to a fairly standard quasiexperimental design. However, Berg's design does not provide for explanations about *why* inhalers were or were not used. She could have obtained such information with focus groups.

In this instance, Berg might have divided her two groups, experimental and control, each into three focus groups. In each of these six focus group interviews, the moderator could have explored how subjects viewed their medication and why they did or did not use the inhalers as prescribed.

As illustrated above, samples for focus groups in the social sciences derive from a wide variety of types. Standard sampling procedures can improve the validity of group interview results. The main question that remains is, When should a focus group strategy be used?

While this is not its primary purpose, you might consider using a version of focus group interviews to pilot an interview schedule. In this instance, you would have members of the focus group read through the instrument under consideration. Next, the group would discuss the usual concerns researchers have about such research instruments: the level of language, comprehensibility of the questions, question order, affected wording of questions, and so forth.

As suggested throughout the examples offered in this chapter, there are numerous other occasions when a focus group could be used. This is, of course, true with many data-collection strategies. As suggested in the first chapter of this book, triangulation in qualitative research can be important to issues of validity. Whenever you can demonstrate corroboration of information you have obtained, you are on solid ground. Whether focus group techniques are used will depend on several issues. These issues have been mentioned in the preceding chapter, but they bear some reiteration.

First, you must decide whether information gathered through the focus group interview will inform the research questions. There is no point in conducting focus groups if the results are superfluous.

Second, you may want to consider aspects of time and cost effectiveness. Will focus group interviews allow you to obtain the best data for the time and money they will require?

Third, is the study population one that requires a faster data-collection strategy that might be provided by another technique? Naturally, this is related to the issue of your research questions as well as to the quality of the data. This may involve decisions about your willingness to make tradeoffs between data precision and gains in data acquisition.

Last, you should consider whether using focus groups might enhance a project by adding another line of action to the study. This additional line of action may, in fact, offer either corroboration of other data or insights into areas other data fail to illuminate.

CONFIDENTIALITY AND
FOCUS GROUP INTERVIEWS

One final issue requires discussion: the problem of confidentiality of information obtained through the use of focus group interviews. While it is easy to ensure that the researcher will maintain confidentiality, what can be done among the participants? Ensuring confidentiality is critical if the researcher expects to get truthful and free-flowing discussions during the course of the focus group interview. If group members feel apprehensive or inhibited by fear of somehow being exposed, they will not fully disclose their feelings and perceptions.

In marketing research situations, this issue of confidentiality may not be viewed as terribly significant. After all, who really cares if the car manufacturer learns that someone thinks their automobile is ugly or fails to perform well? What difference does it make to have some cereal company learn that someone thinks the picture on the box is childish or the taste of the product is awful? While executives need this information to improve product quality, none of these comments is very self-disclosing.

When focus groups are used for social scientific research, however, a different kind of information is obtained. A focus group interview among rapists, for example, could reveal very sensitive pieces of information. Discussion among obese focus group members about why they eat obsessively may not be the kind of information members want to be identified with. Conversations among elementary school teachers about how they discriminate against particular ethnic groups or against girls could be very troublesome if revealed. Thus, certain procedures must be taken to ensure confidentiality.

The logical course to take is to have every member of the focus group sign a statement of confidentiality. In other forms of research, such as individual interviews, this is fairly common practice. The difference, however, is that in the individual interview, this contractual agreement is between researcher and subject. In the focus group situation, the agreement must be among *all* group members and the moderator/researcher. An example of such an agreement is offered in Figure 5.2.

Enforcement of this agreement, as with all confidentiality agreements in research, largely is one of honor rather than law. Use of this sort of document, however, does allow the participant an opportunity to think about issues of confidentiality. If a participant believes he or she will not be able to keep material confidential, this is the opportunity to withdraw. Similarly, if a group member is fearful about confidentiality, he or she can drop out of the group.

FIGURE 5.2 Group Agreement for Maintaining Confidentiality

This form is intended to further ensure confidentiality of data obtained during the course of the study entitled [place title of research here]. All parties involved in this research, including all focus group members, will be asked to read the following statement and sign their names indicating that they agree to comply.

I hereby affirm that I will not communicate or in any manner disclose publicly information discussed during the course of this focus group interview. I agree not to talk about material relating to this study or interview with anyone outside of my fellow focus group members and the researcher [or moderator].

Name: _____

Signature: _____

Project Director's Signature: _____

Allowing concerned or unwilling subjects to withdraw is an important ethical element in all research. It is also important for the quality of your focus group data. Having an unwilling participant in the group could prove to be very disruptive or problematic for a moderator. The discussions, topics, and solutions the group might be able to develop could be seriously compromised.

CONCLUSION

The focus group interview is an innovative strategy for gathering sometimes difficult-to-obtain information. Although it is newly reborn in the social sciences, it promises to quickly become an integral data-collection technology among qualitative researchers. It operates well either as a stand-alone means for data collection or as an additional line of action. The limitations of focus group interviews must be weighed against the advantages they offer in a given research situation.

TRYING IT OUT

Suggestion 1

This suggestion is intended to allow students an opportunity to work in an unguided focus group. Divide the class into groups of approximately six or seven students. Each group begins discussing each of the following topics: how to select a course, how group members chose the college they are attending, and what types of vacations are best during spring break. Allow only 15 minutes or so for each topic. If possible, have each group tape record their session. If recording isn't possible, have one or two members of each group take notes.

Suggestion 2

Develop a means for identifying participants for a focus group study on fear of crime among juveniles. Be certain you consider basic issues of sampling, including representation of both genders and a variety of ethnic groups, ages, and educational levels.

NOTES

1. There is wide disagreement in the literature about what exactly constitutes a *small group* for focus group interviews. Some sources suggest six to nine subjects (Pramualratana et al., 1985, p. 204); others recommend six or eight to ten group members (Morgan, 1989, p. 43); still others claim that six to twelve participants (Lengua et al., 1992, p. 163) may be the ideal size. One thing seems certain: The more complex the research problem, the more effective it is to have smaller size (5–7 people) focus groups.

2. A colleague of mine, W. Timothy Austin, reminds me of an interesting point. While most mainstream writing on focus groups similarly identifies post–World War II as a general time point of origin for the technique, this is somewhat questionable. In fact, for several hundred years, anthropologists conducted what could be described as focus group interviews when they sat around tribal campfires. However, the systematic technique and the label *focus group* do appear to emerge in the literature shortly after World War II.

3. Census samples include all the people who fit a certain characteristic or who exist in a specific location. For instance, a nurse researcher might use such a sampling procedure to study *all* the patients being treated at a single hemodialysis center. Any potential subject who does not want to participate in the research falls into the researcher's rejection rate. Typically, this procedure is used when the total number of potential subjects is not very large.

REFERENCES

Axelrod, M. (1975). 10 essentials for good qualitative research. *Marketing News 8,* 10–11.

Bartos, R. (1986). Qualitative research: What it is and where it came from. *Journal of Advertising Research 26,* RC3–RC6.

Basch, C. E. (1987). Focus group interviews: An underutilized research technique for improving theory and practice in health education. *Health Education Quarterly 14,* 411–448.

Basch, C. E., DeCicco, I. M., & Malfetti, J. L. (1989). A focus group study on decision processes of young drivers: Reasons that may support a decision to drink and drive. *Health Education Quarterly 16,* 389–396.

Berg, J. (1995). *Evaluation of a self-management program for adults with asthma.* Doctoral dissertation, University of Pittsburgh.

Byers, B., & Byers, P. Y. (1996, March). *Focus group research and juries: Literature and applications.* Paper presented at the annual meeting of the Academy of Criminal Justice Sciences, Las Vegas.

Callahan, J. T. (1983). *Upward mobility from the inside: A phenomenological study of female psychologists from working-class backgrounds.* Doctoral dissertation, Massachusetts School of Professional Psychology, Boston.

Denzin, N. K. (1989). *Interpretive Interactionism.* Applied Social Research Methods Series, Vol. 16. Newbury Park, CA: Sage.

Fern, E. F. (1982). The use of focus groups for idea generation: The effects of group size, acquaintanceship, and moderator on a response quality and quantity. *Journal of Marketing Research 19,* 1–13.

Fern, E. F. (1983). Focus groups: A review of some contradictory evidence, implications, and suggestions for future research. *Advances in Consumer Research 10,* 121–126.

Flaskerund, J. H., & Calvillo, E. R. (1991). Beliefs about AIDS, health and illness among low-income Latina women. *Research in Nursing and Health 14,* 431–438.

Grant, B. C. (1993). Focus groups versus mock trials: Which should you use? *Trial Diplomacy Journal 16,* 15–22.

Gubrium, J. F. (1987). *Oldtimers and Alzheimer's: The Descriptive Organization of Senility.* Greenwich, CT: JAI Press.

Hagan, F. E. (1993). *Research Methods in Criminal Justice and Criminology* (3rd ed.). New York: Macmillan.

Hanrahan, K. J. (1990). *Exploring fear of crime among elderly urban females: An application of focus and intensive interview techniques.* Doctoral dissertation, Rutgers University, Newark, NJ.

Hayes, T. J., & Tathum, C. B. (1989). *Focus Group Interviews: A Reader* (2nd ed.). Chicago: American Marketing Association.

Hochschild, A. R. (1983). *The Managed Heart: Commercialization of Human Feelings.* Berkeley: University of California Press.

Husserl, E. (1913). *Ideas: General Introduction to Pure Phenomenology* (Reissued 1962). New York: Collier.

Kramer, T. (1983). The diary as a feminist research method. *Newsletter of the Association for Women in Psychology* Winter, 3–4.

Krueger, R. A. (1994). *Focus Groups: A Practical Guide for Applied Research* (2nd ed.). Thousand Oaks, CA: Sage.

Lengua, L. J., Roosa, M. W., Schupak-Neuberg, E., Michaeles, M. L., Berg, C. N., & Weschler, L. F. (1992). Using focus groups to guide the development of a parenting program for difficult-to-research, high-risk families. *Family Relations 41,* 163–168.

Libresco, J. D. (1983). Focus groups: Madison Avenue meets public policy. *Public Opinion* August/September, 51–53.

Longmire, D. R. (1991). Ethical dilemmas in the research setting: A survey of experiences and responses in the criminological community. In M. D. Braswell, B. R. McCarthy, & B. J. McCarthy (Eds.), *Research Methods in Criminal Justice.* Cincinnati, OH: Anderson Publishing.

McSkimming, M. J., Drach-Brillinger, P., & Hiatt, M. D. (1994, March). *Research ethics: What are we teaching and why?* Paper presented at the annual meeting of ACJS, Chicago.

Merton, R. K. (1987). The focused interview and focus groups. *Public Opinion Quarterly 51,* 550–566.

Merton, R. K., Fiske, M., & Kendall, P. L. (1956). *The Focused Interview.* Glencoe, IL: Free Press.

Merton, R. K., & Kendall, P. L. (1946). The focused interview. *American Journal of Sociology 51,* 541–557.

Moloney, L. (1994). *Women and children: Family perspectives among incarcerated women.* In process doctoral dissertation, Indiana University of Pennsylvania, Indiana, PA.

Moran, W. T. (1986). The science of qualitative research. *Journal of Advertising Research 26,* RC16–RC19.

Morgan, D. L. (1989). *Focus Groups as Qualitative Research.* Newbury Park, CA: Sage.

Morgan, D. L., & Spanish, M. T. (1983). *Focus groups and health beliefs: Learning from others' heart attacks.* Paper presented at the meeting of the American Sociological Association, Detroit.

Morgan, D. L., & Spanish, M. T. (1984). Focus groups: A new tool for qualitative research. *Qualitative Sociology 7,* 253–271.

Oakley, A. (1981). Interviewing women: A contradiction in terms. In H. Roberts (Ed.), *Doing Feminist Research* (pp. 30–61). London: Routledge and Kegan Paul.

Pramualratana, A., Havanon, N., & Knodel, J. (1985). Exploring the normative basis for age at marriage in Thailand: An example from focus group research. *Journal of Marriage and the Family,* February, 203–210.

Reinharz, S. (1992). *Feminist Methods in Social Research.* New York: Oxford University Press.

Roth, J. (1966). Hired hand research. *The American Sociologist 1,* 190–196.

Stewart, D. W., & Shamdasani, P. M. (1990). *Focus Groups: Theory and Practice.* Newbury Park, CA: Sage.

Sussman, S., Burton, D., Dent, C. W., Stacy, A. W., & Flay, B. R. (1991). Use of focus groups in developing an adolescent tobacco use cessation program: Collection norm effects. *Journal of Applied Social Psychology 21,* 1772–1782.

Twiggs, H. F. (1994). Do-it-yourself focus groups: Big profits, modest cost. *Trial 30*(9), 42–117.

Tynan, A. C., & Dryton, J. L. (1989). Conducting focus groups: A guide for first-time users. In T. J. Hayes & C. B. Tathum (Eds.). *Focus Group Interviews: A Reader* (2nd ed., pp. 30–34). Chicago: American Marketing Association.

Wimmer, R. D., & Dominick, J. R. (1987). *Mass Media Research.* Belmont, CA: Wadsworth Publishing.

ETHNOGRAPHIC
FIELD STRATEGIES

ALTHOUGH ETHNOGRAPHY HAS BEEN around for a long time, particularly as practiced by cultural anthropologists, sociologists differ
sharply on both the conceptual meaning of ethnography and its application.
Researchers frequently use the term in seemingly different ways. Spradley
(1979, p. 3), for example, explains that "ethnography is the work of describing a culture. The essential core of this activity aims to understand another
way of life from the native point of view." Zigarmi and Zigarmi (1980) refer
to ethnographers as virtually anyone who enters the natural setting in order
to conduct *field research*, a concept that itself suffers from confused understanding (see Guy et al., 1987). Some researchers, for example Ellen (1984)
and Stoddart (1986), suggest that ethnography involves the end product of
field research, namely, the written account of observations. Other authorities, Preble and Casey (1969), Agar (1973), Weppner (1977), and Johnson et
al. (1985) for instance, describe ethnography as an extremely effective
method for studying illicit drug use and users. In an attempt to differentiate
this style of research from anthropological ethnography, many drug
researchers have called it *street ethnography* or *urban ethnography*. Leininger
(1985, p. 33) coined the term *ethnonursing* to describe ethnography conducted by nurses.

More recently, Lofland (1996, p. 30) describes the strategy of *analytic
ethnography*:

> I use the term "*analytic ethnography*" to refer to research processes and prod-
> ucts in which, to a greater or lesser degree, an investigator (a) attempts to pro-
> vide generic propositional answers to questions about social life and organiza-
> tion; (b) strives to pursue such an attempt in a spirit of unfettered or
> naturalistic inquiry; (c) utilizes data based on deep familiarity with a social
> setting or situation that is gained by personal participation or an approxima-

tion of it; (d) develops the generic propositional analysis over the course of doing research; (e) strives to present data and analyses that are true; (f) seeks to provide data and/or analyses that are new; and (g) presents an analysis that is developed in the senses of being conceptually elaborated, descriptively detailed, and concept-data interpenetrated.

However, the various ways researchers speak about ethnography may amount to little more than terminological preferences. Agar (1986) came to this conclusion in his examination of the language differences among various ethnographers and ethnographic traditions in his book *Speaking of Ethnography.*

Nonetheless, the important point about the concept of ethnography, regardless of one's language and terminological preference, is that the practice places researchers in the midst of whatever it is they study. From this vantage, researchers can examine various phenomena as perceived by participants and represent these observations as accounts.

Wolcott (1973) captures the essence of most of these variations by defining ethnography as the science of *cultural description*. Clearly, ethnography is primarily a process that attempts to describe and interpret social expressions between people and groups. Or as Geertz (1973) suggests, the researcher's task is to convey *thick description*, such that a wink can be distinguished from a twitch, and a parody of a wink is distinguishable from an actual wink (see Wilcox, 1988, p. 458).

Some researchers, Ellen (1984) for example, describe the ethnographic process as *subjective soaking*. According to Ellen (1984, p. 77) this occurs when the researcher "abandons the idea of absolute objectivity or scientific neutrality and attempts to merge him/herself into the culture being studied." Other subjectivist and existential approaches have given rise to the notion of fieldwork as *translation*, in which cultural elements (including human ideas and perceptions) are considered *opaque texts*. From this vantage, the primary objective of ethnography is to read the text. The text, however, is not some abstract concept or idealized heuristic model. Instead, the text should be considered the literal textual content of the ethnographer's notebooks, memos, and the like. This orientation toward ethnography, then, can be understood as the product of interaction between the observer and the observed (Clifford, 1980).

The more traditional anthropological approach of ethnography, as represented by the works of Malinowski, Evans-Pritchard, and Boas, has been primarily concerned with this type of subjectivist translation. During the past 35 years, however, anthropological methods, like sociological ones, have undergone considerable advancement, refinement, and change (see, for example, Adler & Adler, 1987). Ellen (1984) points out that these changes have provided no less than a *quiet revolution*, resulting in a *new ethnography*.

The field of the new ethnography, as suggested in the opening paragraphs of this chapter, has experienced considerable confusion, both conceptually and methodologically. One major result of adaptation to the new ethnography has been a redefining of *ethnography* as a set of highly formal techniques designed to extract cognitive data (Ellen, 1984; Spradley, 1980; Van Maanen, 1982). Another consequence of this quiet revolution is what Spindler (1988) describes as the meteoric rise of <u>educational ethnography</u> during the past decade, particularly the past several years. As Spindler (1988, p. 1) explains: "Ethnography has become virtually a household word in professional education, and it is the rare research project today that does not have somewhere in the table of operations at least one ethnographer and somewhere in the research design some ethnographic procedures."

During the past 15 years, this new ethnography has grown popular among nursing researchers. Frequently, one finds this technique referred to as *ethnonursing research* (Burns & Grove, 1993; Leininger, 1985; Polit & Hungler, 1993). This is given to mean "the study and analysis of the local or indigenous people's viewpoints, beliefs and practices about nursing care behavior and processes of designated cultures" (Leininger, 1985, p. 38). More recently, in nursing, Francke et al. (1996) demonstrate the benefits of observational (ethnographic) research even by staff members.

The principal concern in this chapter is to examine the new ethnography as an extremely effective research strategy. Van Maanen (1982, p. 103) suggests that ethnography has become the method "that involves extensive fieldwork of various types including participant observation, formal and informal interviewing, document collecting, filming, recording, and so on." It is not, however, the intent of this chapter to diminish the significant contribution made by the more traditional (textual) orientation. In fact, a section of this chapter on ethnography as a narrative style discusses the more traditional ethnographic orientation.

One other significant aspect of ethnography is the distinction sometimes made between <u>micro-</u> and <u>macroethnography</u> (sometimes referred to as <u>general ethnography</u>). One obvious difference is the scope of a given investigation. Macroethnography attempts to describe the entire way of life of a group. In contrast, microethnography focuses on particular *incisions* at particular points in the larger setting, group, or institution. Typically, these specific points are selected because they in some manner represent salient elements in the lives of participants and in turn, in the life of the larger group or institution.

A second fundamental difference between micro- and macroethnography is that the former analytically focuses more directly upon the face-to-face interactions of members of the group or institution under investigation. By examining these interactions, their implications (or as Mehan [1978] suggests, their *outcomes)* can be considered. For example, Wolcott's (1973) *The Man in the Principal's Office* was intended to offer an accurate description of the real world of one elementary school principal and, by extension, to identify the various behaviors, attitudes, and processes shared by other elementary school principals.

In spite of various differences, both micro- and macroethnography share the overarching concern for assessing everyday community life from the perspectives of participants. From detailed examinations of people and their social discourse and the various outcomes of their actions, underlying principles and concepts can be identified. As a result, neither micro- nor macroethnography is fully understandable individually without some consideration of the other. For example, it would be impossible to understand the concept of classroom management in relation to the concept of learning without some consideration of how this relates to learning environments in general (see Allen, 1986).

This chapter is divided into five sections: "Accessing a Field Setting: Getting In," "Becoming Invisible," "Other Dangers During Ethnographic Research," "Watching, Listening, and Learning," and "Disengaging: Getting Out." Each section discusses issues related to these five basic segments of ethnographic research.

ACCESSING A FIELD SETTING: GETTING IN

As Shaffir et al. (1980) suggest, one central problem shared by all field investigators is the problem of *getting in*. This particular problem begins at the design stage. It involves consideration of who the subjects are and the nature of the setting. For example, Spencer (1991) describes the problems he and others have had trying to study certain bureaucratic institutions such as the military. Spencer (1991) outlines the mechanisms such institutions possess for avoiding or controlling access to research data. Even when a researcher is given permission to conduct a study in an institution such as a prison, a mental hospital, or as Spencer (1991) did, at the U.S. Military Academy, where a researcher can go and with whom he or she can speak may be controlled.

Hertz and Imber (1993) similarly detail the problems associated with conducting field studies in *elite settings*. As they suggest, there are very few studies of elites because elites are by their very nature difficult to penetrate. Unlike some other segments of society, elites often are visible and fairly easy to locate. Yet, because they are able to establish barriers and obstacles and because they can successfully refuse access to researchers, many elites are difficult to study.

How might you gain access to difficult-to-reach groups? As simplistic as it may seem, the answer lies in reading the literature. While various settings and groups are *difficult* to access, most are not impossible. Ostrander (1993) says she found it rather simple to gain access to upper-class women. She further suggests that sometimes a bit of luck, taking advantage of certain relationships, considerable background work, and making the right contacts frequently aids an attempt to access restricted groups. While researching restricted settings or groups may involve more work initially, the directions for this work can be found by reviewing the literature on such settings and groups. Spencer (1991), for example, offers a series of possible ways to access bureaucratic institutions.

It is also important during the design stage of your research to consider several other important points. For example, since most ethnographic research involves human subjects, researchers must give considerable thought to ways they can protect the subjects from harm and injury. This is especially true when dealing with restricted groups or settings. You must be mindful not to bar future researchers' access by careless protection of subjects' rights and privacy. In addition, researchers must consider how they will go about gaining permission or consent of the subjects. Of course, this itself requires a decision about whether to enter the field as an announced researcher (overtly) or as a secret researcher (covertly).

Most sources on gaining access to the field agree on one thing: Whether it is a highly accessible or a very restricted setting, decisions made during the early stages of research are critical. This is true because such decisions will lay both the conceptual and methodological foundation for the entire project. This can be likened to what Janesick (1994, pp. 210–211) describes as choreographing the research design. In other words, just as an expressive dancer might ask, "What statement do I want to say through my dance?" an ethnographer must consider the question, "What do I want to learn from this study?"

Toward this end, the decision to enter the field overtly or covertly as an investigator is important. Each style of entrance encompasses certain problems, and regardless of the style you choose, you must address these problems.

Similarly, in either style of entrance, researchers must consider that their very presence in the study setting may taint anything that happens among other participants in that setting. As Denzin (1970, pp. 203–204) suggests: "Reactive effects of observation are the most perplexing feature of participant observation, since the presence of an observer in any setting is often a 'foreign object.' The creation of the role of participant observer inevitably introduces some degree of reactivity into the field setting."

Spindler and Spindler (1988, p. 25) similarly express their concerns about intruding by participating in the "life of the school" during their research. As a partial solution, they strive to "melt" into the classroom as much as possible. This attempt to "become invisible" will be discussed in greater detail later in this chapter.

An argument can be made for both covert and overt stances when conducting ethnographic research. For instance, a study on casual homosexual encounters such as Humphreys's *Tearoom Trade* (1975) simply could not have been undertaken if he had formally announced his identity as a researcher. Briefly, Humphreys found a public bathroom where men met for brief homosexual encounters. Standing as lookout and assumed to be a voyeur or "watch queen," Humphreys managed to learn that many of these men had wives and families. They lived heterosexual lives but occasionally had homosexual encounters. His research demonstrated rather clearly that homosexuality was not a disease, as many people had previously believed, but a life style.

Similarly, in studies about people who frequent so-called adult movie theaters and book stores, the identification of an observing ethnographer might result in little information about such persons. It is also likely that such an announcement would create uncontrollable reactivity to the presence of the researcher. For example, nurses conducting ethnographic research with the intention of investigating drug theft practices of hospital staff members might create conflicts between themselves and others on the staff. Thus, a major argument for covert ethnographic research is the sensitivity of certain topics that might make it impossible to do research by other means. Naturally, in making such a case, you must additionally justify the undertaking of such research by some actual social or scientific benefit.

Scientific benefits notwithstanding, some serious ethical questions arise when covert research is conducted on human subjects. Among other concerns is the possibility that this type of research might abuse the rights and privacy of the research subjects, thereby causing them harm. For many scholars, there can be *no* justification for knowingly harming subjects.

On the other hand, entering an ethnographic study as a known researcher has several benefits. For example, in his study of medical students, Becker (1963) noted that his status as an identified researcher allowed him to ask questions of various hospital personnel more effectively. Similarly, Berg et al. (1983), in a study of adolescent involvement in alcohol, drugs, and crime, suggest that by having entered the field overtly, they succeeded in locating guides and informants (discussed in detail later). Many of these adolescents might otherwise have thought the two field ethnographers were narcs—people who are or work for the police. By having established who they were and what they were doing in the field, the two ethnographers managed to gain considerable rapport with their subjects.

Because of the ethical concerns associated with the overt/covert controversy, and in light of heightened concern over falsification of research findings in scientific communities, this chapter primarily considers *getting in* as an overt activity. Issues commonly associated with determining a balance between covert and overt research techniques were more comprehensively considered in Chapter 3.

The Attitude of the Ethnographer

The researcher's frame of mind when entering a natural setting is crucial to the eventual results of a study. If you strike the wrong attitude, you might well destroy the possibility of ever learning about the observed participants and their perceptions. Matza (1969) similarly identifies researcher attitude as a crucial element in field studies. According to Matza (1969), one must enter *appreciating* the situations rather than intending to *correct* them. This sort of neutral posture allows researchers to understand what is going on around them rather than become either advocates or critics of the events they witness. In addition, appreciation does not require the interviewers to agree with or even to accept the perceptions of their subjects but merely to offer empathy.

Although many students might think it is unnecessary to suggest that ethnographers should conduct research with an appreciative attitude, in actuality it is an important recommendation.

The Researcher's Voice

Many researchers—both quantitative and qualitative alike—recommend that social science research maintain a *value neutral* position. From this perspective, social scientists are expected to study the world without imposing their own views or taking stands on social or political issues. This style of research tends to lend itself to a fairly positivist approach. During the recent past, a number of social researchers have argued against this facade of value neutrality. Among the most vocal have been feminist researchers (cf., Reinharz, 1992). Feminists have worked out a research methodology that is comfortable for both the researcher and the subjects. It tends to involve strategies that listen more and talk less, that humanize the research process, and that insist that the ethnographic researcher become involved with his or her subjects.

Objectively, social scientists should recognize that research is seldom, if ever, really value neutral. After all, the selection of a research topic typically derives from some researcher oriented position. As previously implied in this chapter, topic selection occurs because of an interest in the subject matter, or because it is a politically advantageous area to receive grant monies, because of some inner humanistic drive toward some social problem, or because one has personal experiences or what Lofland (1996, p. 44) calls "deep familiarity" with the subject area. The fact is, research is seldom undertaken for a neutral reason. Furthermore, all humans residing in and among social groups are the product of those social groups. This means that various values, moral attitudes, and beliefs orient people in a particular manner.

For instance, a person's selection of certain terms indicates the kind of influences that person's social groups have on him or her. During the early

1980s, I thought nothing of using the pronoun he consistently and exclusively in my writing. Similarly, I often used the words *policeman, chairman, postman,* and similar types of terms. By the mid-1980s, however, with the press for political correctness, my orientation changed and I began using the convention of writing *he or she,* and using terms such as *police officer, chair,* and *postal worker.* The point here is that my basic orientations were affected, not merely my semantics. How I viewed social worlds was now different, and it is such differences that affect the possibility of value neutrality in research.

More recently, and again following from feminist researchers' lead, my writing has begun to incorporate the use of first person singular. In other words, I use the word *I.* Particularly when writing ethnographic reports, it began to be apparent that using the first person singular was more direct. Rather than saying, "The researcher began to recognize blah, blah, blah . . ." it seemed more forthright to simply say, "I began to recognize. . . ." In this manner, a researcher can take both ownership and responsibility for what is being stated. Furthermore, it becomes far less cumbersome to write, and often avoids passive and convoluted sentences.

Along similar lines, the use of personal biography or deep familiarity with a subject has become more common and accepted by ethnographers. One excellent example of this is Phil Brown's exploration of the culture of the Catskill Mountains' resort area (Brown, 1996). The "Borscht Belt" as the area is known, is a Jewish resort location where mainly metropolitan Jews fled New York and New Jersey for a summer retreat (Brown, 1996). On the other side of the coin, it was a place where young, often Jewish, college students went to work in order to earn their way through school. A number of well-known and large hotels, bungalow colonies, and camps grew up during the 1940s, and the largely Jewish resort area flourished until about the 1970s. Brown (1996, p. 84) writes from the perspective of an observer who grew up within this Catskill culture, as well as one who writes from the orientation of first-person deep familiarity:

> *I grew up in a family of "mountain rats," a Catskill term for those who lived and worked in "the Mountains" over many years. My parents began in 1948 as owners of a small hotel, Brown's Hotel Royal, on White Lake. . . . In 1948 the chef quit at the start of the season. Unable to find a replacement, my mother, Sylvia Brown, gave herself a crash course in cooking and never left the kitchen again. After our hotel went broke two years later, she spent the rest of her working years as a chef.*

Maintaining the facade of neutrality prevents a researcher from ever examining his or her own cultural assumptions (Rubin & Rubin, 1995) or personal experiences. Subjective disclosures by researchers allows the reader to better understand why a research area has been selected, how it was studied, and by whom. If a nurse studies cancer patients, and explains that his or her selection of this topic resulted after a family member contracted the disease, this does not diminish the quality of the research. It does, however, offer a keener insight about who is doing the research, and why. It may even provide the reader with greater understanding about why certain types of questions were investigated, while others were not.

Similarly, when a researcher reveals that he or she was tempted to, or did, intervene in the lives of his or her subjects, the reader gets a different image of both the researcher and the research. It is likely that anyone who has ever undertaken drug research among children, at the very least, has been tempted to try to convince some child that using heroin or crack cocaine is not a good thing to do. From a strictly positivist value neutral position, of course, one cannot do this. This activity is the work of social workers and not social scientists. From a softer, more humane perspective, however, it seems a reasonable activity along with the field work. Having the researcher reveal that he or she did try to intervene, or even the inner battle the researcher may have had resisting intervening are important pieces of information. This information allows the reader to better understand the true face of both the researcher and the study results.

Finally, presenting subjective disclosures, or giving voice to the researcher, provides insights into the world of research for the reader. Rather than merely heaping results, findings, and even analysis upon the reader, the researcher can share a small portion of the research experience.

Subjective Motivational Factors

Frequently, qualitative studies report in considerable detail the autobiographical motivations that led investigators to conduct their research as they did. These sorts of "true confessions," as Schwartz and Jacobs (1979) call them, are apparently designed to describe the initial biases, values, and theoretical orientations that eventually produced the project. As Johnson (1975) suggests, some researchers may have been motivated or inspired to conduct research in the hopes that such a project would offer positive steps toward realizing some abstract ideal (for example, advancing scientific knowledge, alleviating human misery, resolving some specific social problem, and so on).

External Motivating Factors

Conversely, Punch (1986, p. 210) suggests that the gamut of possible personal motivational factors that leads investigators to conduct research of one type or another may not result from high ideals at all. A number of features—not articulated in the researcher's confessions—may have been critically influential in the decision to study a given phenomenon or to do so in a particular manner. Certainly the personality of the researcher may have an effect. Not all investigators are willing to associate with certain types of deviants or enter into some specialized natural settings (for example, investigating inmates in correctional institutions or drug addicts in the South Bronx).

Another simple factor, seldom discussed in detail yet perhaps responsible for much research, is geographic proximity and access opportunities. The Adlers (Adler, 1985), for example, indirectly explain that their study on drug dealers and smugglers arose almost serendipitiously. After moving to California to attend graduate school and renting a condominium townhouse on the beach, they met a neighbor identified as Dave. Later, the Adlers learned that Dave was a member of a smuggling crew that imported "a ton of marijuana weekly and 40 kilos of cocaine every few months" (Adler, 1985, p. 14). The friendship that developed between Dave and the Adlers provided access to the world of high-level drug dealers and smugglers.

In a similar manner, Peshkin (1986) reports that he began his study of a fundamentalist Christian school largely as a matter of circumstance. As Peshkin (1986, p. 11) describes it:

> *By means of an event which my Christian friends would call providential, and everyone else I know would call coincidental, I came to my present study. The event: a midwinter blizzard, an evening class, and a student in need of a ride home. The student was the Reverend David Householder, whose son attended a local Christian school and who assured me, when I expressed a fascination with religious schools, that he would help in every way he could to arrange for me to study his son's school.*

Certainly there is something romantic and exciting about the image of an ethnographer spending time with potentially dangerous people, in interesting, albeit grimy, bars, gambling houses, and after-hours spots. Ethnography can be, as Lofland and Lofland (1984) describe it, an "adventure." Yet, it is also rigorous, time-consuming, and often boring, tedious work.

Many researchers study certain settings simply because of their convenience or special ease of accessibility. Later, they endeavor to justify their choice on the basis of some grand ideal or spurious theoretical grounds (Punch, 1986). Yet what these researchers apparently fail to recognize is that everyday realities are heavily influenced by human feelings, and presentation of these feelings is legitimate!

The omission of the ethnographers' feelings for and about their research inevitably creates what Johnson (1975, p. 145) describes as "the fieldworker as an iron-willed, steel-nerved, cunning Machiavellian manipulator of the symbolic tools of everyday discourse." Including some indication of why researchers have undertaken a particular project along with the methodological procedure provides a means for making the research come alive, to become interesting to the reading audience. When research is interesting, as Lofland and Lofland (1984, p. 127) indicate, it is not only instrumental but may be expressively aesthetic. In consequence, researchers may produce what Stinchcombe (1975, p. 32) expresses as "the experience [of] a thrill at a beautiful idea."

Unfortunately, in their attempt to objectify their research efforts, many investigators ignore, omit, or conceal their feelings since such emotions are not typically considered capable of independent verification by others. Yet it is important to remember that overrationalized, highly objectified, nearly sterile methodological accounts of field work efforts are not complete descriptions of the research enterprise. Mentions of researchers' personal feelings are not wholly absent from the research literature, but they are relatively rare and are frequently made anecdotally rather than with a substantive purpose in mind (Johnson, 1975).

Gaining Entry

Accounts of how ethnographers gained entry to research settings vary from situation to situation. Researchers need to remain flexible concerning entry tactics and strategies (Shaffir et al., 1980), yet they also need to plan these strategies and tactics in advance—in short, to be prepared!

Ethnographers can borrow Schatzman and Strauss's (1973) general recommendation to field workers to use a *casing and approaching* style. In addition to considering the suitability of the chosen setting and its appropriateness for the study's research goals, ethnographers must consider their strategies for and their feelings about operating in that setting. This aspect of the process includes determining how much they already know about the people in the setting and how much more they will need to learn in order to operate effectively. Johnson (1975) and Lincoln and Guba (1985) similarly stress paying special attention to preparations before entering the research setting.

Knowledge about the people being studied and familiarity with their routines and rituals facilitate entry as well as rapport once entry has been gained. For example, Philips (1972, 1975) investigated the cultural organization of social relationships in classrooms and homes on the Warm Springs Indian Reservation in central Oregon. Eventually, Philips found that differences did exist between behaviors of Indian and non-Indian adults. These behavioral differences were found to depend largely on the setting—the home (a private setting) or the classroom (a public setting). However, in order to appreciate what this meant, Philips had to learn about the Warm Springs Indian culture.

As a starting point, then, it is wise to begin in the library and to locate as much information about a group as possible before attempting to gain entry. Even when little literature exists on a specific topic, there is often considerable literature on a related one. For example, in a recent study of volunteer police officers (a nonethnographic study), Berg and Doerner (1987) learned that little empirical research has been conducted directly on this group. Yet volumes have been written on the police per se and on voluntarism. They also found considerable research undertaken among similar types of volunteer organizations (for example, volunteer firemen and ambulance drivers). Reviewing these areas of the literature would provide sufficient indirect knowledge about volunteer police to get started locating informants and guides in the setting.

Developing Research Bargains

Gaining entry into various settings is also affected by the kinds of arrangements or *bargains* made between researchers and subjects. Many researchers' accounts about how they gained entry to their research settings demonstrate that the type of bargain struck may either constrain or improve their ability to operate in the setting (Guy et al., 1987; Haas & Shaffir, 1978; Whyte, 1955).

Gatekeepers

Gatekeepers can be critical in terms of accessing a research setting or reaching research subjects. These gatekeepers may be formal or informal watchdogs who protect the setting, people, or institution sought as a target for research. Gaining access, then, may require some sort of mediation with these individuals. Research bargains with these people may be necessary before one begins the actual research project. Once a gatekeeper sees the research favorably, he or she may be willing to go to bat for the researcher. Conversely, if the gatekeeper disapproves of the project, he or she may quickly become an obstacle for the researcher to overcome.

For instance, while developing a current research proposal investigating the initiation of cigarette smoking and alcohol use among junior and senior high school students, I sought the assistance of several school principals as gatekeepers. The plan was to have ethnographers introduced to the student bodies at a school assembly, so youths would not fear these individuals as police, or molesters. My intention was to additionally include these gatekeepers in the research plan and attempt to have them endorse the research.

Two of the three principals I spoke with immediately agreed, and saw the research project as one seeking important information. In fact, I had already solicited and received the backing of the local school district's superintendent, thinking that he would be the primary gatekeeper.

Unfortunately, the third principal became very concerned that the introduction of the ethnographers in the school might be seen by parents as an endorsement of the project. He contacted the superintendent, and expressed his concern. This concern revolved around the fact that to assure subject confidentiality we would not provide the school or parents with information about the identities of cigarette and alcohol users. Thus, he feared, implying some sort of condoning, or permissiveness, of these behaviors by the school and school district. The principal suggested that the project proposal be presented to the local school board. Of course, he raised his concerns with them as well. As a result, in a near state of panic, the school board refused to allow any involvement of the district schools in this project. The proposal was changed to bypass the school introduction and instead a plan to use newspaper stories in advance of the fieldwork, to assure both parents and adolescents of the legitimacy of the ethnographers and the project, was developed. Nonetheless, as a gatekeeper, the third principal had halted the research as originally planned.

Guides and Informants

One way to handle initial relationships is to locate *guides* and *informants*. Guides are indigenous persons found among the group and in the setting to be studied. These persons must be convinced that the ethnographers are who they claim to be and that the study is worthwhile. The worth of the study must be understood and be meaningful to the guides and their group. Similarly, these guides must be convinced that no harm will befall them or other members of the group as a result of the ethnographers' presence. The reason for these assurances, of course, is so the guide can reassure others in the group that the ethnographers are safe to have around.

Horowitz (1983, p. 6), who describes herself as a "Jewish, educated, small, fairly dark woman," obviously needed a guide when she studied a Chicano neighborhood. She describes her initial encounter with the Lions (a Chicano gang) and the fortuitous identification of a guide (Horowitz, 1983, p. 7):

> *I chose to sit on a bench in a park where many youths gathered from noon until midnight. On the third afternoon of sitting on the bench, as I dropped a softball that had rolled toward me, a young man came over and said, "You can't catch" (which I acknowledged) and "you're not from the hood [neighborhood], are you?" This was a statement, not a question. He was Gilberto, the Lions' president. When I told him I wanted to write a book on Chicano youth, he said I should meet the other young men and took me over to shake hands with eight members of the Lions.*

Sometimes persons who are willing to be guides or informants turn out to be restricted in their groups. Perhaps they are resented or disliked by others in the group. Consequently, several guides and the snowballing of guides and informants may assist ethnographers in their maneuverability while in the field. *Snowballing,* in the sense it is being used here, refers to using people whom the original guide(s) introduces to the ethnographer as persons who can also vouch for the legitimacy and safety of the researcher.

The larger the ethnographers' network of reliable guides and informants, the greater their access and ability to gain further cooperation. Eventually, the need for specific guides decreases as subject networks grow in size, and the ethnographers are able to begin casual acquaintanceships by virtue of their generally accepted presence on the scene. This will be further discussed in the next section of this chapter, "Becoming Invisible."

Peshkin (1988, p. 51) describes how he and his research team developed their network of guides for his previously mentioned "Mansfield" study by building on the initial guide, Mr. Tate:

> *I joined him [Mr. Tate] at church and at the Kiwanis meetings. By attending all local football games, other social events, and as many community activities as I thought would welcome me, I meant to become visible and known, and thereby to facilitate my access to other activities and many people I planned to interview.*

The preceding guidelines and illustrations suggest some broad considerations and tactics ethnographers may use in order to gain entry to a specific setting. Similar accounts of entry may be found throughout the literature on ethnography and field research. However, some accounts also suggest that entry is determined by the innate abilities and personalities of the ethnographers. This attitude is comparable to the notion that only certain innately gifted people can conduct effective depth interviews—and it is likewise inaccurate (see Chapter 4 for a comprehensive examination of this argument regarding interviewing). A more accurate description of the effects of persona may be effects from the type of role and personality an ethnographer projects. In other words, just as the characterizations and social roles played out by the interviewer affect the quality of the interview performance, so too do these activities affect the ethnographer's performance.

Naturally, indigenous ethnographers—persons who already are members of the group to be studied—possess certain strategic advantages, but as several nurses who conduct ethnography have suggested, neither their indigenous status nor special knowledge about the health care profession made conducting their research any easier (Ostrander, 1993; Peterson, 1985; Quint, 1967).

In some instances, researchers may be able to gain entry more quickly because of their indigenous status. Unfortunately, this is sometimes mistaken for an innate ability (Hoffmann, 1980). Certainly, a clumsy ethnographer, regardless of personal contacts, will produce flawed ethnographies.

BECOMING INVISIBLE

As mentioned previously, one obstacle to conducting ethnographic research is the very presence of the ethnographer in the field. Early in the history of field research, Roethlisberger and Dickenson (1939) identified a phenomenon now commonly called the *Hawthorne effect*. Briefly, the Hawthorne effect suggests that when subjects know they are subjects in a research study, they will alter their usual (routine) behavior. Fortunately, this effect is typically short lived, and the behavior of subjects eventually returns to a more routine style. But the persistent presence of ethnographers in a social setting might certainly reactivate the Hawthorne effect in varying degrees every time someone new is introduced to the researchers. Ethnographic accounts, therefore, understandably offer readers explanations of how the ethnographers' presence was made *invisible* to the subjects.

The status as an *invisible researcher*, as Stoddart (1986) describes it, is the ability to be present in the setting, to see what's going on without being observed, and consequently, to capture the essence of the setting and participants without influencing them. Stoddart[1] (1968, pp. 109–113) identifies six possible variations on this theme of invisible status:

1. *Disattending: Erosion of visibility by time.* When the ethnographers have been present in a domain for a long time, the inhabitants tend not to be aware of them anymore. The notice inhabitants initially took of them has eroded or worn off.

2. *Disattending: Erosion of visibility by display of no symbolic detachment.* The second variation on the theme differs slightly from the first. In this instance, a specific condition believed to facilitate ethnographer invisibility is offered—namely, the assertion that displaying no symbolic detachment from the ways of the domain promotes normalization of the ethnographers' presence. In short, ethnographers eventually just fit into the domain they are studying.

3. *Disattending: Erosion of visibility by display of symbolic attachment.* In contrast to variation 2, in which the ethnographers eventually fit in, the third variation suggests that researchers should actively work toward invisibility by displaying attachment to the domain under study. This kind of attachment typically involves participating with ordinary inhabitants in their everyday routines. By working shoulder to shoulder with inhabitants, it is asserted, the researchers' ethnographer status becomes less of a focal point for members of the study.

4. *Disattending: Erosion of visibility by personalizing the ethnographer-informant relationship.* In the fourth variation, the relationship between ethnographers and inhabitants provides the researchers with their invisible status. Simply stated, the ethnographers become invisible because their informants suspend concern over the research aspect of their identity in favor of liking the researcher as a person.

5. *Misrepresentation: Masking real research interests.* This fifth variation is based on the premise that the greatest areas of inhabitant reactivity will be in the areas the ethnographers announce to be their interest. Thus, if the ethnographers suggest false areas of interest, the assumption is that their real interest areas will be performed as though they were not present.

6. *Misrepresentation: Masking identity as ethnographer.* In the final variation suggested by Stoddart (1986), ethnographers do not represent them-

selves to the normal inhabitants as ethnographers: In other words, they conduct covert ethnography. Since the normal inhabitants of the domain under examination are not aware of the ethnographers' real activities in the setting, the ethnographers are socially invisible.

Dangers of Invisibility

From the ethnographers' perspective, it may seem ideal to obtain invisible status, but several ethical—or real—dangers exist. At least three types of dangers are inherent in conducting research invisibly. These include researcher-originated or intentional misidentification, accidental misidentification, and learning more than you want to know.

Intentional Misidentification

The first potential danger results when the ethnographers' intentional attempts to misrepresent their identity as researchers successfully isolate the subjects of a study. As Thomas's (Thomas & Swaine, 1928) frequently quoted statement expresses, "If men define situations as real, they are real to them in their consequences." In other words, when researchers misrepresent themselves and become invisible to normal inhabitants in a study domain, their assumed role as something else may be taken for real! For example, Rosenhan (1973), in a study of psychiatric hospitals, describes how he and several research associates became psychiatric patients (actually pseudopatients) by acting out various schizophrenic symptoms during intake assessments. By misrepresenting their role as researchers, Rosenhan and his associates managed to have themselves committed.

From the assumed identity of psychiatric patient, Rosenhan and his associates were able to observe and record the behavior of the hospital staff (nurses, aides, psychiatrists, and so on). Although after being admitted all of the researchers discontinued their simulation of symptoms, each had difficulty convincing doctors that they were not crazy! The length of stay in the hospitals ranged from 5 days to 52 days, with an average stay of 19 days. Eventually, each researcher was released with the discharge diagnosis of schizophrenia in remission.

Rosenhan's original purpose of demonstrating the effects of labeling in psychiatric facilities was accomplished, but this study further illustrates another point—the dangers for researchers of misidentifying themselves as other than ethnographers.

Accidental Misidentification

In contrast to intentional misidentification as researchers, ethnographers who gain invisible status may be found guilty by association. Persons outside the immediate domain under investigation may not know who the ethnographers are and simply assume they belong to the group. Although this may allow accurate assessment of many social interactions among the various participants, it is also potentially dangerous.

Particularly when investigating certain so-called deviant groups (for example, violent youth gangs, drug dealers or smugglers, car thieves) even if the ethnographers are socially invisible (as researchers) to members of this group, they may be taken as actual group members by others outside this group.

If, for example, ethnographers studying some youth gang were treated as invisible by members of this group, these interactions could be misinterpreted by members of a rival youth gang. As a result, the ethnographers' personal safety could be jeopardized in the event of a violent confrontation between the gangs. If the ethnographers are with one gang, they may be guilty of membership through association in the eyes of the rival gang.

Learning More Than You Want to Know

Another danger of researcher invisibility is learning more than you might want to know. During the course of an ethnographic study on adolescent involvement in alcohol, drugs, and crime (Berg et al., 1983), field ethnographers found that their presence was often invisible. It was common for the ethnographers to be present, for example, during criminal planning sessions. Often, the ethnographers had information concerning planned burglaries, drug deals, shoplifting sprees, car thefts, and fights several days before the event. In the case of this particular study, possession of this knowledge presented more of an ethical problem than a legal one, since the study group also possessed a Federal Certificate of Confidentiality.

Federal Certificates of Confidentiality ensure that all employees of a research study and all research documents are protected from subpoena in civil or criminal court actions. The certificate also specifies that the researchers cannot divulge confidential material. Thus, the field ethnographers could not divulge their knowledge of impending crimes without violating this agreement. Nonetheless, it was sometimes difficult for the field ethnographers to maintain their personal sense of integrity knowing in advance that certain crimes would occur and knowing also they could do nothing to stop them. One partial solution to the ethical/moral dilemma was an agreement among all of the study participants concerning special circumstances. Under certain special circumstances—that is, if information were obtained that convinced the ethnographers that someone's life or limb could be saved (for example, if a contract were placed on someone's life, or if plans were made to break someone's arm or leg)—appropriate authorities would be notified.

The question of divulging information on illegal activities uncovered during the course of ethnographic research is an ethical and legal problem researchers must decide for themselves. Polsky (1969, pp. 133–134) succinctly states:

If one is effectively to study adult criminals in their natural settings, he must make the moral decision that in some ways he will break the law himself. He need not be a "participant observer," and commit the criminal acts under study, yet he has to witness such acts or be taken into confidence about them and not blow the whistle. That is, the investigator has to decide that when necessary he will "obstruct justice" or have "guilty knowledge" or be an "accessory" before or after the fact, in the full legal sense of those terms.

Taking the other side of this ethical/legal question, Yablonsky (1965) suggests that researchers should not conduct participant observation among criminally deviant persons. Yablonsky says that offering such a research focus serves to justify and reinforce the criminality of these deviants.

A New Problem in Data Protection: The Case of Mario Brajuha

Recently, with the case of Mario Brajuha, new concerns about the ability of researchers to protect themselves, their notes, and their subjects arose. Brajuha had worked for many years as a waiter in various restaurants throughout New York. His personal knowledge and experiences led him to begin to conduct a systematic investigation of the restaurant business as part of his Ph.D. studies in sociology (see Brajuha & Hallowell, 1986).

While working as a waiter in a Long Island restaurant, Brajuha began to systematically gather data for his dissertation. Then, in March 1983, a suspicious fire that caused extensive damage to the restaurant-research site altered things entirely. Fire marshals and police detectives had learned that Brajuha was conducting research and had been keeping notes. Suspecting arson, and believing that Brajuha's notes might contain information leading to the arsonist, detectives approached him and requested that he show them his notes. Brajuha was opposed to showing anybody his research notes and refused. As Brajuha and Hallowell (1986, p. 456) explain it, "This was not just an abstract commitment to lofty ideals but a concrete feeling about himself and his informants' well-being." Brajuha believed that if a social scientist specifically promises not to reveal information about his subjects, he simply cannot do so!

Ultimately, after two years of court battles to resist revealing his field notes, the case reached the bench of federal judge Jack Weinstein in 1984. The judge not only quashed the subpoena ordering Brajuha to deliver his notes but stated that "serious scholars are entitled to no less protection than journalists" (Brajuha & Hallowell, 1986, p. 461). Unfortunately, this decision was subsequently reversed by the U.S. Court of Appeals, Second Circuit, in December 1984. Although the court did not entirely accept the argument that Brajuha's notes were protected under his scholarly status as a researcher, nor did it entirely reject his assertion for a need to protect subjects. As Brajuha and Hallowell (1986, p. 461) explain: "In their view, Mario could not declare his field notes as protected by themselves but only parts of the notes that involved confidentiality or privacy claims. This was so because it was not the notes per se that were protected, but the relationships represented by the privileged data."

Finally, the U.S. Attorney's office agreed to accept notes edited to remove all claimed confidential material as evidence of Brajuha's fulfilling his subpoena. The precise ramifications from the Brajuha case remain to be worked out during future litigation involving other scholars, but his effort made large strides toward assuring researchers some protection against government intrusions into the confidentiality of their research.

Regardless of the ethical/legal resolutions determined by particular ethnographers, personal safety in the field must be considered. Being visible may provide certain elements of personal safety, albeit at the expense of nonreactivity. Ideally, ethnographers must balance moral conscience, the law, and the amount of invisibility they want to achieve in the field.

OTHER DANGERS DURING
ETHNOGRAPHIC RESEARCH

Most novice researchers do an effective job of protecting the rights and safety of their subjects. Less common among inexperienced researchers, however, are serious concerns during the design stage of research about the investigator's own personal safety. Some research, especially ethnographic research, may be in dangerous places or among dangerous people (Williams et al., 1992). Howell (1990), for example, discusses a number of crimes one is apt to encounter in the field (e.g., robbery, theft, rape, assault). Field investigators have encountered illness, personal injury, and even death during the course of ethnographic research.

Interestingly, the potential for personal or emotional harm to subject is extensively covered in virtually all research methods books. The problem of personal or emotional harm to *researchers*, however, is seldom discussed (Sluka, 1990; Williams et al., 1992). Some basic elements about caution when conducting research in general and ethnographic research in particular can be found—indirectly—in the broad methodological literature on ethnography (Adler, 1985; Adler & Adler, 1987; Broadhead & Fox, 1990; Fetterman, 1989; Johnson, 1990; Rose, 1990).

Yet, contemporary ethnographers often work in settings made dangerous by violent conflict, or with social groups among whom interpersonal violence is commonplace. As Lee (1995, p. 1) suggests, "In many cases, it is the violence itself, or the social conditions and circumstances that produce it, that actively compel attention from the social scientist. Understanding that there are potential dangers and risks to the ethnographer, therefore, is an important lesson. Knowing about these risks allows the novice researcher to determine how best to deal with them, what precautions to take, and perhaps how to avoid them.

It is possible to identify at least two distinct forms of danger that may arise during the course of ethnographic research. These include: *ambient* and *situational* risks. Similar distinctions have been offered by Lee (1995), Brewer (1993), and Sluka (1990).

Ambient dangers arise when a researcher exposes himself or herself to otherwise avoidable dangers, simply by having to be in a dangerous setting or circumstance to carry out the research. Nurses who conduct research in infectious disease wards, for example, place themselves in ambient danger.

Situational danger occurs when the researcher's presence or behaviors in the setting trigger conflict, violence, or hostility from others in the setting. For instance, an ethnographer researching tavern life, who engages in alcohol consumption as a means of gaining greater acceptance by regular participants, may also evoke trouble among the regular drinkers.

Often, the safety precautions you must take in research amount to little more than good common sense. For instance, you should never enter the field without telling someone where you will be and when you expect to leave the field. You must learn to be aware of your environment. What's going on around you? Is it nighttime and dark out? Is it nighttime but well lighted? Are there other people around? Being aware of your environment also means knowing your location and the locations where help can be obtained quickly (e.g., locations of telephones, police stations, personal friends, etc.).

It is important for the researcher's personal safety that he or she have insiders who are ready to vouch for him or her. Often a quick word from an established insider will reassure others in a group of the researcher's sincerity or purposes.

Additionally, there are places one should avoid if possible. For example, often I send my classes out to shopping malls to practice their observational skills. The single proviso I admonish students with is: Do not conduct observations in the public bathrooms! I do this not merely because public bathrooms are designed as places for private activities (although one could argue that ethical case). I do this because public bathrooms are potentially very dangerous places for researchers. Usually, they are unmonitored and secluded from the view of others. They are sometimes frequented by thieves trying to deal stolen property or drug dealers trying to sell their wares. In other words, public bathrooms may draw a variety of undesirable and dangerous people. If you are conducting actual research on activities in public bathrooms, of course, they cannot be avoided. However, in such a situation, you are likely to take proper safety precautions. For the casual practice of observational skills, however, bathrooms are simply too risky a setting.

It is also important to note that while potential risks to researchers clearly exist, only a very small proportion of researchers has ever actually been seriously injured or killed as a direct result of research (Williams et al., 1992). Perhaps one reason for this low injury rate is that experienced researchers do recognize the potential dangers and develop plans and procedures to reduce or avoid the risks involved.

WATCHING, LISTENING, AND LEARNING

Much ethnographic research involves entering the setting of some group and simply watching and listening attentively. Because it would be virtually impossible to observe everything or hear all that is going on at one time, ethnographers must watch and listen only to certain portions of what happens. One solution to this problem is to determine exactly what the researchers want to learn about at various points in the research.

Once the ethnographers have determined their essential aims, it should be possible to partition off the setting. This may be accomplished by bracketing certain subgroups of inhabitants of the domain and observing them during specific times, in certain locations, and during the course of particular events and/or routines. Frequently, a given partitioning snowballs into other relevant locations, subgroups, and activities. For example, during an ethnographic study of adolescents' involvement in alcohol, drugs, and crime (Carpenter et al., 1988), a central focus was how adolescents structured their leisure time. The ethnographers spatially began by spending time with adolescents during their free periods in local junior and senior high schools. Temporally, this meant during the time before classes in the morning (approximately one hour), during their lunch periods (approximately two hours), and after school was dismissed (approximately one hour).

In addition to learning how the observed youths structured their leisure time during these free-time periods on and around school campuses, the ethnographers began to learn where, when, and how youths spent their time outside of school. New spatial partitioning began to emerge and snowball. In addition to continuing their observations of the youths at and around school campuses, the ethnographers followed various subgroups of youths in other areas of the community and during various activities (both routine and special ones).

By the conclusion of 18 months of ethnography, the field workers had observed youths in parks, skating rinks, people's homes, school dances, video arcades, bars, movie theaters, local forests, and an assortment of other locales.

Verenne (1988) similarly writes about how youths formed cliques and made use of various spaces throughout their high school and community. Describing the availability of spaces throughout the high school, Verenne (1988, p. 216) says:

The adults gave the students a complex building which, surprisingly for a modern construction, offered various types of spaces that various groups could call their own. For example, there were many tables in the cafeteria, there were nearly a dozen small and only intermittently occupied offices in the library, there were the guidance office and the nurses' office. There were bathrooms, isolated stairway landings, the backstage area in the auditorium. There were hidden spots on the grounds—behind bushes, in a drainage ditch.

Regarding some of the times and ways students used various spaces, Verenne (1988, p. 216) explains:

During the times when they were not required to be in class, the students thus continually had to make decisions about where to go or where to sit. By ordinary right they could be in only three places: the "commons" [the cafeteria was so designated when not in use for lunch], the library, or a study hall. By extraordinary right, most often by virtue of membership in some special "club," students could be found in the private offices in the back of the library, in the coordinator's office, in the room where the audiovisual equipment was kept. . . . By self-proclaimed right, students might also be found in the bathrooms for very long periods of time not solely dedicated to the satisfaction of biological functions, or on the stairway landing from which the roof could be reached.

As indicated by the above illustrations, often subjects group themselves in meaningful ways, which allows the ethnographer to observe them more systematically.

In some instances, the researchers can partition or restrict certain places where they watch and listen and increase observational capabilities through filming or videotaping the area. This style of observation has grown increasingly popular in educational settings. For example, in a study by Hart and Sheehan (1986), social and cognitive development among children during preschool years was investigated in relationship to play activities. To accomplish their study, Hart and Sheehan (1986, p. 671) restricted the use of the playground to two groups of preschoolers and videotaped the children at play:

For seven weeks from the beginning of the preschool year in the fall before the observations began, children from each of the two groups had equal access to both sides of the playground during their 30-minute outdoor play period each day. During the observational period, barricades were placed in the access

routes between the two playgrounds and children from each separate class . . .
were asked to stay on an assigned side.

Videotaped observations then took place over a four-week period on
fair weather days while preschool activities were conducted as usual. In general, the use and versatility of videotaping during research have increased
enormously as the costs of doing so have continued to fall. Other uses of
videotape in research are discussed in Chapter 8.

How to Learn: What to Watch and Listen For

When inexperienced ethnographers enter the field for the first time, they are
impressed by the sheer number of activities and interactions going on in the
setting. The initial activities of ethnographers frequently involve getting
acclimated to the setting. This involves four general aspects:

1. Taking in the physical setting
2. Developing relationships with inhabitants (locating potential guides
   and informants)
3. Tracking, observing, eavesdropping, and asking questions
4. Locating subgroups and stars (central characters in various subgroups)

Taking in the Physical Setting

During the first few days, ethnographers usually wander around the general
location they plan to use as the setting. As they walk around the area, they
should begin to map the setting carefully. This may mean literally drawing
an accurate facsimile of the various physical locales in the setting (that is, the
streets, the buildings, the specific rooms where inhabitants pass their time,
and so on). It may mean writing detailed field notes (to be discussed later)
that describe the setting. Or it may mean some combination of both mapping and detailing in field notes.

Several purposes are served by this initial task of taking in the physical
setting. First, while mapping out the spatial elements of the setting, researchers can begin to think about how to cover these areas in the most efficient and effective manner (for example, the number of hours required,
which days or which hours during the day or night are best, and so forth).

Second, wandering around the area allows the ethnographers to begin
getting acquainted with inhabitants and vice versa. Frequently, a smile or
greeting during this initial phase will pay back tenfold later during the
research.

Third, often merely by walking around and watching and listening,
important first impressions are drawn. The first impressions may not be
entirely accurate, but they will become *points of reference* later as the

researchers become more familiar and knowledgeable about the setting and its inhabitants (Guy et al., 1987).

Developing Relationships with Inhabitants

During the initial phase of research in the field, researchers typically rely heavily on *guides*. Guides may have been located before the research through friends, acquaintances, or colleagues who knew someone among the group the researchers planned on studying. Alternatively, in the event that no guides can be identified before entering the field, one or more guides simply must be located during the early period following entry (Peshkin, 1986).

Concerning this latter form of locating guides, researchers may find that having smiled and greeted several inhabitants while taking in the setting actually becomes an essential means of beginning relationships. Although it is more difficult than simply walking up and introducing oneself, ethnographers are better advised to assume a more passive role until some relationships have been established.

The amount of receptivity shown by inhabitants varies (Argyris, 1952; Bogdan & Taylor, 1975). Frequently, inhabitants will respond to the ethnographer's greeting gestures with an inquiry about what the researchers are doing or who they are. This provides an opportunity for the researchers to explain their presence and strike an arrangement, perhaps, with the inquiring individual(s).

Researchers should remember that when they explain their presence in the field to locals, it is not a good idea to elaborate on technical details of the study. Generally, inhabitants are only interested in hearing a cursory answer to the questions, What are you doing here? and Who are you? A brief response typically will suffice. It is important, however, to answer any questions these inhabitants may ask about the project as clearly and truthfully as possible.

Another important point to impress upon locals is that all information collected during the research study will be held in strict confidence. Similarly, it is critical to impress on potential guides that the researchers are who they claim to be. This may be simply accomplished by carrying a letter of introduction and photographic identification or it may require a more extensive process of having the potential guides check you out through either official channels (calling the sponsoring institution) or, in some situations, the guides' own channels!

Finally, researchers should assure potential guides that their extensive knowledge of the people and domain will make them extremely valuable to the study. Certainly, researchers should be cautious not to become overtly insincere in their flattery. But, in truth, guides do possess certain expert knowledge and are virtually invaluable to the ethnographers for helping them gain access.

Having established a rapport with one or more guides, ethnographers can begin snowballing additional relationships with other inhabitants. The most direct way to accomplish this is to gain permission from the guides to spend some time hanging around the setting with them. As others begin to pass time in proximity, the ethnographers can ask questions of their guides about these others and may possibly obtain an introduction—including having the guides reassure newcomers of the legitimacy of the ethnographers.

Tracking, Observing, Eavesdropping, and Asking Questions

Having established relationships with several guides and inhabitants, ethnographers are free to begin really learning what goes on among the inhabitants of their study domain. This is done by tracking, observing, eavesdropping, and asking questions.

Tracking literally means following the guides around during their usual daily routines and watching their activities and the other people they interact with. As researchers follow and observe, they can also eavesdrop on conversations. Although social norms typically prohibit eavesdropping, such a proscription is untenable when conducting ethnography. Bogdan (1972) similarly suggests that although eavesdropping is necessary, it is also sometimes difficult to accomplish for people who have been reared in a noneavesdropping society. Nonetheless, researchers often learn a great deal about a phenomenon or an event simply by overhearing several people discussing it.

On some occasions, during the process of eavesdropping, researchers hear terms or learn about situations that may be important but that fall upon deaf ears. In other words, the ethnographers do not understand the significance of what they hear. On these occasions, ethnographers must ask questions, but, again, they should consider taking a passive role during such informal questioning. Perhaps jotting a cryptic note to ask the guide at a later time would serve better than interrupting the ongoing action with a question. Or perhaps arranging another meeting with some participant in the conversation (other than the guide) would offer a more fruitful approach. Decisions about how to pursue information will vary from situation to situation.

Locating Subgroups and Stars

During the course of tracking and observing, ethnographers are able to identify certain inhabitants who tend to spend more time with one another than with others. These subgroupings may or may not represent formal groups but certainly suggest a kind of social networking. Among these social networks, researchers can sociometrically identify individuals who appear to be more or less the central figures in a given network of inhabitants. Such central figures may be referred to as *stars*. Although ethnographers may not always need to establish a guide-type relationship with a star, it is sometimes necessary to obtain his or her goodwill.

In a manner similar to what Bogdan and Taylor (1975, pp. 30–33) describe as accessing *gatekeepers*, developing a relationship with a star may be a critical element in an ethnographic project. Even when ethnographers locate a guide and gain access to the basic setting, a star may hold the key to deeper penetration into the lives and perceptions of inhabitants of that setting. Sometimes a single gesture or word from a star will open more doors than weeks and weeks of attempts to gain access to these portals. Conversely, that same single gesture can slam doors that took months for the ethnographer to get opened. Whenever possible, it is advisable to find and gain the confidence of a star as soon as possible after entering the field.

Field Notes

The central component of ethnographic research is the *ethnographic account*. Providing such narrative accounts of what goes on in the lives of study subjects derives from having maintained complete, accurate, and detailed field notes. From the approach endorsed here, field notes should be completed immediately following every excursion into the field, as well as following any chance meeting with inhabitants outside the boundaries of the study setting (for example, at the supermarket, in a doctor's office, at a traffic light, and so on).

There are many variations on how to go about taking field notes. Some researchers wait until they have left the field and then immediately write complete records (Bogdan, 1972). Others take cryptic notes covertly while in the field, and later translate these into complete field notes (see Festinger et al., 1956). Burgess (1991, p. 192) suggests that "note-taking is a personal activity that depends upon the research context, the objectives of the research, and the relationship with informants."

Nonetheless, Burgess (1991) also suggests that there are some general rules for note-taking. Among these rules are recommendations for establishing a regular time and place for writing up one's notes (including the date, time, and location of the observations) and duplicating notes for safety reasons.

There are various ways to keep field notes. For example, some ethnographers carry tape recorders and periodically enter their own notes or record various conversations they witness. Other researchers carry slips of paper or index cards and simply jot notes and verbatim quotes periodically throughout the field excursion. Once out of the field, the researchers can use these notes and sketches to write full accounts. Given the advances in computers and computer software (as well as the radical cost reduction in highly sensitive and powerful personal computers), many modern-day ethnographers store their field notes on computer disks. In addition to the advantage of compact storage, word processing and utility programs allow ethnographers to move rapidly from one location in the notes to another to reconstruct sequences of events over time by copying and editing out extraneous elements, and to produce copies of portions of full notes at the press of a button.

Regardless of these note-style variations (as well as others), it is important to remember that field notes represent an attempt to record everything about an observation period in the field. Particularly concerning conversations, it is crucial that note reproduction be as close to verbatim as possible. Sometimes jotting down a key word or phrase will assist ethnographers later when they attempt to reproduce conversations. Field notes should also include details of the physical appearance of inhabitants: their clothes, hair styles and hair color, age, ethnic background, and so on.

Several additional elements to include in field notes are the time and duration of the field excursion and a consistent alteration of names and places. Concerning the former, in addition to indicating the time researchers enter and exit the field, it is important to make note of the time at which conversations, events, or activities occurred throughout the field session. These temporal sequencing marks allow ethnographers to recreate more systematically the field session. With regard to the latter issue of altering the names of people and places, the point is to protect the identities of inhabitants. Toward this end, it is advisable for ethnographers to maintain a continuous list of pseudonyms assigned to every person and location recorded in their field notes. This will assist both confidentiality and systematic retrieval of data during later analysis phases of the research.

Finally, even the opinions, preconceived notions, and general feelings about certain observed situations are also legitimate entries in field notes. However, these ethnographer-originated entries should always be bracketed and identified so that they are not mistaken as actual observations or perceptions the inhabitants themselves made.

Erosion of Memory

Individuals vary in the extent and degree of accuracy with which they can remember—in detail—events and conversations witnessed during a field excursion. Through repetition, concentration, and sincere effort, the researchers' ability to retain even minute elements, such as facial grimaces, tongue clicks, and even belt-buckle ornaments, begins to increase greatly. In addition, carefully concentrating on remembering elements of observed situations assists ethnographers in maintaining their role as researchers.

Clues and Strategies for Recalling Data

Although precise reproduction of every nuance of behavior, conversation, and event during a field excursion is impossible, highly accurate, detailed field notes can be produced. Novice ethnographers are frequently quite amazed to learn just how much material they can recall (over a short period of time) even without any specific training.

According to Bogdan and Taylor (1975), many field observers use the analogy of a *switch* to describe their procedure for remembering people, conversations, and details of a setting. These individuals suggest that they can literally turn on and turn off the intense concentration necessary for good-quality recall.

Of course, as they gain experience, ethnographers tend to develop their own cryptic note-taking styles for use in the field. Nonetheless, several general suggestions can be offered to novice ethnographers to facilitate their recollection of events that occur during a field session. Some suggestions have been implied or mentioned previously in this chapter, but will be summarized here for the sake of convenience.

1. *Record key words and key phrases while in the field.* It would be ill advised to try to stop the participants in a conversation and attempt to write down their every word. It would also be distracting to pull out a tape recorder and place it between the participants in a natural conversation. On the other hand, it may be possible during the course of their conversation to abstract certain key terms or sentences and jot these down. Whether researchers write these phrases on a napkin, an index card, or a scrap of brown paper bag is unimportant. What is important is that these phrases are taken down. It is also advisable to indicate the time the conversation occurred. Interestingly, later, in the privacy of their offices, ethnographers can usually reconstruct almost the entire conversation simply by rereading these cryptic key terms and sentences. Researchers typically will have a certain amount of memory erosion, but because of the memory-triggering effects of the key words and phrases, this erosion should be lessened.

2. *Make notes about the sequence of events.* From one perspective, activities occurring during a field session are beyond the control of the ethnographers and are consequently unstructured. However, if ethnographers gain a certain perspective, it is possible to apply a kind of pseudostructure: identifying a sequence of events. As researchers jot brief, cryptic notes, they should indicate their observed sequence of events: what occurred before the noted action, what was observed, and what occurred following this noted event. Researchers frequently find it useful, when sorting through their scraps of in-field notes, to lay them out in sequence. By rethinking the field session, following the sequence in which it actually occurred, researchers are able to recall the details and substance of even very long conversations.

3. *Limit the time you remain in the setting.* Field-note writing operates at approximately a 4:1 ratio with the time in the field. If researchers spend two hours in the field, it may require as long as eight full hours to write comprehensive field notes. Particularly for novice ethnographers, whose skill at recall may not be fully developed, only very short (15–30 minute) intervals in the field should be attempted at first. Although it is sometimes tempting to remain in the field for hours and hours, researchers must remember that in doing so, they reduce the likelihood of producing high quality, detailed field notes.

On occasion, of course, ethnographers may be willing to forego comprehensive notes in order to gain entry to some special event or ceremony. On these occasions, researchers actually turn off their intentional field concentration until the special event occurs. This, too, should be mentioned in the notes, in order to account for the two or three hours during which nothing has been annotated in the field notes.

4. *Write the full notes immediately after exiting the field.* While this may seem obvious, it still needs to be mentioned. As previously indicated, erosion of memory begins immediately and progresses rapidly. The longer researchers wait to translate their cryptic notes to full notes, the greater the likelihood of contamination from erosion. It is advisable to schedule field sessions in such a manner that full notes can be written immediately after exiting the field. Even the interruption for a meal could be sufficient to flaw the full notes.

5. *Get your notes written before sharing them with others.* Ethnographic research is often very exciting. Ethnographers frequently observe some event or conversation that so excites them that they simply need to share it with someone (often a colleague). The basic rule of thumb here is to refrain from talking; write it up and talk about it later. Besides possibly forgetting important details from a time lag before writing up notes, researchers may also accidentally embellish events. Although this embellishment may be completely unintentional, it can still flaw and contaminate otherwise important data.

What Complete Notes Should Look Like

Both in order to increase the systematic structure of later data retrieval and in order to ensure comprehensive detail without loss of quality, field-note pages should be standardized as much as possible. This means that every sheet of field notes should contain certain consistent elements: the time the ethnographer entered and exited the field; the date of the field session; a brief, descriptive topic label that captures the essence of the field session; and a page number.

As an illustration, consider the following field-note excerpt, which represents approximately two or three minutes in the field setting:

April 8, 1981, Eddie's Bar
Time In: 9:10
Time Out: 10:10
TIME: 9:10   I left the meeting with the parents' advisory group and Barry a
              few minutes past 9:00 p.m. I went directly to Eddie's Bar. After

parking my car directly in front of the bar, I started toward the door. I immediately noticed Olaf hurrying in. I followed him inside the bar. The inside of Eddie's consists of three separate rooms. The first room one enters is the main bar room. It is set up like a traditional neighborhood bar: one long bar counter (to the right of the entrance), a television up on the wall at the far end of the bar, and a few booths set along the left side of the room. To the immediate left, as one faces the wall with the booths, there is a doorway leading to a small room (approximately 10 by 10). This room contains a small billiard table, a football table, and five or six chairs and small tables. Off this smaller room is a much larger one (perhaps twice the size). There is also an entrance into this larger room through the rear of the main bar room. This larger room contains 14 long picnic tables. There are two large stereo speakers on the wall to the extreme left, and a small D.J. booth in the far left corner. The lights were very dim in this room, and the music being played (rock and roll) was very loud.

When I first walked into the main bar room, I noticed four very young-looking kids seated in the first booth (they may have been 14 or 15 years old). I didn't know any of them. I continued looking for faces I recognized. At the bar counter, several older men stood or sat on stools, drinking. Toward the back of the main bar room, where there were several small tables, I could see several more young-looking kids sitting around, some on the tables themselves and others in chairs. I still saw no one I knew.

I walked through the entrance into the large room off the rear of the bar room. Sitting on what appeared to be a bar counter (much smaller than the one in the main bar room and not in use this evening) were three girls I recognized from Oxford High School. I smiled at them, waved a greeting and said hello as I approached them. One of the girls (the one seated in the middle) leaned over to the girl to her left and audibly whispered, "Do you know this guy?" The girl being asked nodded her head yes, and said, "Yeah, I met him at the school play rehearsal the other day." I walked on past these three girls as I spotted Audrey Miller drinking a beer and sitting on top of one of the other small tables. Audrey was sitting with her right arm draped over the shoulder of some guy sitting next to her (I didn't know him). As I moved closer to her, she looked up and said, "Hello, Bruce." Her eyes widened, and she appeared a little surprised to see me. She got up off the table and walked over to me. She asked if I was there doing research or just out socializing. I told her I was doing research. She remarked, "Well, you've certainly come to the right place, this whole room is filled with Oxford kids." She was just slightly slurring her words, suggesting that the beer she held in her right hand was not her first. She said, "I'll see you later," and walked back to the group of kids with whom she had been sitting.

As illustrated in the preceding field-note excerpt, much observed detail about the physical setting is included, as well as assessments of people in the setting. After reading ethnographers' full field notes, it should be possible for a person to visualize exactly what the ethnographers saw and heard during the field session.

Having concluded their field sessions (the data-gathering phase of the project) the ethnographers will have presumably amassed hundreds or even thousands of pages of field notes. These field notes will take up considerable space and an even longer time to read. Organizing large quantities of such notes is very time consuming and both physically and mentally exhausting. It is desirable, then, to amass these notes in some systematic fashion and perhaps even to reduce their bulk for analytic purposes (Becker, Gordon, & LeBailly, 1984).

To accomplish the dual task of keeping large quantities of field notes and reproducing them in reduced form, many researchers rely upon computers. An additional advantage to using computers, beyond storage and reproduction, is their ability to allow textual material to be retrieved in an efficient and speedy manner. There are several ways one can make use of computers when developing field notes. The most obvious is to use any commercial word processing program. Word processing programs are designed to handle, store, and retrieve textual material or, in this case, data. Alternately, one might choose one of the commercial programs designed for qualitative data storage and analysis (see for examples Dennis, 1984; Tallerico, 1991). These programs provide a structure into which novice researchers can pour their field notes. As well, they provide a method by which to efficiently create a duplicate set or a data-reduced set of field notes.

You must be cautious when reducing qualitative data such as field notes. If you reduce too much, details and nuance of the data may be lost, impairing if not ruining the analysis. As well, some studies will require greater amounts of detail than others (Becker, Gordon, & LeBailly, 1984). In these cases, field notes will need to be kept closer to their original form. In most cases, however, various aspects of field notes may be redundant. For example, descriptions of the same individuals, locations, and settings need not be reproduced in full every time they arise. Researchers may find it better to briefly summarize such material or cite it only once. Similarly, many researchers find it more effective for analytical purposes to create a set of summarized field notes that are keyed or cross indexed to their original lengthier versions. Thus, two or three pages of notes may be reproduced to perhaps a half page of summary. Since the full notes are cross indexed to this summary, the researcher can fairly easily retrieve these lengthier versions during analysis. The use of computers in qualitative analysis is discussed in somewhat greater detail in Chapter 11. For now, it is sufficient to suggest that computers do aid significantly in the storage, duplication, and data-reduction portions of field note generation.

The obvious next question becomes, What do you do now? You have completed all your field work, recorded these full notes on a computer, perhaps even created reduced summaries to assist in managing the bulk. But how will you actually go about analyzing this material? Although there are certainly no easy answers to how you go about abstracting meaning from ethnographic research, researchers may draw on several potentially useful analytical strategies.

Analyzing Ethnographic Data

Analysis of data is not an exact science. With some types of data (particularly survey questionnaire data), there are many different ways to make sense of the information once the data are collected, organized, and coded. However, when dealing with ethnographic data, researchers must make somewhat narrower choices. For example, even though it is certainly possible to test hypotheses using ethnographic data, the process differs somewhat from research that uses survey data. Ethnographic research can potentially demonstrate the plausibility of a hypothesis, but it cannot actually prove its validity. Using reductionistic procedures to cull numbers from the ethnographic data is not really in keeping with the ethnographic process. Thus, two effective ways remain to analyze ethnographic research while preserving the rich textual detail of the data: inductive content analysis and ethnographic narrative accounts.

Systematic analysis of ethnographic data typically begins by reading the field notes—whether one wants to produce ethnographic accounts or a content analysis of the data. The purposes of this initial reading of the notes are to reinforce any hypotheses or themes developed during the data-collection phase and to generate new hypotheses and themes previously unrealized—in short, to ground themes and hypotheses to the data (Glaser & Strauss, 1967). During this initial coding, researchers undertake what is called *open coding* (explained comprehensively in Chapter 11). Briefly, open coding allows researchers to identify and even extract themes, topics, or issues in a systematic manner.

Next, ethnographers should begin to notice and systematically create records of patterns in the conversations and activities of people depicted in the notes. This *coding* process is discussed more completely in Chapter 11.

At this juncture, the researchers must decide whether to undertake a comprehensive content analysis or to rely on lengthy textual accounts to document themes and patterns observed in the data. Although both procedures are certainly similar, there is at least one important difference, which concerns whether, conceptually, ethnography is viewed strictly as a means for collecting data or as both the means and the product of the ethnographic process (Stoddart, 1986). In the first instance, researchers may easily accomplish a comprehensive content analysis, but if the second conceptual stance is taken, the researchers must demonstrate topics and patterns by presenting appropriate (and often lengthy) narrative textual accounts from the field notes.

As with all analytic strategies, strengths and weaknesses are associated with each approach. The most important problem commonly associated with qualitative data of any type is the question of confidence in the accuracy of suggested patterns. In the case of content analysis, researchers might manage to convince their audience by suggesting the magnitude (frequency) of a given theme or pattern (see Chapter 11). In the case of ethnographic narratives, researchers must rely on the pattern being sufficiently clear in itself (as presented in the field notes) to convince an audience of its accuracy (Stoddart, 1986).

Burns (1980) illustrates how one effectively uses ethnographic narrative accounts in his "Getting Rowdy with the Boys." Burns offers a detailed examination of the drinking behavior of a single group of young working-class males. His procedure involves describing the sequence of events and interactions experienced by these young men during one evening in several different drinking environments. As Burns indicates, his analysis of the ethnographic narrative account offered may be termed *thick description* (Geertz, 1973). This type of analysis is directed toward drawing out a complete picture of the observed events, the actors involved, the rules associated with certain activities, and the social contexts in which these elements arise. Burns (1980) accomplishes this by first presenting the narration (chiefly the detailed field notes of his ethnographic experience during the observed evening). Next, Burns steps out of the field and, in his role as a social scientist, analyzes the narrative contents, highlighting apparent structural components of situations, meanings suggested by actors and events, and patterns that emerge during the course of the narrative. To some extent, this lengthier narrative technique is justified in the following passage from Festinger et al. (1956, p. 252):

> *Our material is largely qualitative rather than quantitative, and even simple tabulations of what we observed would be difficult. Owing to the complete novelty and unpredictability of the movement, as well as the pressure of time, we could not develop standard categories of events, actions, statements, feelings, and the like, and certainly could not subject the members of the group to any standardized interview, in order to compare indices before and after disconfirmation.*

In a similar manner, Humphreys (1970, p. 22) states:

My concern in this study has been with the description of a specific style of deviant behavior and of the population who engage in that activity. Beyond such systematic, descriptive analysis, I have tried to offer, in the light of deviance theory, some explanation as to why, and how these people participate in the particular form of behavior described [namely, casual homosexual encounters].

Traditionally, the researches of Humphreys (1970) and Festinger, Riecken, and Schlacter (1956) are described as *participant observational* studies, but their techniques are chiefly consistent with ethnography. This, of course, draws attention once more to the conceptual confusion that surrounds the general sociological understanding of ethnographic research.

DISENGAGING: GETTING OUT

Although it is certainly possible to maintain complete professional distance when distributing questionnaires to anonymous subjects, it is not as easy during ethnography. Because relationships are virtually the stock and trade of a good ethnographer, care must be taken when leaving the field.

Exiting any field setting involves at least two separate operations: first, the physical removal of the researchers from the research setting and second, emotional disengagement from the relationships developed during the field experience. In some situations *getting out* is described as a kind of mechanical operation, devoid of any (personal) emotional attachments on the part of the ethnographer. Concern is sometimes shown, and efforts made, to avoid distressing a research community. However, negative repercussions can occur in the forms of possible effects on the group(s) as a whole or the possible reception future field investigators might expect (Chadwick et al., 1984; Shaffir et al., 1980).

Even when the emotions of field relationships are mentioned, they frequently are described exclusively as concern over the perspective of the inhabitant of the natural setting. For example, Shaffir et al. (1980, p. 259) state:

Personal commitments to those we study often accompany our research activity. Subjects often expect us to continue to live up to such commitments permanently. On completing the research, however, our commitment subsides and is often quickly overshadowed by other considerations shaping our day-to-day lives. When our subjects become aware of our diminished interest in their lives and situations, they may come to feel cheated—manipulated and duped.

The point is not to underplay the possible emotional harm a callous investigator might cause a research group, but it should be noted that relationships are two-way streets. Subjects make personal emotional commitments, and so, too, do many researchers—even without actually going native! Consequently, when it comes time to leave the field, researchers have developed some deep feelings for their subjects. These feelings may not always be positive but are nonetheless psychologically taxing.

Ethnographers can certainly absent themselves from the field and simply dismiss the subjects from their minds, but it is likely that the ethnographers will continue to hold at least some proprietary interest in the welfare of the subjects. For example, during the course of conducting the research discussed in Carpenter et al. (1988), the ethnographers commonly spoke about "their" kids with almost parental concern or, on occasion, with almost parental pride in certain accomplishments.

A strong commitment and attachment developed between many of the youthful subjects and the ethnographers. When it came time to leave the field, the ethnographers informally continued to keep an eye on many of the subjects for over a year. This essentially amounted to asking about specific kids when they accidentally ran into mutual acquaintances or getting involved in the lives of these special kids when their paths crossed by chance (for instance, in a supermarket or shopping mall). Other field investigators have indicated similar prolonged interest in research subjects, even many years after physically leaving the setting. Letkemann (1980, p. 300), for instance, indicates that even 10 years after exiting the field, and more than 800 miles away from the site, he continued to stay informed about the welfare of his subjects.

Because of the uniqueness of every field situation, there are different nuances to exiting. Ethnographers, however, must always be mindful that the time will come to leave—at least physically. Toward this end, researchers must prepare both the community members and themselves for the exit. Perhaps a quick exit will work in some cases (Festinger et al. 1956; Rains, 1971), whereas a more gradual drifting off may be required in other circumstances (Glaser & Strauss, 1967). Unfortunately, these research-related decisions are not easily made.

TRYING IT OUT

As with all research methods, researchers must practice, stumble, and even sometimes fail to accomplish the research project in order to appreciate how ethnographic strategies operate. Several suggestions follow for brief microethnographic projects. Again, as with the practice interviewing topics (see Chapter 4), these suggestions are intended as exercises, not necessarily full-blown projects in themselves.

The first project suggestion sounds deceptively simple, but be mindful and attentive while in the field. This suggestion borrows from Garfinkel's (1967) conceptualization of how people make sense of things around them (reflexively) and adjust their meanings to fit their observations (creating indexes of things). This general theoretical area is more commonly called *ethnomethodology* (see Schwartz & Jacobs [1979] for elaboration of this term). These suggestions properly belong in the category of ethnomethodological experimentation. Stated simply, students/researchers will be asked first to violate intentionally some social norm. Next, the students/researchers should carefully watch, listen, and take note of how people around them process the norm violation. In doing this, they will gain considerable practice in many of the methods associated with ethnographic research.

Suggestion 1

In a crowded elevator, begin systematically to violate elevator rituals. For example, on entering, do not turn around and face the front. Rather than stand silently, strike up a conversation with the people around you. Ask strangers in the elevator such personal questions as "So, how's the family?" "How have things been at work for you?" and so forth.

Be sure to record in your field notes, both verbal responses and facial grimaces. Be attentive to details. It may be wise to work in teams so that as one student violates the norms, the other can more comprehensively observe the responses of people attempting to process the event.

Suggestion 2

After carefully walking through a supermarket and loading up a cart, begin systematically to walk backward through the store, replacing every item previously placed in the cart in its original location on the shelves. Again, this project might be better accomplished with both a watcher and a norm violator.

Inexperienced researchers will probably be a bit skittish at first. Therefore, in order to allow these students/researchers an opportunity to practice and gain confidence in their researching skills, consider the next practice suggestion (and its obvious possible extensions).

Suggestion 3

Position yourself in a location where many people congregate. (Shopping malls, bus terminals, and airports are good examples of the sorts of places.) Next, simply sit and watch and listen. Construct field notes of the observations and what you have heard (from conversations and the like). Repeat this activity for several different days. Be certain that you write up full notes when you leave the field each day. Bear in mind that the time spent in the field geometrically increases when you write up your full notes. Initially, spend no more than 15 or 20 minutes at a time in the field.

NOTE

1. Stoddart, Kenneth, The presentation of everyday life, *Urban Life*, 15(1) (1986), pp. 103–121.

REFERENCES

Adler, P. A. (1985). *Wheeling and Dealing.* New York: Columbia University Press.

Adler, P. A., & Adler, P. (1987). *Membership Roles in Field Research.* Newbury Park, CA: Sage.

Adler, P. A., Adler, P., & Rochford, E. B., Jr. (1986). The politics of participation in field research. *Urban Life 14*(4), 363–376.

Agar, M. H. (1973). *Ripping and Running: A Formal Ethnography of Urban Heroin Addicts.* New York: Seminar Press.

Agar, M. H. (1986). *Speaking of Ethnography.* Beverly Hills, CA: Sage.

Allen, J. D. (1986). Classroom management: Students' perspectives, goals, and strategies. *American Educational Research Journal 23*(3), 437–459.

Argyris, C. (1952). Diagnosing defenses against the outsider. *Journal of Social Issues 8*(3), 24–34.

Becker, H. S. (1963). *Outsiders: Studies in the Sociology of Deviance.* New York: Free Press.

Becker, H. S., Gordon, A. C., & LeBailly, R. K. (1984). Field work with the computer: Criteria for assessing systems. *Qualitative Sociology 7*(1/2), 16–33.

Berg, B. L., & Doerner, W. G. (1987, November). *Volunteer police officers: An unexamined aspect of police personnel.* Paper presented at the annual meeting of the American Society of Criminology, Montreal, PQ.

Berg, B. L., Ksander, M., Loughlin, J., & Johnson, B. (1983, August). *Cliques and groups: Adolescents' affective ties and criminal activities.* Paper presented at the annual meeting of the Society for the Study of Social Problems, Detroit.

Bogdan, R. (1972). *Participant Observation in Organizational Settings.* Syracuse, NY: Syracuse University Press.

Bogdan, R., & Taylor, S. (1975). *Introduction to Qualitative Research Methods.* New York: Wiley.

Brajuha, M., & Hallowell, L. (1986). Legal intrusion and the politics of fieldwork. *Urban Life 14*(4), 454–479.

Brewer, J. D. (1993). Sensitivity as a problem in field research: A study of routine policing in Northern Ireland. In C. M. Renzetti & R. M. Lee (Eds.), *Researching Sensitive Topics.* Newbury Park, CA: Sage.

Brown, P. (1996). Catskill culture: The rise and fall of a Jewish resort area seen through personal narrative and ethnography. *Journal of Contemporary Ethnography 25*(1), 83–119.

Broadhead, R. S., & Fox, K. J. (1990). Takin' it to the streets: AIDS outreach as ethnography. *Journal of Contemporary Ethnography 19,* 322–348.

Burgess, R. G. (1991). Keeping field notes. In R. G. Burgess (Ed.), *Field Research: A Sourcebook and Field Manual.* New York: Routledge.

Burns, N., & Grove, S. K. (1993). *The Practice of Nursing Research.* Philadelphia: W. B. Saunders.

Burns, T. F. (1980). Getting rowdy with the boys. *Journal of Drug Issues 80*(1), 273–286.

Carpenter, C., Glassner, B., Johnson, B., & Loughlin, J. (1988). *Kids, Drugs, and Crime.* Lexington, MA: Lexington Books.

Chadwick, B. A., Bahr, H. M., & Albrecht, S. L. (1984). *Social Science Research Methods.* Englewood Cliffs, NJ: Prentice Hall.

Clifford, J. (1980). Fieldwork, reciprocity and the making of ethnographic texts: The examples of Maurice Leenhardt. *Man 15*, 518–532.

Dennis, D. L. (1984). Word crunching: An annotated bibliography on computers and qualitative data analysis. *Qualitative Sociology 7*(1/2), 148–156.

Denzin, N. K. (1970). *Sociological Methods: A Sourcebook.* Chicago: Aldine.

Denzin, N. K. (1978). *The Research Act.* New York: McGraw-Hill.

Ellen, R. F. (1984). *Ethnographic Research.* New York: Academic Press.

Festinger, L., Riecken, H. W., & Schacter, S. (1956). *When Prophecy Fails.* New York: Harper and Bros.

Fetterman, D. M. (1989). *Ethnography: Step by Step.* Newbury Park, CA: Sage.

Francke, A. L., Garssen, B., Abu-Saad, H. H., & Grypdonck, M. (1996). Qualitative needs assessment prior to a continuing educational program. *Journal of Continuing Education in Nursing 27*(1), 34–41.

Garfinkel, H. (1967). *Studies in Ethnomethodology.* Englewood Cliffs, NJ: Prentice Hall.

Geertz, C. (1973). Thick description: Toward an interpretive theory of culture. In C. Geertz (Ed.), *The Interpretation of Culture.* New York: Basic Books.

Glaser, B. G., & Strauss, A. (1967). *The Discovery of Grounded Theory: Strategies for Qualitative Research.* Chicago: Aldine.

Guy, R. F., Edgley, C. E., Arafat, I., & Allen, D. E. (1987). *Social Research Methods.* Boston: Allyn and Bacon.

Haas, J., & Shaffir, W. (August 1978). *Do new ways of professional socialization make a difference? A study of professional socialization.* Paper presented at the Ninth World Congress of Sociology, Uppsala, Sweden.

Hart, C. H., & Sheehan, R. (1986). Preschoolers' play behavior in outdoor environments: Effects of traditional and contemporary playgrounds. *American Educational Research Journal 23*(4), 668–678.

Hertz, R., & Imber, J. B. (1993). Fieldwork in elite settings (Introduction). *Journal of Contemporary Ethnography 22*(1), 3–6.

Hoffmann, J. E. (1980). Problems of access in the study of social elites and boards of directors. In W. Shaffir, R. Stebbins, & A. Turowetz (Eds.), *Fieldwork Experience.* New York: St. Martin's Press.

Horowitz, R. (1983). *Honor and the American Dream.* New Brunswick, NJ: Rutgers University Press.

Howell, N. (1990). *Surviving Fieldwork: A Report of the Advisory Panel on Health and Safety in Fieldwork.* Washington, DC: American Anthropological Association.

Humphreys, L. (1970). *Tearoom Trade.* Chicago: Aldine.

Humphreys, L. (1975). *Tearoom Trade: Impersonal Sex in Public Places* (Enl. ed.). Chicago: Aldine.

Janesick, V. J. (1994). The dance of qualitative research design. In N. K. Denzin & Y. S. Lincoln (Eds.), *Handbook of Qualitative Research.* Thousand Oaks, CA: Sage.

Johnson, B., Goldstein, P. J., Preble, E., Schmeidler, J., Lipton, D. S., Spunt, B., & Miller, T. (1985). *Taking Care of Business.* Lexington, MA: Lexington Books.

Johnson, J. C. (1990). *Selecting Ethnographic Informants.* Newbury Park, CA: Sage.

Johnson, J. M. (1975). *Doing Field Research.* New York: Free Press.

Lee, R. M. (1995). *Dangerous Fieldwork.* Thousand Oaks, CA: Sage.

Leininger, M. M. (Ed.). (1985). *Qualitative Research Methods in Nursing.* Orlando, FL: Grune & Stratton.

Letkemann, P. (1980). Crime as work: Leaving the field. In W. Shaffir, R. Stebbins, & A. Turowetz (Eds.), *Field Work Experience*. New York: St. Martin's Press.

Lincoln, Y. S., & Guba, E. G. (1985). *Naturalistic Inquiry*. Beverly Hills, CA: Sage.

Lofland, J. (1996). Analytic ethnography: Features, failings, and futures. *Journal of Contemporary Ethnography 24*(1), 30–67.

Lofland, J., & Lofland, L. H. (1984). *Analyzing Social Settings: A Guide to Qualitative Observation and Analysis*. Belmont, CA: Wadsworth Publishing.

Matza, D. (1969). *Becoming Deviant*. Englewood Cliffs, NJ: Prentice Hall.

Mehan, H. (1978). Structuring school structure. *Harvard Educational Review 48*(1), 32–64.

Ostrander, S. A. (1993). Surely you're not in this just to be helpful: Access, rapport, and interviews in three studies of elites. *Journal of Contemporary Ethnography 22*(1), 7–27.

Peshkin, A. (1986). *God's Choice: The Total World of a Fundamentalist Christian School*. Chicago: University of Chicago Press.

Peshkin, A. (1988). The researcher and subjectivity: Reflections on an ethnography of school and community. In G. Spindler (Ed.), *Doing The Ethnography of Schooling*. Prospect Heights, IL: Waveland Press.

Peterson, B. H. (1985). A qualitative clinical account and analysis of a care situation. In M. L. Leininger (Ed.), *Qualitative Research Methods in Nursing*. Orlando, FL: Grune & Stratton.

Philips, S. (1972). Participant structures and communicative competence: Warm Springs children in community and classroom. In C. Cazden, D. Hymes, and V. John (Eds.), *Functions of Language in the Classroom*. New York: Columbia University Teachers College Press.

Philips, S. (1975). *The invisible culture: Communication in classroom and community in Warm Springs Reservation*. Doctoral dissertation, University of Pennsylvania, Philadelphia.

Polit, D. F., & Hungler, B. P. (1993). *Essentials of Nursing Research*. Philadelphia: J. B. Lippincott.

Polsky, N. (1969). *Hustlers, Beats, and Others*. Garden City, NY: Doubleday.

Preble, E., & Casey, J. J. (1969). Taking care of business: The heroin user's life on the street. *International Journal of Addiction 4*, 1–24.

Punch, M. (1986). *The Politics and Ethics of Field Work*. Newbury Park, CA: Sage.

Quint, J. C. (1967). *The Nurse and the Dying Patient*. New York: Macmillan.

Rains, P. (1971). *Becoming an Unwed Mother*. Chicago: Aldine.

Roethlisberger, F. J., & Dickenson, W. J. (1939). *Management and the Worker*. Cambridge, MA: Harvard University Press.

Rose, D. (1990). *Living the Ethnographic Life*. Newbury Park, CA: Sage.

Rosenhan, D. L. (1973). On being sane in insane places. *Science 179*(19), 250–258.

Rubin, H. J., & Rubin, I. S. (1995). *Qualitative Interviewing: The Art of Hearing Data*. Thousand Oaks, CA: Sage.

Schatzman, L., & Strauss, A. (1973). *Field Research: Strategies for a Natural Sociology*. Englewood Cliffs, NJ: Prentice Hall.

Schwartz, H., & Jacobs, J. (1979). *Qualitative Sociology: A Method to the Madness*. New York: Free Press.

Shaffir, W. B., Stebbins, R. A., & Turowetz, A. (1980). *Fieldwork Experience: Qualitative Approaches to Social Research*. New York: St. Martin's Press.

Sluka, J. A. (1990). Participant observation in violent social contexts. *Human Organization 49*(2), 114–126.

Spencer, G. (1991). Methodological issues in the study of bureaucratic elites: A case study of West Point. In R. G. Burgess (Ed.), *Field Research: A Sourcebook and Field Manual*. New York: Routledge.

Spindler, G. (1988). *Doing the Ethnography of Schooling*. Prospect Heights, IL: Waveland Press.

Spindler, G., & Spindler, L. (1988). Roger Harker and Schonhausen: From familiar to strange and back again. In G. Spindler (Ed.), *Doing the Ethnography of Schooling*. Prospect Heights, IL: Waveland Press.

Spradley, J. P. (1979). *The Ethnographic Interview*. New York: Holt, Rinehart & Winston.

Spradley, J. P. (1980). *Participant Observation*. New York: Holt, Rinehart & Winston.

Stinchcombe, A. C. (1975). Merton's theory of social structure. In L. Coser (Ed.), *The Idea of Social Structure*. New York: Harcourt Brace Jovanovich.

Stoddart, K. (1986). The presentation of everyday life. *Urban Life 15*(1), 103–121.

Strauss, A. L. (1987). *Qualitative Analysis for Social Scientists*. New York: Cambridge University Press.

Tallerico, M. (1991). Application of qualitative analysis software: A view from the field. *Qualitative Sociology 14*(3), 275–285.

Thomas, W. I., & Swaine, D. (1928). *The Child in America*. New York: Knopf.

Van Maanen, J. (1982). Fieldwork on the beat. In J. Van Maanen, J. Dabbs, Jr., & R. R. Faulkner (Eds.), *Varieties of Qualitative Research*. Beverly Hills, CA: Sage.

Verenne, H. (1988). Jocks and freaks: The symbolic structure of the expression of social interaction among American senior high school students. In G. Spindler (Ed.), *Doing the Ethnography of Schooling*. Prospect Heights, IL: Waveland Press.

Weppner, R. S. (1977). *Street Ethnography*. Beverly Hills, CA: Sage.

Whyte, W. F. (1955). *Street Corner Society*. Chicago: University of Chicago Press.

Wilcox, K. (1988). Ethnography as a methodology and its applications to the study of schooling: A review. In G. Spindler (Ed.), *Doing the Ethnography of Schooling*. Prospect Heights, IL: Waveland Press.

Williams, T., Dunlap, E., Johnson, B. D., & Hamid, A. (1992). Personal safety in dangerous places. *Journal of Contemporary Ethnography 21*(3), 343–373.

Wolcott, H. F. (1973). *The Man in the Principal's Office: An Ethnography* (Reprint, 1984). Prospect Heights, IL: Waveland Press.

Yablonsky, L. (1965). Experience with the criminal community. In A. W. Gouldner & S. M. Miller (Eds.), *Applied Sociology*. New York: Free Press.

Zigarmi, D., & Zigarmi, P. (1980). The psychological stresses of ethnographic research. *Education and Urban Society 12*(3), 291–322.

SOCIOMETRY

WHAT IS SOCIOMETRY?

Sociometry is a procedure that allows the researcher to make assessments about the affinity or disdain members of some group have toward one another. It allows you to consider friendship patterns, social networks, work relationships, and social distance in general. Sociometry can be described as a means of assessing group relational structures such as hierarchies, friendship networks, and cliques. Sociometry can also indicate a group's social dynamics and influence structure.

Sociometry has been used in organizational settings to assess power relationships, especially those with superordinate and subordinate power arrangements. It also has been used to examine classroom and playground interactions and associations, in social psychological settings, and fairly extensively in social network research (Asher & Hymel, 1981; Hampson, 1984; Hartup, 1976; Newcomb & Bukowski, 1983).

Sociometric techniques have been used to examine the social skills of preschoolers and, increasingly during the past decade, to categorize children with difficulties in peer relations (Hymel & Rubin, 1985; Rubin, 1982). However, during the past 40 years or so, fewer and fewer qualitative researchers have recognized the utility of sociometry. One possible reason for this may be the attempt by some users to make sociometry more mathematical than is necessary (see, for examples, Arabie, 1984; Leedy, 1993; Schwartz & Sprinzen, 1984; Skvoretz, 1985, Wilson, 1982).

This notion of mathematizing sociometry suggests that users have tried to claim precision akin to more sophisticated statistical measures of association (Berg & Rounds, 1992). Were this mathematizing activity merely a dramaturgic attempt to play the part of scientist—the pretense of positivism to obtain federal funding or greater acceptance in the publication arena—one might understand such behavior (Glassner, 1990; Lidz & Ricci, 1990). Unfortunately, mathematizing sociometric techniques is a genuine attempt to convert a strategy once rich with grounded theoretical orientations into little more than another analytic formula stripped of its connections to social reality. Let us consider the origins of sociometry and perhaps better understand how it can be used effectively in qualitative research.

THE HISTORY AND PURPOSE
OF SOCIOMETRIC STRATEGIES

Often, sociometry is credited with having been popularized by Moreno in *Who Shall Survive?* (1934). This book, however, was published after Moreno and others in the field of social psychology and sociology had themselves used sociometric strategies in elementary school settings for many years. During the early years of sociometry's development and refinement, it rapidly expanded its scope and application areas. Social scientists of varied interest areas began incorporating sociometric techniques in their research. These areas included such diverse research topics as corporate organizational structures, children, and even the military. In 1952, Moreno observed that while there was a rapid assimilation of sociometry's techniques, operations, and methods, there was a parallel ignorance of and resistance to its theories (Moreno, 1952, p. 148).

In hindsight, it seems sad and ironic that sociometric techniques have somehow been lost to contemporary qualitative researchers and found by quantitative ones. Worse yet is the reality that many of the contemporary sociometric strategies have been taken for granted: methodological activities that have been undertaken in a theoretical void, techniques whose qualitative and social psychological theoretical histories have been taken lightly or forgotten. This is a serious problem for several reasons. First, the techniques used in sociometric strategies were not developed in a vacuum. Rather, they are intricately related to empirical evidence established as a result of the repeated testing of theories and concepts. These empirical tests bear directly on the validity and reliability of each technique. Second, understanding the theoretical origins of sociometry is an important prerequisite for the proper use of sociometric tests and the effective understanding of sociometric drawings or sociograms.[1] In other words, if you do not understand the theoretical underpinnings, you do not actually understand the reasons that certain techniques are used. Nor, for that matter, can you actually understand the meaning of the outcomes when you use these sociometric strategies.

What appears to have occurred during the past 60 years is that researchers have used sociometric techniques but have separated these techniques from their meanings and theories. This has created a kind of vacuous mechanical activity in which the technique becomes an end in itself.

Consequently, sociometric tests and sociograms have been used to produce research in a kind of theoretical abyss.

In this void, people were asked in a gamelike fashion whom they liked and disliked. Then, lines of connection were drawn to represent their answers and to describe the group's structure. In addition, as sociometric strategies moved away from their traditional meanings and theories, the differences between these and observational practices in general became blurred. Sociometric strategies certainly may be used during the course of observational research. They are not, however, synonymous with strategies usually associated with observational field research (Berg & Rounds, 1992).

Sociometry, in its traditional sense, is a means of measuring social distance between group members. More directly, it concerns assessing attractions and repulsions between individuals in a group and within the group structure as defined by these feelings. Jennings (1948, p. 11) describes the method as follows, "Stated briefly, sociometry may be described as a means of presenting simply and graphically the entire structure of relations existing at a given time among members of a group. The major line of communication, or the pattern of attraction and rejection in its full scope, are made comprehensive at a glance."

However, Jennings (1948, p. 11) also states that the sociometric test and sociograms are not the end point of research but only the beginning. She says, "It should, of course, be said at once that the sociometric test and diagram do not suffice to explain the motives underlying the choices made. . . . As a starting point, however, the chief significance of a sociogram lies in its comprehensive revelation of the group structure and its clear direction toward the next steps for study or investigation."

The study of social structure long has been a central focus of researchers in the social sciences. Investigations such as Sutherland's (1939) *differential association*, Cohen's (1955) study of delinquent boys, Sykes's (1958) examination of correctional officers, Coleman's (1961) consideration of adolescent culture, and Alpert and Dunham's (1988) study of community policing strategies all examine social structure. In any social structure, we find positions held by incumbents that form systematic patterns of social relations between other positions and incumbents in the group. Even in the study of social networks, where individuals may have fairly loose connections to the network, social pressure may be exerted to divert network members away from social norm violation. Conversely, social pressure may be exerted to support and encourage norm violations by social network members (Schwartz & Sprinzen, 1984). Thus, identification of a subject's relative social position in a group through sociometric tests can assist a researcher in identifying key elements of the social structure. This technique also provides a means for field researchers to identify *key individuals*, those people who can serve as guides or informants for the researcher. Finally, this technique identifies *stars*, persons able to wield considerable influence over others in the group (Leedy, 1993).

Sociometric techniques allow considerable latitude in their application and flexibility in how they can be used in research settings. For example, consider a large city hospital's intensive care unit that may be plagued with internal complaints, low morale, and intrapersonnel conflict. You could examine the problems in an intensive care unit in a number of ways. Among these would be to begin with a sociometric test (explained in the section that follows) and from this identify the individual or people who possess the greatest influence over others in the work group. Once identified, these sociometric stars could be approached and interviewed, more carefully observed in interaction with others, or even surveyed about their concerns. Identification of the influence structures, then, would provide a first step in better understanding the formal and informal organizations of the intensive care unit.

Perhaps the most widely known applications of sociometric techniques are those used by Whyte (1955) in his *Street Corner Society* study. Whyte studied Doc and his boys, a group of men in their teens and twenties who hung around together in an Italian-American slum neighborhood in Boston during the 1930s. At the time, Whyte was on a fellowship at Harvard University. Whyte, an outsider to this neighborhood and group, needed a guide to assist him in gaining access and insight to the group.

In his examination of Doc's boys, the Nortons, Whyte was able to create a diagram that detailed the relative social status and influence on relationships among this group. This diagram or *sociogram* allowed Whyte to demonstrate that usual expectations about personal and social relationships may not always operate in a rational and predictable manner. For example, among the activities the Nortons regularly participated in was bowling. The group members frequently engaged in matches among themselves and competed in teams on Saturdays. Whyte observed that a member's bowling score did not reflect his athletic abilities. For example, on the basis of sheer athletic abilities, Frank, who had played semiprofessional baseball, should have been the best bowler. Yet he was not the best bowler. In fact, even when he played sandlot baseball with his friends, Frank was not a very good player.

Another member of the Nortons, Alec, excelled at bowling when the group played just for fun on weekdays. However, when the boys got together to compete in teams on Saturday evenings, Alec could not seem to bowl a decent game. Yet Doc and another member, Danny, both of whom were only average bowlers during the week, would defeat the other teams game after game on Saturday evenings.

Whyte eventually learned that a member's bowling ability did not reflect his athletic ability. Rather, bowling scores reflected the social status a member held in the group—the very status Whyte had identified in his sociogram.

HOW SOCIOMETRY WORKS

A sociometric test typically includes three basic characteristics:

1. A specific number of choices are used (varying with the size of the group).
2. A specific number of choices are allowed (varying according to the functions and/or activities of the groups tested).
3. Different levels of preference are assigned to each choice.

Positive Peer Nominations

The early users of sociometric tests typically employed a *peer nomination* version of this test. In this procedure, the group members were asked to name three or more peers whom they liked the most, or whom they best liked working with, or who were their best friends (depending upon the kind of group). A group member's score was then computed as the number of nominations he or she received from other members of the group. This version of the sociometric test is called *positive peer nominations*. As users of sociometric tests refined these procedures, adaptations naturally arose.

Negative Peer Nominations

One such adaptation to peer nominations initially was introduced by Dunnington (1957) and again by Moore and Updergraff (1964). This adaptation involved a request for negative nominations. In other words, in addition to asking for three especially liked peers, a second request was made that members identify the three peers least liked (or least desirable to work with). This strategy was used to identify two groups of peers—namely, a *popular group* (high frequency of positive nominations) and a disliked or *rejected group* (high frequency of negative nominations). Subsequent research in which juveniles are identified as members of these groups indicates that rejected children often are more aggressive and likely to engage in antisocial behavior (Dodge, Coie, & Brakke, 1982; Hartup et al., 1967). This suggests significant utility for those interested in studying delinquents, youth movements, school cliques, and even gang structures.

Peer Rating Procedures

Another adaptation that has come into common use is the *peer rating procedure*, a sociometric test similar in many ways to the nomination procedure. Group members respond to the usual sociometric questions (whom do you like to work with, be with, etc.) for every other member of the group. Each group member is given a list containing the names of all group members and asked to rate every other member using a five-point Likert-like scale. The scale for these five points is typically a graduated series of statements that moves from expressions of favor to expressions of disfavor for members of the group. An example of this sort of scale is shown in Figure 7.1. As in traditional Likert scales, you assess the mean rating score for each person. A mean rating in the low range indicates that the group member is not well liked by others in the group. A mean rating in the high range indicates that the group member is well liked. As Jennings (1948) warned, however, identification of this sociometric pattern *is not* the completion of the research but only the beginning. The use of mathematics to locate sociometric stars, then, should not be overemphasized. It is a convenient tool but not the substantive result of research.

Once you have identified the social relations and social structures that exist, you still must examine the incumbents of positions in this structure. Assisted by the sociometric information, you are better equipped to locate appropriate guides, informants, and gatekeepers of the group. Thus, you might begin an investigation with a sociometric survey and then pursue the research through other ethnographic field techniques, interviews, or even unobtrusive measures. Sociometric choice tests, then, provide yet another line of action you can use in a triangulated research design.

APPLICATIONS OF
SOCIOMETRIC TECHNIQUES

Even the cursory description of sociometric tests offered in this chapter should demonstrate the utility of this strategy in social scientific research. For instance, you can easily imagine how a study of police officers might be enhanced by considering their social structure. This is particularly true since police officers do not all occupy the same positions in the group. Police agencies are composed of persons in such positions as dispatchers, line officers, sergeants, lieutenants, detectives, and so forth. There is no way to presuppose any particular pattern of affective relations among occupants of these different positions.

For example, most line officers have their performance monitored and supervised by a sergeant, not by other line officers. While some may have a special relationship with the sergeant that allows them to engage in idle conversation or joking, many will not. Thus, line officers may interact with one another very differently from the way they interact with their supervisors. Certain types of relations, then, are seen as appropriate only between

FIGURE 7.1 A Sample Sociometric Assessment

(Question/Choices)

Directions: On a separate sheet, write the name of everyone in your group or organization. Read the following paragraphs and place their corresponding numbers in front of every name for which they apply. You may use the number <u>one</u> only once, and please place only a single number by each name. By your own name, please place a zero.

My Very Best Friend

1. I would like to have this person as one of my very best friends. I would like to spend a great deal of time with this person. I think I could tell some of my problems and concerns to this person, and I would do everything I could to help this person with his or her problems and concerns. I will give a number 1 to my very best friend.

My Other Friend(s)

2. I would enjoy working and doing things with this person. I would invite this person to a party in my home, and I would enjoy going places with this person and our other friends. I would like to talk and do a variety of things with this person and to be with this person often. I want this person to be one of my friends. I will give a number 2 to every person who is my friend.

I Do Not Know This Person

3. I do not know this person very well. Maybe I would like this person if I got to know him or her; maybe I would not. I do not know whether I would like to spend time or work with this person. I will place a number 3 in front of the name of every person I do not know very well.

I Do Not Care for This Person

4. I will greet this person when I see him or her around school or in a store, but I do not enjoy being around this person. I might spend some time with this person—if I had nothing to do, or I had a social obligation to attend where this person also was in attendance. I do not care for this person very much. I will place a number 4 in front of the name of every person I do not care for very much.

I Dislike This Person

5. I speak to this person only when it is necessary. I do not like to work or spend time with this person. I avoid serving on the same groups or committees with this person. I will place a number 5 in front of the name of every person I do not like.

specific structural positions in this group. In short, sociometric tests could assist an investigator who is attempting to study police organizations by identifying differential relations among officers.

You might just as easily imagine the usefulness of sociometric techniques in a study of health professionals working in a hospital. You can certainly conceive of reasons you might want to know the formal hierarchical relations among workers. You might also find it useful, however, to learn sociometrically what the informal social status structure might be. Again, what officially serves as the hierarchical arrangement between these hospital coworkers may not accurately reflect their informal social influence structure.

Consider another example of the utility of sociometry in field research. Austin and Bates (1974) studied the hierarchical social structure of inmates in a Georgia prison bullpen. They observed the inmates at work and at leisure and noticed that in the evenings they clustered around a single television set. Austin and Bates also established that inmate proximity to the direct line of sight of the television was based upon an inmate's social position in the group's hierarchy. Inmates with the highest status had their bunks virtually in front of the television screen. Those with lower status were further from the television and not in direct line with the screen. Those with little status were out of good viewing position entirely. Austin and Bates (1974) suggested that aggressive acts between inmates throughout the day served to maintain this hierarchical arrangement during the evenings.

In the Austin and Bates (1974) study, the use of more abstract mathematical sociometric techniques and rating questionnaires would not have been nearly as effective as methods of direct observation. As in any good piece of research, the setting and research questions should direct the data-collection and analytic strategies used by the researcher.

Sociometric techniques are also useful for assessing patterns within and among youthful groups, cliques, and gangs. During the recent past, considerable attention has been drawn toward the activities of youth gangs. A number of researchers have sought to investigate delinquent gang behavior. Sociometric techniques offer a conceptual or analytical tool that provides a framework for examining social relations among gang members and different gangs. Several theories about gangs suggest that friendship patterns and social cohesion relate to delinquent behavior (Giordano et al., 1986; Hansell & Wiatrowski, 1981; Hirschi, 1969; Yablonsky, 1966).

A simple application of a sociometric test might be to ask members of a gang to identify other members of that gang with whom they are friendly. In some cases, we will find that friendship choices are reciprocated, while in others they are not. It can be reasoned that friendship relationships that are reciprocal indicate greater cohesion than one-sided or unreciprocated arrangements. Thus, gangs that contain overlapping or numerous reciprocal relationships can be described as densely cohesive. Conversely, gangs with few reciprocal relationships can be seen as compartmentalized, perhaps even disorganized.

Application of similar sociometric techniques might also allow one to assess the leadership patterns in simple social clubs or organizations. Does the official leadership structure—the president, vice-president, secretary, and treasurer—actually represent those who lead the group? Are there, perhaps, others with as much or more influence among the general membership? Answers to such questions are quickly obtained through sociometry.

THE SOCIOGRAM

Another way to use sociometry is to create a sociogram. A *sociogram* is a graphic display of the peer rating choices. Figure 7.2 contains imaginary data from a social acceptance scale. In this example, the imaginary students were instructed to use the numbers corresponding to questions in Figure 7.1 once only. This means that peer raters had to identify the best fit to the scale. This results in many blanks in the matrix but fewer lines to graph in the sociogram, making it somewhat clearer to visualize as an example.

The summary totals at the bottom of the matrix in Figure 7.2 show the frequency of being chosen at various levels of choice. This, in turn, provides a means of scaling the social acceptability of each of the individuals in the class. Since, however, our imaginary example restricted the choosers from using numbers corresponding to question choices more than once, scaling would not be a very effective strategy with these data. If the instructions in Figure 7.1 had been followed, every identified cell of the matrix would contain an entry, and the total row at the bottom would show the relative position of each chooser in terms of being accepted.

One can also create a choice status index for each member of the group at every choice level. A *choice status* is a numerical value for each individual; it is derived by taking the sum of choices found in the summary or total row at the bottom of the matrix and dividing the individual's column total by n-1. The n-1 is used since an individual does not choose himself or herself, and there are no values for this relationship in the matrix.

For example, if you applied this to person C in the imaginary data matrix of Figure 7.2, one would divide C's best friend score of 1 by 11 (the total n minus one). C's choice status then is 0.09. If one does the same thing for F's score, the choice status is 0.64 (7 divided by 11). Thus, the relative choices can be placed along a continuum of best friend acceptability, where 1 equals the most acceptable best friend and 0 the least acceptable within the group.

The relationships represented by the entries in the matrix have been plotted as a *sociogram* shown in Figure 7.3. The purpose of this sociogram is to make clear the network of social acceptances in a graphic way. When

FIGURE 7.2 Sociometric Scoring Sheet
(Sample Scoring Sheet for Social Acceptance)

Person Choosing	A	B	C	D	E	F	G	H	I	J	K	L
A		1	2	3	5		6		4			
B	2		1	3	4			6	5			
C	2	1		3	5			4		6		
D	3	2				1	5		6			4
E	5			2		1			6	3		
F	4	1		2			5	6		3		
G		4		2		1		6		3		5
H		4		2		1	5			3		6
I		3		2		1		3		6	5	
J	6		4	3		1		2				5
K		2			5	1		4	6	3		
L	6	2			5	1		4		3		
Best friend (1)		3	1			8						
Other friends (2)	2	3	1	5				1				
All right (3)	1	1		4				1		6		
Totals	3	7	2	9		8		2		7		

169

**FIGURE 7.3   Example of Sociogram Representing the
Sample Social Acceptance Scale**

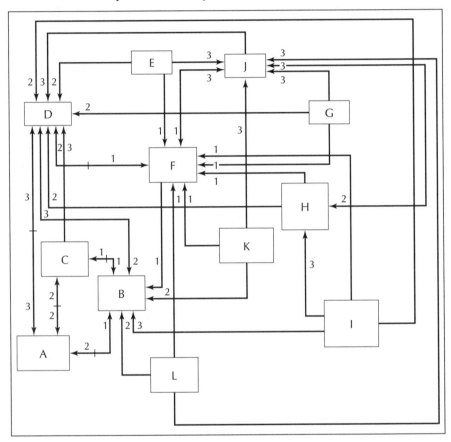

analyzing the acceptability network shown in this sociogram, certain elements must be made clear. First, sociograms are useful for identifying informal influence or leadership patterns. In the present case, and owing to his or
her popularity, F clearly surfaces as the most influential member of the
group. A quick look at the sociogram in Figure 7.3 shows that eight of the
choosers have identified F as their best friend (designated by the number 1).
As mentioned, such informal leaders often are referred to as *stars*.

Second, the sociogram reveals that several of the group members are
also influenced by B (but to a lesser extent than F). In this case, three individuals identified B as their best friend, three as other friends, and only one
chooser identified B as someone he or she doesn't really know (a number 3).

This indicates that B is considerably attractive to members of the group. B, then, forms what may be called an *island* or a *satellite*.

Third, the sociogram shows a number of stable relationships, such as J being identified by six of the eleven choosers (J cannot choose himself) as all right. Similarly, D has been identified as an other friend by five members and as all right by four members. These sorts of relationships suggest cohesion in this group of individuals.

Fourth, several members of the group have received no choices as 1, 2, or 3. This suggests that while they may not be disliked, they have very little influence in the group.

Mapping and the Creation of Sociograms

Another way you can create sociograms is to do them in the field. In this case, you use direct observations of individuals and objects as they are arranged in the setting. Essentially, this involves the creation of social/environmental maps and from these, sociograms.

This strategy of sociometric mapping depends upon a fairly stable setting, and as such, it is not always applicable. Often, this type of sociometric mapping is used in social psychological applications of organizational research. For example, how executives place themselves around a board meeting table may be mapped and may delineate power and informal influence structures. By knowing this information, a researcher (or executive) can interrupt or weaken the amount of influence emanating from certain segments of the members. For instance, by placing himself or herself or a nonmember of some informal influence clique between several actual members, he or she can affect the ability of those members to wield influence and authority during a board meeting.

Similarly, knowledge about sociometric body language and even furniture placement can influence interactions. For example, when you enter someone's office, how is it arranged? Is there a chair near the desk, inviting you to sit near the desk's occupant? Or is the chair far from the desk, perhaps across the room, requiring a guest to physically move it to be near the desk's occupant? Usually, when you move furniture in another person's office, you must first ask permission. Thus, tacitly, you hold a subordinate role in the relationship. Alternately, you might choose to stand while the other party sits. This, of course, immediately shifts the power structure to the seated occupant of the office because he or she is able to leave you standing or suggest you pull up a chair. This situation is also somewhat reminiscent of school days, when you were called before the school's principal where you stood, at the foot of the desk, being scolded.

The arrangement of people and objects in a setting may have an impact on interactions and relationships. This, in turn, can be a useful tool in research. This type of applied sociometric strategy frequently begins with a *mapping* of the setting. This sort of mapping is also useful in other types of institutional investigations. For example, it could prove useful in a study of how inmates use environmental space in a prison or a study of the effect of environmental design on inmates. Alternatively, it might prove fruitful in an examination of how children use and perhaps territorially divide playground space. It might even be useful in a study of a game arcade located in some mall or in similar studies of leisure-time activities in amusement parks. Again, sociometric strategies are extremely flexible. They are limited only by your imagination.

To describe how you might develop the sort of sociometric maps discussed above, let us assume an investigator wants to study some group of youths in a particular neighborhood. One way to begin this task is to create a drawing or *map* of the setting. This map would contain all the stable physical elements observed in the setting: access ways, trees and shrubs, buildings, stores, street lamps, public telephones, and so forth all should be included. Next, this map might be duplicated a number of times so that every time the researcher enters the field, he or she can work on a fresh map.

While in the field, the researcher can add symbols to represent individual gang members, dyads (groups of two), triads (groups of three), gender, leadership roles, and so forth. Over time, and by assessing the successive annotated maps and actual field notes, the researcher will be able to identify the star and any satellite cliques that constitute the groups under study. Stars will become apparent *over time* when you use observation to create a sociogram. Typically, you find only one or two stars in a given group. Even when you locate several stars, typically one will demonstrate himself or herself to hold some degree of influence over the others.

Satellite cliques are sometimes mistaken as representing a star and his or her followers. In fact, satellite cliques usually contain several members influenced by what appears to be a single individual. However, this individual frequently is himself or herself influenced by a more centralized star.

Sociometric maps also can assist the investigator in understanding how a group uses its environmental space and maintains territorial control over areas, the locus of control in various power and influence arrangements, and the social space (proximity) between different members and nonmembers of the group(s).

As with other types of data-collecting strategies, sociometric data is strengthened by using multiple methods. Thus, the existence of social distance or social acceptability identified through sociometric techniques can be accepted as valid only insofar as they remain constant when observed (measured) by other lines of action. For example, once a group's sociometric structure is identified, informal interviews with members to check out relationships would increase validity.

Sociometric strategies provide a number of ways to access important and useful qualitative structures in groups. They offer a technique for both diagraming and understanding organizations and organizational influence configurations not easily identified in other ways. Yet caution is necessary when using sociometric strategies. It is very tempting to think that once you have calculated a sociometric index or created a sociogram, you have completed the research. However, as important as this information may be, this is only a first step in fully researching some group. As with the reporting of descriptive statistics in qualitative research, seldom are these *findings* in themselves. Rather, they provide a convenient method for the researcher to organize and showcase material. Findings and analysis will still require an unfolding of the textures and details of the research.

During the last several decades, sociometric applications have found a home among organizational, educational, and social psychological researchers. Yet often these applications are practical rather than research oriented and limited to single-shot peer nomination tests. However, recently, the techniques have also begun moving back into mainstream research texts (Leedy, 1993; Salkind, 1991). The real test will be watching to see if qualitative researchers recognize the usefulness of these tests for their research.

TRYING IT OUT

Write the names of everyone in your class on a sheet of paper. Read over the paragraphs listed as Questions/Choices in Figure 7.1 and place the corresponding numbers in front of every name for which they apply. You may use the number one only once. Place only a single number by each name. By your own name, place a zero.

Once the students in your class have been assigned their appropriate numbers, cast these into the matrix shown in Figure 7.4. For the purpose of this exercise, the summary totals should be limited to only the first three category choices. For practice, you might want to summarize category choices 4 and 5 at a later time.

Once totals are calculated, you can begin to consider the social acceptance structure of the class by identifying individuals most frequently selected number 1, number 2, and number 3.

NOTE

1. The terms and theoretical origins of actor in situ, the alter and the auxiliary ego, spontaneity training, the social atom, social dynamics, derive from sociodrama and psychodrama. As techniques in themselves, sociodrama and psychodrama, too, are frequently credited to the work of Moreno (1952, 1977). These concepts, however,

FIGURE 7.4 Sociometric Scoring Sheet
(Sociometric Matrix)

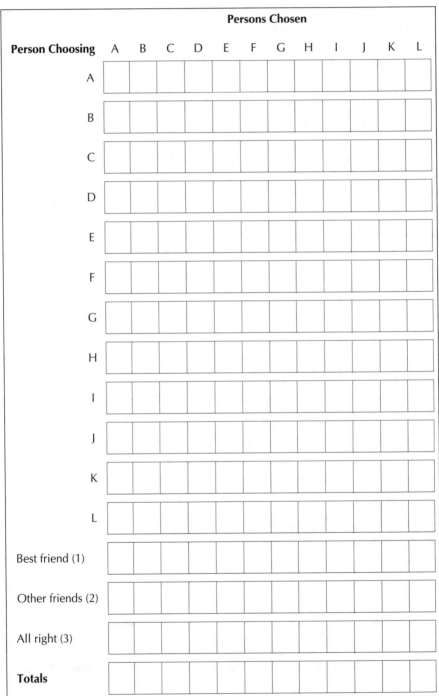

owe their roots to the more general theoretical base of symbolic interaction (Cooley, 1926; Mead, 1934) and from the more theatrical base of dramaturgy (Burke, 1966; Goffman, 1959).

REFERENCES

Alpert, G., & Dunham, R. (1988). *Police and Multi-Ethnic Neighborhoods*. New York: Greenwood Press.

Arabie, P. (1984). Validation of sociometric structure by data on individuals' attributes. *Social Networks 6*, 373–403.

Asher, S. R., & Hymel, S. (1981). Social competence in peer-relations: Sociometric and behavioral assessment. In J. D. Wine & M. D. Smye (Eds.), *Social Competence*. New York: Guilford Press.

Austin, W. T., & Bates, F. L. (1974). Ethological indicators of dominance and territory in a human captive population. *Social Forces 52*(4), 447–455.

Berg, B. L. (1989). *Qualitative Research Methods for the Social Sciences*. Boston: Allyn and Bacon.

Berg, B. L., & Rounds, D. (1992). Sociometric applications in criminology and other settings: A reexamination of a traditional method. *Sociological Practice Review 3*(3), 126–132.

Burke, K. (1966). *Language as Symbolic Action: Essays on Life, Literature, and Method*. Berkeley: University of California Press.

Cohen, A. (1955). *Delinquent Boys*. New York: Free Press.

Coleman, J. S. (1961). *The Adolescent Society*. New York: Free Press.

Cooley, C. H. (1926). The roots of social knowledge. *American Journal of Sociology 32*, 59–79.

Denzin, N. K. (1978). *The Research Act*. Chicago: Aldine.

Dodge, K. A., Coie, J. D., & Brakke, N. P. (1982). Behavioral patterns of socially rejected and neglected adolescents: The roles of social approach and aggression. *Journal of Abnormal Child Psychology 10*, 389–410.

Dunnington, M. J. (1957). Behavioral differences of sociometric status groups in a nursery school. *Child Development 28*, 103–111.

Giordano, P., Stephen Cernkovick, S., & Pugh, M. D. (1986). Friendship and delinquency. *American Journal of Sociology 91*, 1170–1202.

Glassner, B. (1990). Editorial introduction. *Qualitative Sociology 13*(2), 111–112.

Goffman, E. (1959). *The Presentation of Self in Everyday Life*. New York: Anchor Books.

Hampson, R. B. (1984). Adolescent prosocial behaviors: Peer-group and situational factors associated with helping. *Journal of the American Psychological Association 46*(1), 153–162.

Hansell, S., & Wiatrowski, M. D. (1981). Competing conceptions of delinquent peer relations. In G. F. Jensen (Ed.), *Sociology of Delinquency: Current Issues*. Beverly Hills, CA: Sage.

Hartup, W. W. (1976). Peer interaction and the behavioral development of the individual child. In E. Schoopler & R. J. Reichler (Eds.). *Psychology and Child Development: Research and Treatment*. New York, Plenum Press.

Hartup, W. W., Glazer, J. A., & Charlesworth, R. (1967). Peer reinforcement and sociometric status. *Child Development 38*, 1017–1024.

Hirschi, T. (1969). *Causes of Delinquency*. Berkeley: University of California Press.

Hymel, S., & Rubin, K. H. (1985). Children with peer relationship and social skills problems: Conceptual, methodological, and developmental issues. In G. I. Whitehurst (Ed.), *Annals of Child Development* (Vol. 2, pp. 251–297). Greenwich, CT: JAI Press.

Jennings, H. H. (1948). *Sociometry in Group Relations*. Washington, DC: American Council on Education.

Leedy, P. D. (1993). *Practical Research: Planning and Design*. New York: Macmillan.

Lidz, C. W., & Ricci, E. (1990). Funding large-scale qualitative sociology. *Qualitative Sociology 13*(2), 113–126.

Mead, G. H. (1934). *Mind, Self, and Society*. Chicago: University of Chicago Press.

Moore, S. G., & Updergraff, R. (1964). Sociometric status of preschool children related to age, sex, nurturance giving, and dependence. *Child Development 35*, 519–524.

Moreno, J. L. (1934). *Who Shall Survive?* Beacon, NY: Beacon House.

Moreno, J. L. (1952). Current trends in sociometry. *Sociometry: A Journal of Inter-Personal Relations and Experimental Design 15*(1–2), 146–163.

Moreno, J. L. (1977). *Psychodrama*, Vol I. Beacon, NY: Beacon House.

Newcomb, A., & Bukowski, W. (1983). Social impact and social preference as determinants of children's peer group status. *Developmental Psychology 19*, 856–867.

Rubin, K. H. (1982). Non-social play in preschoolers: Necessary evil? *Child Development 53*, 651–657.

Salkind, N. J. (1991). *Exploring Research*. New York: Macmillan.

Schwartz, J., & Sprinzen, M. (1984). Structures of connectivity. *Social Networks 6*, 103–140.

Skvoretz, J. (1985). Random and biased networks: Simulations and approximations. *Social Networks 7*, 225–261.

Strauss, G. (1952). Direct observation as a source of quasi-sociometric information. *Sociometry: A Journal of Interpersonal Relations and Experiential Design 15*(1–2), 141–145.

Sutherland, E. (1939). *Principles of Criminology*. Philadelphia: J. B. Lippincott.

Sykes, G. (1958). *The Society of Captives*. Princeton, NJ: Princeton University Press.

Whyte, W. F. (1955). *Street Corner Society: The Social Structure of an Italian Slum*. Chicago: University of Chicago Press.

Wilson, T. P. (1982). Relational networks: An extension of sociometric concepts. *Social Networks 4*, 105–116.

Yablonsky, L. (1966). *The Violent Gang*. Baltimore: Penguin.

UNOBTRUSIVE MEASURES
IN RESEARCH

I N THE PRECEDING FOUR CHAPTERS, research procedures that require an intrusion into the lives of subjects have been discussed. Researcher reactivity—the response of subjects to the presence of an intruding investigator—has been considered as it applies to interviewers and ethnographers. In each case, suggestions have been offered concerning how to make positive use of the reactivity or to neutralize it. In this chapter unobtrusive (nonintruding) research strategies will be examined.

Although such intrusive techniques as direct observation frequently find their way into most conventional research methods books, unobtrusive strategies less regularly do. In fact, when research methods books do mention unobtrusive procedures, they typically define terms (e.g., Frankfort-Nachmias & Nachmias, 1996) or give only a very brief elaboration on the work of Webb et al. (1981). However, unobtrusive measures actually make up a particularly interesting and innovative strategy for collecting and assessing data. In some instances, unobtrusive indicators provide access to aspects of social settings and their inhabitants that are simply unreachable through any other means.

To some extent, all the unobtrusive strategies amount to examining and assessing human traces. What people do, how they behave and structure their daily lives, and even how humans are affected by certain ideological stances can all be observed in traces people either intentionally or inadvertently leave behind. The more unusual types of unobtrusive studies are sometimes briefly highlighted in textbook descriptions of unobtrusive measures—just before dismissing these techniques in favor of measures regarded as more legitimate.

For instance, it is fairly common to hear about how an investigator estimated the popularity of different radio stations in Chicago by having automobile mechanics record the position of the radio dial in all the cars they serviced (Z-Frank, 1962). Or one hears about Sawyer's (1961, cited in Webb et al., 1981) attempts to study liquor sales in Wellesley, Massachusetts—a so-called dry town (i.e., no liquor stores are permitted). To obtain an estimate of liquor sales, Sawyer studied the trash from local Wellesley homes and counted the number of discarded liquor bottles. In some instances, almost absurd situations are ascribed to findings culled from unobtrusive data. For example, Jelenko (1980) describes the observation of a rock on the campus of Wright State University that is regularly painted by students. Accretion of paint each time the rock has been painted has been determined, and Jelenko calculates that in another 7,778 years the rock will have grown (from layers of paint) to a size that will encroach on the gymnasium located 182 meters away.

More recently, Brown (1995) explored the expression of freedom and growing influence of Western cultural ideas in Hungary by examining graffiti on Hungarian building walls. Among commonly found stenciled images was one of Garfield, the cartoon cat.

Although perhaps amusing and indeed somewhat trivial in substance, each of the preceding illustrations demonstrates that information can be culled from various traces left by humans. It would be a mistake, however, to conclude that unobtrusive measures in general are restricted to trivial subjects. Furthermore, as Schwartz and Jacobs (1979, pp. 183ff) so articulately point out in their discussion on the sociology of everyday life: Formal sociology's study of the trivia and minutiae of everyday life will prove to be no easy task. By the very act of making trivia a topic of study and recognizing its prevalence and importance in everyday life, formal sociologists change the very thing they seek to study. That is, trivia is no longer trivial; it now becomes important.

In this chapter, several broad categories of unobtrusive strategies are examined in detail. This approach is not meant to suggest that the various unobtrusive techniques are necessarily ordered in this manner. It is intended, rather, to simplify presentation by simultaneously discussing similar techniques under like headings. The categories will be considered under the headings "Archival Strategies" and "Physical Erosion and Accretion."

ARCHIVAL STRATEGIES

As Denzin (1978, p. 219) remarks, archival records can be divided into two sets: public archival records and private archival records. In the case of the former, *records* are viewed as prepared for the expressed purpose of examination by others. Although access to public archives may be restricted to certain groups (for example, certain law enforcement records, credit histories, school records, and so on) they are typically prepared for some audience. As a result, public archival records tend to be written in more or less standardized form and arranged in the archive systematically (for instance, alphabetically, chronologically, or numerically indexed).

In contrast to these public orientations and formal structures, private archival records typically are intended for personal (private) audiences. Except for published versions of a diary or personal memoirs (which in effect become parts of the public archival system), private archival records reach extremely small—if any—audiences.

Public Archives

Traditionally, the term *archive* brings to mind some form of library. Although libraries are indeed archives, so too are graveyard tombstones, hospital admittance records, computer-accessed bulletin boards, motor vehicle registries, newspaper morgues, arrest records, and even credit companies' billing records. As Webb et al. (1981) suggest, virtually any *running record* provides a kind of archive.

In addition to providing large quantities of inexpensive data, archival material is virtually nonreactive to the presence of investigators. Many researchers find archival data attractive because public archives utilize more or less standard formats and filing systems, which makes locating pieces of data and creating research filing systems for analysis easier.

Naturally, as in any research process, serious errors are possible when using archival data. However, if this possibility is recognized and controlled, through data triangulation, for example, errors need not seriously distort results (Webb et al., 1981).

Modifying and modernizing the four broad categories suggested by Webb et al. (1966, 1981), results in a three-category scheme. This second scheme identifies varieties of public archival data as commercial media accounts, actuarial records, and official documentary records.

Commercial Media Accounts

Commercial media accounts represent any written, drawn, or recorded (video or audio) material produced for general or mass consumption. This may include such items as newspapers, books, magazines, television program transcripts, videotapes, drawn comics, maps, and so forth.

When Johannes Gutenberg developed the movable type printing press, he could not have foreseen the advances in the technology of writing and publishing that are commonplace today. With the assistance of microchips, microprocessors, and laser printers, the only limitations on writing, storage, and printing are now time and inclination. Similarly, with technical developments in video cameras and recorders making such equipment affordable, new worlds of running records have been opened to both official agencies and private citizens.

One excellent illustration of the use of television program transcripts as a type of public archival record is Molotch and Boden's (1985) examination of the congressional Watergate hearings of 1973. In their effort to examine the way people invoke routine conversational procedures to gain power, Molotch and Boden (1985) created transcriptions from videotapes of the hearings. By examining the conversational exchanges between relevant parties during the hearings, Molotch and Boden (1985) manage to develop a blow-by-blow account of domination in the making.

In a similar vein, following the O. J. Simpson trial, Frank Schmalleger (1996) offered a commentary on the exchanges between the defense and prosecution based upon court transcripts he downloaded from the Internet.

Molotch and Boden (1985) are primarily concerned with the audio portion of the videotapes. Schmalleger (1996), is similarly interested only in the written transcript of verbal exchanges. Other researchers, however, have concentrated on visual renderings, such as still photographs. Jackson (1977), for example, used photographs to depict the prison experience in his *Killing Time: Life in the Arkansas Penitentiary.* Another example of the use of still photographs is Goffman's (1979) examination of gender in advertisements. Goffman's research suggests that gender displays, like other social rituals, reflects vital features of social structure—both negative and counterbalancing positive ones.

An another illustration, Gottschalk (1995) recently used photographs as an intricate element in his more ethnographic exploration of the "Strip" in Las Vegas. Gottschalk's (1995) use of photos evokes an emotional sense about the Strip not actually possible in their absence. Their inclusion, then, significantly heightens the written account of his ethnography.

Actuarial Records

Actuarial records also tend to be produced for special or limited audiences but are typically available to the public under certain circumstances. These items include birth and death records; records of marriages and divorces; application information held by insurance and credit companies; title, land, and deed information; and similar demographic or residential types of records.

Private industry has long used actuarial information as data. Insurance companies, for example, establish their price structures according to life expectancy as mediated by such factors as whether the applicant smokes, drinks liquor, sky dives (or engages in other life-threatening activities), works in a dangerous occupation, and so forth. Similarly, social scientists may use certain actuarial data to assess various social phenomena and/or problems. Although each of these preceding categories of public archival data may certainly be separated conceptually, it should be obvious that considerable overlap may occur.

Although archival information is a rich source of primary data, albeit underused, such data frequently contain several innate flaws as well. For example, missing elements in an official government document may represent attempts to hide the very information of interest to the investigators, or missing portions of some official document may have merely resulted from the carelessness of the last person who looked at the document and lost a page.

It is sometimes difficult to determine possible effects from editorial bias and control over selection of what gets published and what does not. Bradley et al. (1979) expressly mention this element as one of two weaknesses in their study of men's magazine cartoons in relation to changing natures of male sexual mores and prostitution. In addition, Bradley et al. (1979) indicate as a second weakness their inability to measure precisely audience reaction merely from examining cartoons that appeared in *Esquire* and *Playboy* over a 40-year period.

When dealing with aggregate statistical data, missing values or nonresponses to particular questions can be accounted for. In some instances, data sets can be purchased and cleaned of any such missing pieces of information. Unfortunately, when using archival data, it may sometimes be impossible to determine, let alone account for, what or why pieces of data are missing. This again suggests the need to incorporate multiple measures and techniques in order to reduce potential errors, but it should not prevent or discourage the use of archival data.

Formal actuarial records (for instance, birth, death, and marriage records) have been used frequently as data in social science research. Such aggregated data as aptitude test scores, age, income, number of divorces, smoker or nonsmoker, gender, occupation, and the like are the lifeblood of many governmental agencies (as well as certain private companies).

Among the more interesting variations on unobtrusive actuarial data are those described by Warner (1959). As part of Warner's larger classic five-volume series on "Yankee City" (the other volumes include Warner & Lunt, 1941, 1942; Warner & Srole, 1945; Warner & Low, 1947), he offered *The Living and the Dead: A Study of the Symbolic Life of Americans.*

In his study, Warner (1959) used official cemetery documents to establish a history of the dead and added interviewing, observation, and examination of eroded traces as elements in his description of graveyards. From his data, Warner was able to suggest various apparent social structures present in graveyards that resembled those present in the social composition of Yankee City (Newburyport, Massachusetts). For instance, the size of headstones typically was larger for men than for women, plots were laid out so that the father of a family would be placed in the center, and so forth.

Webb et al. (1981, p. 93) point out that tombstones can themselves be interesting sources of data. Webb et al. (1981) also mention the possible analysis of different cultures by, for example, considering the relative size of the headstones of men as compared to women.

In fact, tombstones often reveal several other interesting things. For example, most tombstones contain birth and death dates, and many include social role information (for example, "beloved son and father," "loving wife and sister"). In some cases, the cause of death may even be mentioned (for instance, "The plague took him, God rest his soul" or "Killed by Indians"). In consequence, tombstones cease to be merely grave markers and become viable actuarial records. Examination of information in a given cemetery can reveal waves of illness, natural catastrophes, relative social status and prestige, ethnic stratification, and many other potentially meaningful facts.

Official Documentary Records

Schools, social agencies, hospitals, retail establishments, and other organizations have reputations for creating an abundance of written records, files, and communications (Bogdan and Biklen, 1992). Many people regard this mountain of paper—or electronic records—as something other than official documents. In fact, *official documentary records* are originally produced for some special limited audiences, even if they eventually find their way into the public domain. These records may include official court transcripts, police reports, census information, financial records, crime statistics, political speech transcripts, internally generated government agency reports, school records, bills of lading, sales records, and similar documents. Official documents may also include less obvious, and sometimes less openly available, forms of communications such as inter-office memos, printed e-mail messages, minutes from meetings, organizational newsletters, and so forth. These materials often convey important and useful information that a researcher can effectively use as data.

Official documentary records may offer particularly interesting sources of data. Blee (1987), for example, bases her investigation of gender ideology and the role of women in the early Ku Klux Klan on a content analysis of official documentary records. As Blee (1987, p. 76) describes it, "The analysis of the WKKK [Women's Ku Klux Klan] uses speeches and articles by the imperial commander of the women's klan, leaflets and recruiting material and internal organizational documents such as descriptions of ceremonies, rituals and robes and banners, membership application forms and the WKKK constitution and laws."

In a study by Melichar (1987), the evolution of the Montana Clean Air Act of 1967 was investigated by examining social definitions surrounding the issue of air pollution. In his study, public documents and depth interviews provide the primary data. Among the documents utilized by Melichar (1987, p. 52) are "legislative committee records, written testimony, house and senate journals, personal files, Montana Power Company's legislative files, and newspapers."

Naturally, not all research questions can be answered through the use of archival data, or at least not archival data alone. Some studies, however, are so well suited to archival data that attempts to examine phenomena in another manner might not prove as fruitful. For example, Poole and Regoli (1981) were interested in assessing professional prestige associated with criminology and criminal justice journals. In order to assess this, they counted the number of citations for various journals (in the *Index of Social Science Citations*) and ranked each cited journal from most to least citations. The operative assumption was that the journals with the greatest frequency of citation reflected the subjective preference of professionals working in the field. In consequence, those journals that enjoyed the most frequent reference in scholarly works possessed the greatest amount of prestige.

In a similar fashion, Thomas and Bronick (1984) examined the professional prestige of graduate criminology and criminal justice programs by ranking each on the basis of volume of publication citations per faculty member during a single year (1979–1980). Thomas and Bronick examined both the total number of citations of faculty in each department studied and the number of citations per each experience year of faculty members in each department. By assessing both the quantity of publications and publication weight (by considering proportions of publications in prestigious journals) Thomas and Bronick managed to rank the graduate programs.

Although most archival data can be managed unobtrusively, researchers must sometimes be cautious regarding certain ethical concerns. For example, since some archives include certain identifiers such as names and addresses, their use requires that researchers take steps to ensure confidentiality. For instance, police complaint records typically are open to the public (with the exception of certain criminal complaints involving minors) and contain much identifying information. Similarly, during the recent past, a growing number of newspapers have begun publishing police blotter sections. These typically indicate the names, addresses, occupations, charges, and frequently the case dispositions of crimes committed during the day or evening preceding the published account. Certainly these types of data could prove valuable in a variety of studies. But care is necessary if you are to avoid identifying the individuals depicted in these press accounts or crime reports.

A simple removal of certain particularly sensitive identifiers (for example, names and addresses) and aggregation of the data according to some nonidentifying factor might be sufficient. For instance, in a study of crime in relation to geographic-environmental factors that was mapped by C. Ray

Jefferys, particulars of identity were unnecessary. Using official criminal reports occurring in Atlanta during 1985 and 1986, Jefferys annotated a map of the city and identified high-risk locations for particular categories of crime.

Social scientists have traditionally used a variety of official types of reports and records. Several governmental agencies exist literally in order to generate, assess, and disseminate research information. In many cases, in addition to straightforward statistical analysis, detailed reports and monographs are made available. Further, and because of the technological advances in audio- and videotaping devices, it is becoming increasingly possible to obtain verbatim accounts of governmental hearings, congressional sessions, and similar events.

Burstein and Freudenberg (1978), for example, were interested in how public opinion influenced legislative votes. Although legislators certainly possess the right to vote their consciences even against the general wishes of their constituents, they do not usually do so. Burstein and Freudenberg examined 91 bills and motions concerning the issue of the Vietnam War submitted both before and after the 1970 invasion of Cambodia. These bills were compared against public opinion poll information that had been conducted throughout the war years and ranged from opinions against the war from the beginning to those opinions that approved of and supported the ways the president handled the situation.

Stated simply, Burstein and Freudenberg (1978) found that before the 1970 invasion of Cambodia, public opinion had an influence on some of the dovish (antiwar) legislators but that hawkish (prowar) legislators were generally unaffected. Similarly, funding the Vietnam War, although not a particularly important dimension in affecting vote outcomes before 1970, did become relevant in votes after the 1970 invasion. The explanation offered by Burstein and Freudenberg suggests that while the financial costs of Vietnam were bearable before the invasion of Cambodia, these costs became insupportable after the invasion.

Today, in addition to voting records, the behavior of Congress and state legislatures can be unobtrusively assessed through other traces. Because of technological innovations and increased permissiveness on the part of state and federal legislators (perhaps in response to the secretiveness that surrounded Watergate) many congressional and state legislature debates and votes are televised.

Videotape can now capture the kind of joke-making at one another's expense that is rather common in state legislature committee meetings, as well as the various symbolic gestures and ceremonial rituals that typically occur but have gone unrecorded for years. Analysis of these types of interactions may reveal some interesting and telling things about how both politics and votes actually operate.

For example, Masters and Sullivan, professors at Dartmouth College, have begun to examine meanings encoded in the facial grimaces and symbolic gestures of politicians during speeches. In order to study the various clucks, furrowed brows, smiles, head tilts, hand motions, and so forth, Masters and Sullivan examine videotapes of speeches made by political leaders (Masters & Sullivan, 1988).

Certain videotapes, in fact, may fast become among the most useful and complete running records available to archival researchers. Examination of videotape records, to quote the Bell Telephone people, "is almost like being there." Many law enforcement agencies, for example, now routinely videotape persons as they are tested for driving while intoxicated and maintain these tapes as components of the official arrest record.

Albrecht (1985) described the uses of videotape and film—for defining social problems (including uncovering secrets about situations), creating records of behavior, testing the representative nature of these records, constructing hypotheses, and building grounded theory.

As noted in Chapter 6, many ethnographies of schooling have been compiled by using videotaping strategies. For example, Erickson and Mohatt (1988) describe their efforts to uncover cultural organizations of participation structure in classrooms. They videotaped both first-grade teachers and their students across a one-year period. In order to capture the students and their teachers in usual interaction routines, each hour-long tape cassette was photographed with a minimum of camera editing. In other words, the camera operator did not pan the room or zoom in and out for close-ups. Rather, wide-angle shots of the classroom and its participants were utilized.

The result was an effective collection of data that gave a microethnographic look at how interactions between teachers and students differ when the two groups belong to different cultural groups (in this case, Native American and non–Native American). Certainly videotapes should prove to be important and useful as audiovisual transcripts of official proceedings, capturing emergent and/or serendipitous acts in various social settings, and creating behavioral records. In fact, in 1987, the *American Behavioral Scientist* devoted an entire issue to the use of videocassette recorders (VCRs) in research. But other video-related official documents may prove equally useful—in particular, the receipt records from sales and rentals of commercial video programs. For example, the issue of whether watching violence on television is related to committing violence in society is a long-standing question. In 1969, the National Commission on the Causes and Prevention of Violence (Eisenhower, 1969, p. 5) concluded: "Violence on television encourages violent forms of behavior, and fosters moral and social values about violence in daily life which are unacceptable in civilized society."

Since 1969, a number of studies have similarly concluded that watching violent television programs encourages violent behavior (see Comstock, 1977; Eron, 1980; Phillips, 1983). Yet the debate over whether watching violence on television encourages violent behavior continues. Central issues in this debate include the question of whether people who became aggressive after viewing violent programs might already have been aggressive; whether the violence depicted on the program was or was not rewarded and/or justified (that is, was it the good guys or the bad guys who were violent?), and whether the viewer was watching a real-life violent event (e.g., hockey, boxing, football) or a fictionalized one.

Although television certainly offers an inexpensive education in a variety of violent techniques, so too can video rental stores. Since videotape rental stores have sprouted up across the nation faster than weeds grow in a vegetable garden, they may offer an efficient measure of popular film genre choices. Whether their records amount to boxes of sales receipts or, more than likely, microcomputer disks, comprehensive records of the titles that are rented or sold and of the frequency of rental or sale are potentially available.

By identifying and tabulating the rental rate of certain movies that depict a range and variety of violence, researchers may be able to discover which dimensions of violence appear the most popular (e.g., vigilante behavior, retaliation, national reprisals, sporting events, and so on).

In addition, since sales slips are keyed to membership's identification numbers (so that store owners can keep tabs on their wares), it may be possible to gain demographic information on who rents what by checking membership application records (another official document record). Estimates of which films are rented how frequently and by whom may allow greater understanding of Eron's (1980) notion that watching violence may encourage desensitization, role-modeling, and approval of violence in others.

Webb et al. (1981) may have been correct at the time when they suggested that videotaped records were disorganized and not widely accessible, but times have changed. Webb et al. (1981, p. 119) note, "As yet newspapers and magazines, the print media, provide the only dependable archives for study since television, radio, movies, and so on, the visual and auditory media, are either not so dependably archived or else archives are not readily available to those who might want to study them."

During the past several years, the use of videotape equipment has grown not only in official circles but also among researchers and private citizens as well. In addition to sales and rental suppliers, most urban library systems now possess fairly sizable collections of videotaped movies and documentaries. Even children's books and games have begun to appear in video format. Supermarkets and convenience stores now carry video libraries. Large video store chains and small mom-and-pop video stores have sprung up across the nation. The array of possible uses and the access to video data have simply grown too large to be overlooked or ignored by researchers any longer.

Although video technology might have us looking toward moving pictorial representation of life, still photography also possesses considerable research value. Analysis of photographs, or *visual ethnography*, as it is sometimes called (Schwartz, 1989), offers yet another interesting avenue for unobtrusive research. The use of photographs as data requires a theory of how pictures should be used by both picture makers and viewers. Photos can be used either as data in themselves (Dowdall & Golden, 1989) or to assist in the conduct of interviews (Musello, 1980; Wagner, 1979). In the former case, photos provide a sense of what existed, perhaps years in the past, as well as a viewpoint—namely, that of the photographer.

Photographs, however, can mean different things to different people. They also may intentionally reflect the photographer's viewpoint and not the viewer's. Thus, many researchers consider photographs somewhat ambiguous. Rather than seeing this ambiguity as a disadvantage, however, visual ethnographers see it as a negotiation of meanings by viewers. These researchers believe that photos can be presented to people and discussed within the comfortable context of a family viewing of pictures. By doing this, visual ethnographers suggest that they can identify a verbal context for delineating what should be seen in a photo and what significance can be attached to various images (Musello, 1980; Schwartz, 1989).

In effect, what arises in some cases is a kind of *photo-interview* (Schwartz, 1989). In this situation, interviews actually center on or around a discussion of photographs. When interviews are held in comfortable locales, such as subjects' homes or lounges, the interaction is quite relaxed. While more intrusive than actual unobtrusive measures, such photo-interviews create the familiar context of friends looking at and chatting about family photos.

Similarly, audio recordings as data also have a wide variety of applications. Audiotapes of natural conversations are typically used by conversational analysts as the sole source of data (Schwartz & Jacobs, 1979).

As Chapter 9 more fully details, oral histories are often recorded or transcribed, creating excellent data for present or future unobtrusive researchers. This form of *history-telling* (Portelli, 1992), creating records of oral histories, also suggests some intrusion into the lives of subjects. However, oral historians and historiographers (discussed in Chapter 9) often create and archive documents that later researchers can use as unobtrusive data.

Other Types of Official Documentary Sources of Data

Webb et al. (1981, pp. 108ff) suggest that researchers have used a variety of interesting official documents as unobtrusive data. Among these are weather report data in relation to bad moods (Persinger, 1975), emotional well-being and altruism (Cunningham, 1979), seasonal effects on panhandlers (Cialdini et al., 1975), and climate in relation to sexual activity (Smolensky, 1980).

Along similar lines, Freedman (1979) indicated that the self-admittance patient census in a New York state psychiatric facility located in Syracuse increased significantly following the first freeze of each winter (late November or early December). Conversely, Freedman suggests, a like number of discharges occurred suddenly around late March and April (after which they tapered off) as the weather grew warmer. Freedman's explanation was that street people checked themselves into the facility to avoid the severely cold winter weather of Syracuse.

Private Archives: Solicited and Unsolicited Documents

Thus far, the discussion has centered on running records prepared primarily for mass public consumption. Other types of archival records, however, are created for smaller, more specific audiences than the public in general. These private archival records include autobiographies (memoirs), diaries and letters, home movies and videos, and artistic and creative artifacts (drawings, sketches). In some cases, these documents occur naturally and are discovered by the investigators (unsolicited documents); in other situations, documents may be requested by investigators (solicited documents). An example of an unsolicited private record might be an existing house log, for instance, of a delinquency group home, which could be used to investigate staff and client relationships in order to determine misbehavior patterns. An example of a solicited document, on the other hand, would be a daily work journal kept by nurses in an intensive care unit at the request of researchers for the purpose of assessing staff and task effectiveness.

Private records are particularly useful for creating case studies or life histories. Typically, owing to the personal nature of private documents, the subjects' own definitions of the situation emerge in their private records, along with the ways they make sense of their daily living routines. Precisely these bits of self-disclosure allow researchers to draw out complete pictures of the subjects' perceptions of their life experiences.

Perhaps the most widely accepted form of personal document is the autobiography. In their discussions of autobiographies, Bogdan and Taylor (1975), Denzin (1978), and Webb et al. (1981) each draw extensively from Allport's (1942) monograph entitled *The Use of Personal Documents in Psychological Science.* Allport distinguishes among three types of autobiography: comprehensive autobiographies, topical autobiographies, and edited autobiographies.

Comprehensive Autobiography

Inexperienced researchers are usually most familiar with the *comprehensive autobiography.* This category of autobiography spans the life of the individual from his or her earliest recall to the time of the writing of the work and includes descriptions of life experiences, personal insights, and anecdotal reminiscences (Smith, 1994).

Topical Autobiography

In contrast to the more rounded and complete description of experiences offered in comprehensive autobiographies, a *topical autobiography* offers a fragmented picture of a life. Denzin (1978, p. 221) suggests that Sutherland's (1937) treatment of "Chic Conwell," who was a professional thief, illustrates this type of autobiographical style. The topical autobiography is an "excision from the life of the subject. As such it invites comparison with other kinds of lives" (Denzin, 1978, p. 221). Other examples of this sort of excision are Bogdan's (1974) examination of "Jane Fry," a prostitute, and Rettig, Torres, and Garrett's (1977) examination of "Manny," a criminal drug addict.

Edited Autobiography
In the case of *edited autobiographies*, researchers serve as editors and commentators, eliminating any repetition in descriptions, making lengthy discourse short and crisp, and highlighting and amplifying selected segments of the material while deleting other segments. Regarding the issue of which segments should be edited and which retained as intended by the author, Allport (1942, p. 78) offers a broad guideline and suggests that all unique styles of speech (for example, slang, colloquialism, street jargon, and the like) remain unedited. Researchers should only edit for the sake of clarity, eliminating repetition, shortening long, convoluted explanations, and so forth.

The intimacy afforded by diaries and personal journals, although conceptually recognized by Allport (1942) and Denzin (1978), remains an underutilized element in research. In diaries, individuals are free to express their feelings, opinions, and understandings fully. In contrast, published autobiographies must maintain the readers' interest or perhaps distort reality in order to project the author's desired public image.

Recently, Reinharz (1992) discussed the use of autobiography by feminist social researchers. Reinharz suggests that some feminist researchers have written full autobiographies (e.g., Hewlett, 1986; Oakley, 1984; Riley, 1988). However, a greater number of feminist researchers have offered self-disclosures in either prefaces or postscripts to their published research. These explanations or expositions into their personal and professional lives can provide subject matter similar to more traditional autobiographical data.

The use of autobiography continues to meet resistance in some academic circles, and has even been called "self-indulgent" (Mykhalovskiy, 1996). In defense of the strategy of autobiography, Mykhalovskiy (1996, p. 134) has written, "The abstract, disembodied voice of traditional academic discourse [is] a fiction, accomplished through writing and other practices which remove evidence of a text's author, as part of concealing the condition of its production." Autobiography, whether offered as a full and lengthy unfolding of one's life or as snippets of disclosure in prefaces and appendices can be extremely useful. This information offers more than simply a single individual's subjective view on matters. An autobiography can reflect the social contours of a given time, the prevailing, or competing ideological orientations of a group, or the self-reflections about one's activities in various roles. In short, autobiographies offer a solid measure of data for the research process.

Another distinct form of intimate private record is the *letter*. In contrast to the autobiography or diary, the letter is not simply a chronicle of past experiences. Letters are designed to communicate something to some other person. As a result, they are geared toward a *dual audience*—namely, the writer and the recipient (Denzin, 1978). The topic of the letter and the social roles and personal relationships of both the writer and receiver must therefore be considered.

The classic example of letters as a source of research data, of course, is Thomas and Znaniecki's (1927) *The Polish Peasant*. In their study, Thomas and Znaniecki learned of an extensive correspondence among recent Polish immigrants in America and their friends and relatives remaining in Poland. As part of their pool of data, Thomas and Znaniecki solicited copies of letters written to Poland as well as those received by Polish immigrants from their homeland. A small fee was offered for each letter submitted. Typically, however, they received only one side of a given letter exchange. In spite of limitations, Thomas and Znaniecki managed to uncover a variety of social values and cultural strains associated with the transition from Poland to America.

More recently, suicide was studied using letters as a viable data source (Garfinkel, 1967; Jacobs, 1967). In one study, Jacobs examined 112 suicide notes and found that the notes could be categorized into six groups, the largest of which was what Jacobs (1967, p. 67) termed *first form notes*. One manifest theme in these notes was the authors' requests for forgiveness or indulgence. From the content of these suicide notes, Jacobs deduced that the authors were involved in long-standing and complex problems. Unable to solve the problems, they found no rational alternative other than taking their own lives. In order to justify this final act, the individuals begged indulgence and forgiveness from the survivors.

Another example of letters as data is Eckberg's (1984) examination of job rejection letters as evidence of bureaucratic propaganda. According to Eckberg (1984), rejection letters reveal how documents may be utilized as propaganda in order to legitimate the work of an organization. The central purpose of such efforts is the creation or maintenance of a definition of the organization's social reality and a projection of this image in the letters.

A Last Remark about Archival Records

Throughout the preceding review of various archival studies, a variety of research topics were related to archival materials. The purpose of this was to suggest the versatility and range of knowledge that can be served by archival research.

An attempt was also made to indicate both the enormous quantity of information and the technological innovations available in connection to archival data. Collections of both privately and publicly held videotaped materials are certainly among the most striking and exciting of recent additions to viable archival sources.

However, researchers should be cautious in the use of archival data. Although an extraordinarily useful source of data for some research questions, archives may be the wrong source of data for some other questions. It is particularly important to use multiple procedures (triangulation) when working with archival data in order to reduce possible sources of error (missing data and so on).

PHYSICAL EROSION AND ACCRETION: HUMAN TRACES AS DATA SOURCES

As implied in the section title, what follows is an examination of various physical traces. Quite literally, traces are physical items left behind by humans, often as the result of some unconscious or unintentional activity, that tell us something about these individuals. Because these traces have been left behind without the producers' knowledge of their potential usefulness to social scientists, these pieces of research information are *nonreactively produced*. Two distinct categories of traces are *erosion measures* (indicators of wearing down or away) and *accretion measures* (indicators of accumulation or build-up).

Erosion Measures

Physical evidence is often the key to solving criminal cases. Similarly, physical evidence is frequently the key to resolving social scientific questions in research. *Erosion measures* include several types of evidence indicating that varying degrees of selective wear or use have occurred on some object or material. In most cases, erosion measures are used with other techniques in order to corroborate one another.

An example of an erosion measure would be using replacement records in order to determine which of a series of high school French language tapes was most frequently used. The hypothesis would be that the tape that required the greatest amount of repair or replacement was the one most frequently used. Unfortunately, several other explanations exist for why a particular tape frequently needs repair. In other words, there can be alternative hypotheses to explain this erosion. Thus, caution is once again advised when using erosion measures.

In spite of their obvious limitations as data sources, erosion measures do contribute interestingly to social scientific research. Perhaps the most widely quoted illustration of how erosion measures operate involves a study at the Chicago Museum of Science and Industry cited by Webb et al. (1981, p. 7):

A committee was formed to set up a psychological exhibit at Chicago's Museum of Science and Industry. The committee learned that the vinyl tiles around the exhibit containing live, hatching chicks had to be replaced every six weeks or so; tiles in other areas of the museum went for years without replacement. A comparative study of the rate of tile replacement around the various museum exhibits could give a rough ordering of the popularity of the exhibits.

Webb et al. (1981) additionally note that beyond the erosion measure, unobtrusive observations (covert observers) indicated that people stood in front of the chick display longer than they stood near any other exhibit. Additional evidence may be necessary to determine whether the wear shown on tiles near the chick exhibit resulted from many different people walking by or smaller numbers of people standing and shuffling their feet over prolonged periods of time. Nonetheless, the illustration does indicate the particularly interesting kinds of information provided by augmenting data sources with erosion measures. This case further illustrates how multiple measures may be used to corroborate one another.

Another example of an erosion measure cited by Webb et al. (1981) involves the examination of wear on library books as an index of their popularity. A variation on this book-wear index might be the examination of textbooks being sold back to a bookstore in order to determine if any signs of use are apparent. For example, if the spine of the book has been broken, it might indicate that the student had actually opened and turned the pages. You might likewise consider whether page corners have been turned down or sections of text highlighted.

Accretion Measures

In contrast to the selective searching out of materials suggested in erosion measures, *accretion measures* represent deposits over time. These trace elements are laid down naturally, without intrusion from researchers.

As an illustration of accretion measures, consider the findings in Siu's (cited in Burgess & Bogue, 1964) study of Chinese laundrymen. Siu (1964) found that calendars with nude female figures were common in certain laundry shops. The study showed that such calendars were more frequently hung in shops run by younger men who were labeled sexual deviants by others. Perhaps more significant, Siu suggested that displays of these calendars were due to the Chinese laundrymen's view that it was legitimate to associate with prostitutes. Siu explained that hanging calendars with nudes merely served to reinforce this general belief pattern.

Although accretion measures may seem more immediately related to the example of paint deposits described in the beginning of this chapter, that is but one form of accretion. As illustrated in the Siu study, the deposit of almost any object or material by humans can be an accretion. In fact, as illustrated by the work of Rathje (1979), even garbage may contain important clues to social culture.

Another illustration of accretion is the examination by Klofas and Cutshall (1985) of graffiti collected from the walls of an abandoned Massachusetts juvenile correctional facility. The graffiti for the study were transcribed verbatim from the walls of the facility (including walls in corridors, bedrooms, the dining hall, and day rooms). Klofas and Cutshall were able to describe juvenile incarceratory culture from this graffiti, as well as shed new light on the influence of the social historical context under which this prison subculture emerged.

Some Final Remarks about Physical Traces

There are several advantages to erosion and accretion measures. Certainly, it should be clear that they are themselves rather inconspicuous and unaffected by researchers who locate and observe them. In consequence, the trace data are largely free of any reactive measurement effects. However, interpreting these physical traces and affixing meaning is problematic and may severely bias the results. Thus, researchers must always remember to obtain corroboration. Similarly, any single trace of physical evidence may have strong *population restrictions* (Webb et al., 1981, p. 32). It is not likely, for example, that a complete description of some group can be accomplished on the merits of some worn spot on a tile or a smudge on some wall. Similarly, physical traces may be selectively found only at certain times and in only certain places. Denzin (1978, p. 260) offers the following example:

> *Chinese laundrymen may no longer display calendars with nude women, or they may only make such displays when their wives are not living with them. In this respect it would be inappropriate to draw conclusions about their relationship to sexual ideology without data on the temporal and spatial dimensions.*
>
> *Certainly, for example, Chinese laundrymen today, to the extent that they still exist, are likely to be considerably different from their counterparts in the 1920s when Siu made his study [actually his dissertation].*

In conclusion, physical traces, although terribly interesting and useful in many ways, are only one of several possible strategies that should be used in concert.

TRYING IT OUT

Researchers can practice using unobtrusive measures in a variety of ways. Some of the unobtrusive data more readily accessible for students/researchers are those offered in the headlines of daily newspapers, the covers of magazines, the commercials on television, the titles of movies they view on their videocassette players, and so forth.

Suggestion 1

One fairly straightforward practice project involves a study of textbook use. By examining the books in school bookstores marked "used," you can get an idea about how well read these used books were. You should note, for example, how many were never opened, as evidenced by uncracked spines. You should consider as well how many have been written in (either with marginal notes or highlight markers) and perhaps whether only certain portions of the books have been read, which may be discerned by looking at the bottom edge of the text.

Look first to see if only segments of the pages have been separated one from the other (as a result of the book being opened and pages turned). Next, notice at what point pages appear to have never been opened (where they fit neatly and flatly together). You might even consider using a ruler and measuring to the place where the pages begin to be neat and flat in order to assess what proportion of each text (in inches) has customarily been read.

Suggestion 2

Another possible practice project using unobtrusive measures might be to examine solicited documents. On a designated day, everyone in a class should be asked to keep a diary. Ask that entries be as detailed as possible and that they include a comprehensive description of activities and events occurring throughout the day. These solicited diary or journal pages will form the base of the practice project's data.

From this data, the researchers may examine entries from an assortment of perspectives. One researcher might, for example, consider similarities or differences that emerge during a given hour or activity—lunch, for instance. Another researcher might look for linguistic characteristics, such as the use of certain types of colloquialisms. Another investigator might even consider reading Chapter 11 (on content analysis) in order to identify a number of other possible practice uses for these particular types of data.

Suggestion 3

A final practice suggestion involves borrowing from Warner's (1959) classic study of "Yankee City." In this case, students should locate a cemetery (preferably an old, established one). Next, read the grave markers and tombstones with the aim of stratifying the cemetery according to information gleaned from these monuments. For instance, based on inscribed phrases, researchers might be able to locate sections of the cemetery containing casualties of some plague or natural disaster. Sizes and styles of markers might be used to identify social and economic stratifications of the cemetery, names might offer a clue to ethnic or religious stratifications, and so forth. It may be helpful to draw a map of the graveyard and to number approximate locations of grave markers. On a separate set of sheets, students can record the phrases inscribed on markers and identify each with a number corresponding to the map location. Other pertinent pieces of information can likewise be annotated on these sheets.

REFERENCES

Albrecht, G. L. (1985). Videotape safaris: Entering the field with a camera. *Qualitative Sociology 8*(4), 325–344.

Allport, G. (1942). *The Use of Personal Documents in Psychological Science*. New York: Social Science Council.

American Behavioral Scientist 30(5). (1987). Special issue on the VCR age.

Blee, K. (1987). Gender ideology and the role of women in the 1920s Klan movement. *Sociological Spectrum 7*, 73–97.

Bogdan, R. (1974). *Being Different: The Autobiography of Jane Fry*. New York: Wiley.

Bogdan, R., & Biklen, S. K. (1992). *Qualitative Research for Education* (2nd ed.). Boston: Allyn and Bacon.

Bogdan, R., & Taylor, S. (1975). *Introduction to Qualitative Research Methods*. New York: Wiley.

Bradley, D. S., Boles, J., & Jones, C. (1979). From mistress to hooker. *Qualitative Sociology 2*(2), 42–62.

Brown, J. C. (1995). The writing on the wall: The messages in Hungarian graffiti. *Journal of Popular Culture 29*(2), 115–118.

Burgess, E. W., & Bogue, D. (Eds.), (1964). *Contributions to Urban Sociology*. Chicago: University of Chicago Press.

Burstein P., & Freudenberg, W. R. (1978). Changing public policy: The impact of opinion, antiwar demonstrations, and war costs on Senate voting in Vietnam War motions. *American Journal of Sociology 84*, 99–122.

Cialdini, R. B., Vincent, E. J., Lewis, S. K., Catalan, T., Wheeler, D., & Darby, B. L. (1975). Reciprocal concession procedure for inducing compliance: The door-in-the-face technique. *Journal of Personality and Social Psychology 34*, 206–215.

Comstock, G. S. (1977). Types of portrayal and aggressive behavior. *Journal of Communication 27*, 189–198.

Cunningham, M. R. (1979). Weather, mood and helping behavior. Quasi experiments with the sunshine Samaritan. *Journal of Social Psychology 37*, 1947–1956.

Denzin, N, K. (1978). *The Research Act*. New York: McGraw-Hill.

Dowdall, G. W., & Golden, J. (1989). Photographs as data: An analysis of images from a mental hospital. *Qualitative Sociology 12*(2), 183–213.

Eckberg, D. L. (1984). Job-related letters as bureaucratic propaganda. *Qualitative Sociology 7*(4), 340–351.

Eisenhower, M. (1969). *Commission Statement on Violence in Television Entertainment Programs.* National Commission on the Causes and Prevention of Violence. Washington, DC: U.S. Government Printing Office.

Erickson, F., & Mohatt, G. (1988). Cultural organization of participation structures in two classrooms of Indian students. In G. Spindler (Ed.), *Doing the Ethnography of Schooling.* Prospect Heights, IL: Waveland Press.

Eron, L. D. (1980). Prescriptions for reduction of aggression. *American Psychologist 35*, 244–252.

Fields, E. E. (1988). Qualitative content analysis of television news: Systematic techniques. *Qualitative Sociology 11*(3), 183–193.

Frankfort-Nachmias, C., & Nachmias, D. (1996). *Research Methods in the Social Sciences* (5th ed.). New York: St. Martin's Press.

Freedman, J. (1979). Lecture notes from a course on clinical sociology. Syracuse University, Syracuse, NY.

Garfinkel, H. (1967). *Studies in Ethnomethodology.* Englewood Cliffs, NJ: Prentice Hall.

Goffman, E. (1979). *Gender Advertisements.* New York: Harper and Row.

Gottschalk, S. (1995). Ethnographic fragments in postmodern spaces. *Journal of Contemporary Ethnography 24*(2), 195–228.

Hewlett, S. A. (1986). *Lesser Life: The Myths of Women's Lives in America.* New York: Morrow.

Jackson, B. (1977). *Killing Time: Life in the Arkansas Penitentiary.* Ithaca, NY: Cornell University Press.

Jacobs, J. (1967). A phenomenological study of suicide notes. *Social Problems 15*, 60–72.

Jelenko, C., III (1980). The rock syndrome: A newly discovered environmental hazard. *Journal of Irreproducible Results 26*, 14.

Klofas, J. M., & Cutshall, C. R. (1985). The social archeology of a juvenile facility: Unobtrusive methods in the study of institutional culture. *Qualitative Sociology 8*(4), 368–387.

Masters, R., & Sullivan, D. (1988). Happy warriors: Leaders' facial displays, viewer's emotions and political support. *American Journal of Political Science, 32*(2), 365–678.

Melichar, K. E. (1987). The making of the 1967 Montana Clean Air Act. *Sociological Perspective 30*(1), 49–70.

Molotch, H., & Boden, D. (1985). Talking social structure: Discourse domination and the Watergate hearing. *American Sociological Review 50*(3), 273–287.

Musello, C. (1980). Studying the home mode: An exploration of family photography and visual communications. *Studies in Visual Communication 6*(1), 23–42.

Mykhalovskiy, E. (1996). Reconsidering table talk: Critical thoughts on the relationship between sociology, autobiography, and self-indulgence. *Qualitative Sociology 19*(1), 131–151.

Oakley, Ann. (1984). *Taking It Like a Woman.* New York: Random House.

Persinger, M. S. (1975). Lag response in mood reports to changes in the weather matrix. *International Journal of Biometeorology 19*, 108–114.

Phillips, D. P. (1983). The impact of mass media violence on U.S. homicides. *American Sociological Review 48*, 560–568.

Poole, E. D., & Regoli, R. M. (1981). Periodical prestige in criminology and criminal justice: A comment. *Criminology 19*, 470–498.

Portelli, A. (1992). History-telling and time: An example from Kentucky. *Oral History Review* 20(1/2), 51–66.

Rathje, R. H. (1979). Trace measures. In L. Sechrest (Ed.), *Unobtrusive Measurement Today*. San Francisco: Jossey-Bass.

Reinharz, S. (1992). *Feminist Methods in Social Research*. New York: Oxford University Press.

Rettig, R. P., Torres, M. J., & Garrett, G. R. (1977). *Manny: A Criminal Addict's Story*. Boston: Houghton Mifflin.

Riley, M. W. (Ed.). (1988). *Sociological Lives*. Newbury Park, CA: Sage.

Sawyer, H. G. *The meaning of numbers*. Paper presented at the annual meeting of the American Association of Advertising Agencies, 1961. Cited in Eugene J. Webb, Donald T. Campbell, Richard D. Schwartz, Lee Sechrest, and Janet Belew Grove, *Nonreactive Measures in the Social Sciences*. Boston: Houghton Mifflin, 1981.

Schmalleger, F. (1996). *The Trial of the Century: People of the State of California vs. Orenthal James Simpson*. Englewood Cliffs, NJ: Prentice Hall.

Schwartz, D. (1989). Visual ethnography: Using photography in qualitative research. *Qualitative Sociology* 12(2), 119–154.

Schwartz, H., & Jacobs, J. (1979). *Qualitative Sociology: A Method to the Madness*. New York: Free Press.

Smith, L. M. (1994). Biographical Method. In N. K. Denzin & Y. S. Lincoln (Eds.), *Handbook of Qualitative Research*. Thousand Oaks, CA: Sage.

Smolensky, M. (1980). To everything there is a season. *Science News 18*, 150–151.

Sutherland, E. H. (1956). *The Professional Thief*. Phoenix, 1937. (Reprint.) Chicago: University of Chicago Press.

Thomas, C., & Bronick, M. J. (1984). The quality of doctoral programs in deviance criminology and criminal justice: An empirical assessment. *Journal of Criminal Justice 12*(1), 21–37.

Thomas, W. I., & Znaniecki, F. (1927). *The Polish Peasant*. New York: Knopf.

Wagner, J. (1979). *Images of Information: Still Photography in the Social Sciences*. Beverly Hills, CA: Sage.

Warner, L. W. (1959). *The Living and the Dead: A Study of the Symbolic Life of Americans*. New Haven: Yale University Press.

Warner, L. W., & Low, J. O. (1947). *The Social System of the Modern Community. The Strike: A Social Analysis*. New Haven: Yale University Press.

Warner, L. W., & Lunt, P. S. (1941). *The Social Life of a Modern Community*. New Haven: Yale University Press.

Warner, L. W., & Lunt, P. S. (1942). *The Status System of a Modern Community*. New Haven: Yale University Press.

Warner, L. W., & Srole, L. (1945). *The Social Systems of American Ethnic Groups*. New Haven: Yale University Press.

Webb, E., Campbell, D. T., Schwartz, R. D., & Sechrest, L. (1966). *Unobtrusive Measures: Nonreactive Research in the Social Sciences*. Chicago: Rand McNally.

Webb, E., Campbell, D. T., Schwartz, R. D., Sechrest, L., & Grove, J. B. (1981). *Nonreactive Measures in the Social Sciences*. Boston: Houghton Mifflin.

Z-Frank stresses radio to build big Chevy dealership. (1962). *Advertising Age 33*, 83.

HISTORIOGRAPHY AND ORAL TRADITIONS

WHAT IS HISTORICAL RESEARCH?

What exactly is meant by historical research? The obvious answer to this question is that *historical research* or *historiography* is an examination of elements from history. Unfortunately, this answer begs the next question—namely, What is history? Often in common parlance the term *history* is used synonymously with the word *past* and, in turn, to refer conceptually to past events during bygone eras (Hamilton, 1993).

You can open textbooks from many disciplines and locate *time lines*, lists or drawings of time-ordered events shown in chronological sequence. This chronology of historical events allows the presenter to describe interesting or important past events, people, developments, and the like. It is a classification system some might call *historical*. Further, it provides the reader with a sense of which things or events came before others. It is not, however, historiography. Historical time lines can be quite illuminating and do have their place. They are, however, passive and somewhat lackluster and lifeless. Historiography, on the other hand, attempts to fashion a descriptive written account of the past. Such a narrative account is flowing, revealing, vibrant, and alive!

Historiography involves far more than the mere retelling of facts from the past. It is more than linking together tired old pieces of information found in diaries, letters, or other documents, important as such an activity might be. Historical research is at once descriptive, factual, and fluid (Matejski, 1986). Historical research is not merely creative nostalgia. In fact, it is important to distinguish nostalgia from historical research.

Nostalgia, or the retelling of comfortable past pleasantries, events, or situations, lacks research rigor. In contrast to nostalgia, *historical research* attempts to systematically recapture the complex nuances, the people, meanings, events, and even ideas of the past that have influenced and shaped the present (Hamilton, 1993; Leedy, 1993). In nursing research, as Burns and Grove (1993) note, historical research provides a means for the history of a profession to be transmitted to those entering the profession. Historical analysis of social knowledge, traditions, and conditions can increase appreciation and understanding of contemporary issues of health, race relations, crime and corrections, education, business trends, and a virtually infinite array of social, political, and spiritual realms.

Notter (1972) points out that historical research extends beyond a mere collection of incidents, facts, dates, or figures. It is the study of the relationships among issues that have influenced the past, continue to influence the present, and will certainly affect the future (Glass, 1989). Ironically, it is only during recent *history* that standard research methods books have begun looking seriously at historical research. Many methods texts continue to omit any consideration of this methodology (e.g., Gilgun, Daly, & Handel, 1992; Bogdan & Biklen, 1992). In some cases, history is mentioned only in terms of its possible threat to internal validity (Shaughnessy & Zechmeister, 1990; Frankfort-Nachmias & Nachmias, 1996); or its effect on construct validity (Taylor, 1994). In other texts, the use of historical research is used synonymously with comparative analysis (see, for example, Babbie, 1995). Sarnecky (1990), however, suggests that there has been an increased interest in historiography during recent years. Sarnecky attributes this growing interest to the move away from a traditional focus on abject positivism and toward a broader perspective that is more generally supportive of the type of knowledge offered by historical research.

Historical research, then, involves a process that examines events or combinations of events in order to uncover accounts of what happened in the past. Historical research allows the contemporary researcher to "slip the bonds of their own time" (Hamilton, 1993, p. 43) and descend into the past. This provides access to a broader understanding of human behavior and thoughts than would be possible if we were trapped in the static isolation of our own time.

Such a tragic isolation is illustrated in the classic H. G. Wells book, *The Time Machine* (published in 1895). When the protagonist arrives in the distant future, a near utopia seems to exist. Yet the people of the future millennia are actually raised as the slaves and food of a group of mutant creatures. When the protagonist tries to learn how such a situation could have developed, no one can tell him. They have no sense of their history. How things had come to be as they are and how things might be changed were concepts lost on these people. They were oblivious to their past, living in the isolation of a single time period—their present.

Most American students are never formally introduced to historical methods of research and analysis. Instead, there seems to be an assumption that one can become expert at historical research through some tacit process, that merely by taking a history course or two, one can automatically gain the ability to perform historical research (Leedy, 1993; Salkind, 1991). This is, of course, not accurate. There is a simple reason one cannot learn how to do historical research and analysis in typical history courses: Such courses present the end product of the research, not the process by which it was uncovered. Hence, many people confuse the study of history with the method of historical research.

Nonetheless, understanding the historical nature of phenomena, events, people, agencies, and even institutions is important. In many ways, it may be as important as understanding these items in themselves. One cannot fully evaluate or appreciate advances made in knowledge, policy, science, or technology without some understanding of the circumstances within which these developments occurred (Salkind, 1991). There is a parallel with dating. When you go out on a first date, there is usually considerable small talk between yourself and your date. Each person attempts to get to know the other. Small talk often centers on your background and the other person's. Where were you born, raised, and educated? What do you like to do in your spare time, and do you have hobbies? What are your favorite foods, colors, and television shows? Do you or your date have brothers or sisters, and how well do you each get along with your parents? All of this information goes into the process of getting to know each other and into decisions about whether to go home early, kiss on the first date, or even continue the relationship. Could you make the decision to continue a relationship and perhaps even to marry without knowing about the other person's background? It is unlikely, and so it is with the importance of historical research. Knowledge of the past provides necessary information to be used in the present in order to determine how things may be in the future. What, then, does historical research involve?

The major impetus in historical research is, as with other data-collection strategies, the collection of information and the *interpretation* or analysis of these data. Specifically, historical research is conducted for one or more of the following reasons: to uncover the unknown; to answer questions; to seek implications or relationships of events from the past and their connections with the present; to assess past activities and accomplishments of individuals, agencies, or institutions; and to aid generally in our understanding of human culture.

As with the example of getting to know your date, a basic assumption underlying historical research is that you can learn about the present from the past. You must use care, however, and avoid imposition of modern thoughts or understanding when considering information about the past (Marshall & Rossman, 1989). Researchers must seek to understand both literal and latent meanings of documents and other historical sources within their historical time frames. Definitions and connotations for terms change over time. A hundred years ago, the word *nurse* conjured up images of hand maidens and subservient clinical helpers to physicians. Today, however, one envisions nurses as health professionals—members of a team that includes physicians.

This is likewise true regarding different cultures and cultural terms and meanings. You must be careful not to impose your own cultural judgments on other cultures' meanings. For example, in Israel today, the common word for *nurse* in Hebrew actually translates to *sister*. It is likely this corresponds more to the connotation in early American history of the subservient hand maiden. Yet it would not be appropriate, as it would not be in other research strategies, to make judgmental statements about the term's connotation.

Passing judgment about the rightness or wrongness of earlier connotations or meanings within other cultures literally misses the point of historical research. What should be of interest and importance to the historiographer is the progression from the older image to the newer one. In the case of different cultures, the historical research is interested in comparisons, not judgments. For example, the historical researcher might be interested in the impact of changed images on modern practices. You might consider how the meaning of *nurse* affects patient care, other health professionals, and medical institutions in general.

Also, historical research provides a window to understanding today various symbols used in the past. Elman (1996) for example, examines the use of pink and black triangles by the Nazis to designate gay men and women respectively. Elman's (1996, p. 3) discussion indicates that the "pink triangles symbolized the femaleness of this group of detainees whose masculinity was diminished within the context of Nazi heterosexism." Lesbians were classified as asocials who were made to wear black turned-down triangles. These asocials were especially despised because the color of their triangle was viewed as an insult to the black uniform of the elite black-uniformed SS *(Schutzstaffel)*.

LIFE HISTORIES AND HISTORIOGRAPHY

Like the confusion between the concepts of history and historiography, there is sometimes a confusion between life histories and historiography. Researchers taking life histories, as a variation on traditional depth interviewing strategies, are sometimes confronted with problems similar to those faced by historiographers. This is because researchers involved in life histories often move beyond the limits of the depth interview and seek external corroborating pieces of evidence. This may be called *construction of a life history* and involves depth interviewing as merely a single line of action. This may also cause confusion because in the construction of a life history, the researcher may find it necessary to assess the motives of authors of crucial documents. This action is quite similar to how historiographers attempt to make such assessments. For example, the comments made in a diary or a suicide note must be assessed in order to ensure who the author is or was and what his or her motive might have been.

These concerns, however, are really issues that lie at the heart of any form of document analysis. As historical methods unfold throughout the remainder of this chapter, readers will also see similarities with previous descriptions of archival unobtrusive strategies.

From the perspective presented in this book, depth interview life histories or constructed documentary-based life histories are merely elements potentially useful as data in the larger historiographic analysis. Thus, any strategies that attempt to collect information from the past and to weave these pieces of information into a meaningful set of explanations fit my perspective on historical research. The reconstruction of the past from such information or data falls under the label *historiography* (Denzin, 1978). Let us further consider the types and sources of data used in historiographies.

WHAT ARE THE DATA OF HISTORICAL RESEARCHERS?

The sources of data used by historiographers parallel those of many other social scientists: confidential reports, public records, government documents, newspaper editorials and stories, essays, songs, poetry, folklore, films, photos, artifacts, and even interviews or questionnaires. The historiographer classifies these various data as either *primary sources* or *secondary sources*.

- *Primary Sources.* These sources involve the oral or written testimony of eyewitnesses. They are original artifacts, documents, and items related to the direct outcome of an event or an experience (Salkind, 1991). They may include documents, photographs, recordings, diaries, journals, life histories, drawings, mementos, or other relics.
- *Secondary Sources.* Secondary sources involve the oral or written testimony of people not immediately present at the time of a given event. They are documents written or objects created by others that relate to a specific research question or area of research interest. These elements represent secondhand or hearsay accounts of someone, some event, or some development. Secondary sources may include textbooks, encyclopedias, oral histories of individuals or a group, journal articles, newspaper stories, and even obituary notices (Brink & Wood, 1989; Leedy, 1993). They may also include information that refers not to a specific

subject but to a class of people (Denzin, 1978). These may involve court records of delinquents, lab information about asthmatic patients, reading scores of an entire grade level in an elementary school, and other aggregated information about some group.

DOING HISTORIOGRAPHY: TRACING WRITTEN HISTORY AS DATA

You begin historical research just as you begin any research project. This was described in detail in Chapter 2 but bears some reiteration here. You begin with an idea or a topic. This may be organized as a research problem, a question, a series of questions, or a hypothesis or series of hypotheses.

Next, you seek basic background information through a literature review. As you create this literature review, your topic and questions may be altered or refined and become clearer and better delineated. As you refine the research focus, you also begin to consider where and what you will use as sources of historical data. You might outline this procedure as follows:

1. Identify an idea, topic, or research question.
2. Conduct a background literature review.
3. Refine the research idea and questions.
4. Determine that historiography will be the data-collection process.
5. Identify and locate primary and secondary data sources.
6. Confirm the authenticity and accuracy of source materials.
7. Analyze the data and develop a narrative exposition of the findings.

As described in Chapter 2, you often begin with a broad idea or question for research. Initially, it may reflect an area of research more than it does a specific research statement: for instance, "women in law enforcement." You then need to begin seeking basic background information about this broad topic, just as you would with any other research problem. As you read the literature, you might begin to refine the topic and realize that how women are treated in police work has changed over time.

For example, you might notice that in 1845, when the first woman was hired by the New York City police department, she was hired as a *matron* (Berg, 1992; Feinman 1986). You might also notice that during the nineteenth century, matrons seemed to fit a social worker role more than they did a law enforcement one. That is, their primary responsibilities were to assist victims of crime, runaways, prostitutes, and children (Feinman, 1986; Hamilton, 1924). Moreover, this general social work orientation carried through until late into the 1960s (Berg, 1992; Berg & Budnick, 1986; Talney, 1969). You might now refine the original research focus to examine the changing role of policewomen. You might also begin to consider historiography as an appropriate way to examine this research problem. Next, you will need to locate sources of data regarding the topic. These will be sorted into primary and secondary classifications. Looking over the various books and journal articles you have already amassed during this preliminary literature review is a good first step. Certainly, many of these documents will fit into the secondary source classification. However, by examining the reference sections in these documents, you might also locate leads to or actual primary data references. These may include references to autobiographies written by people during the period of interest or newspaper stories reporting interviews with people of the time. These may also include references to diaries, letters, notes, or personal journals. They may even include the court transcripts of some hearing or the minutes of some agency's meeting.

In other words, you begin to seek primary sources that contain the descriptions of a witness to the time or event now the focus of the research. You may be able to obtain these documents directly from a library or similar archive, or you may need to contact agencies or organizations. You may even need to directly contact individuals who are still alive and can bear witness to some situation or aspect of interest to the research.

For many, locating and gathering primary data is considered the actual data-collection component of historical research (Glass, 1989). Historical researchers must make serious efforts to locate as much source material related to the original event as possible. These may be memos, diary entries, witnesses' accounts—all of which serve to establish a cohesive understanding of the situation. This will eventually result in insights into the meaning of the event or situation. Metaphorically, this becomes a drawing together of the puzzle pieces to form a complete picture.

However, it also is important to recognize that often secondary sources provide both access to primary ones and details not always immediately apparent in the primary sources. Many different pieces of information—both primary and secondary—will be necessary before the researcher can adequately fit them all together into a cogent exposition.

As you amass the primary data, you also will need to assess each item for its usefulness and in terms of its critical external and internal adequacy: the validity and reliability of the material. This means making notes on each document not only on the content of the material (as detailed in Chapter 2 regarding literature reviews) but on the document itself. Where was it located? What information supports the accuracy or authenticity of the material? What corroboration, if any, can be or has been located? Let's consider external and internal criticism in more detail.

Primary source materials are subject to two kinds of evaluations or criticisms: First, you must determine whether a document or artifact is authentic, which is sometimes referred to as *external criticism* or *validity*. Second, you must determine the accuracy of meaning in the material, which is called *internal criticism* and is related to the document's reliability.

External Criticism

External criticism is primarily concerned with the question of veracity or genuineness of the source material. Was a document or artifact actually created by the author? Wilson (1989, p. 137) suggests that "documents cannot be taken to reflect the truth unless they are really what they appear to be rather than forgeries or frauds. In short, is it a valid piece of primary data? Counterfeit documents are not uncommon. Throughout history, there have been numerous hoaxes perpetrated on the literary, historical, scientific, and social science communities. For example, there been many literary forgeries. Major George de Luna Byron claimed to be the natural son of George Gordon, Lord Byron, and a Spanish countess. He successfully produced and sold many forgeries of works alleged to have been written by Shelley, Keats, and others—including his alleged father, Byron (*Encyclopaedia Britannica*, 1987, p. 136).

More commonly known is the Thomas Chatterton-Rowley Manuscripts incident. In this case, poems written by Thomas Chatterton (1752–1835) were passed off by the young writer as the works of a medieval cleric. Controversy over these poems caused a scholarly feud that lasted for many years. In fact, it has been said that this controversy actually led to the Gothic revival in literature (*Encyclopaedia Britannica*, 1987, p. 136).

An even more bizarre incident occurred in the early 1980s, when two men passed off 60 volumes alleged to be the diaries of Adolf Hitler. They sold them to the German magazine *Stern* for a sum amounting to nearly $3 million. Almost three years later, *Stern* discovered that these diaries were complete phonies, and the magazine sued the sellers. The forgers were forced to return their ill-gotten money and were sentenced to prison ("Hitler Diaries," 1985; "Two Charged," 1984).

In 1993, George Jammal appeared on national television claiming to have obtained a piece of the original Noah's Ark (Jaroff, 1993). Jammal claimed to have obtained the chunk of ark during a 1984 search for the ark on Mount Ararat in Turkey. He explained that he and a friend known only as Vladimir had "crawled through a hole in the ice into a wooden structure. [They] got very excited when [they] saw part of the room was made into pens, like places where you keep animals" (Jaroff, 1993, p. 51). Unfortunately, Vladimir was allegedly killed, and all photographic evidence was lost on the journey. But Jammal had managed to return safely with a piece of the ark.

The television network made no effort to verify Jammal's story. After the story was aired, however, network executives learned that Jammal was an actor who had been telling this and other versions of the ark story for years (Jaroff, 1993). There never was a Vladimir, and the piece of ark is nothing more than a piece of ordinary pine Jammal soaked in fruit juices and baked in his oven (Jaroff, 1993).

Frauds, hoaxes, and forgeries are not uncommon, and this can be particularly problematic for the naïve or novice researcher. It is very important, therefore, that researchers carefully evaluate their sources. You must ensure that the document or artifact is genuine. This is true for credibility of both the research and the historical researcher. Being duped can jeopardize your ability to be taken seriously during later research investigations. Authenticating documents and objects, of course, is a study in itself. Therefore, researchers should not hesitate to seek the assistance of others more proficient than themselves when attempting to authenticate source material. This may mean handwriting experts, scientists for carbon dating, linguists knowledgeable in writing dialects or period styles, and other specialists.

Internal Criticism

The question, Is this material genuine? is separate from the question, What does this document mean? Important collateral questions include: What was the author trying to say? Why did the author write the document? and even, What inferences or impressions can be taken from the contents of the document? (Leedy, 1993).

For example, what exactly did Mary Hamilton (1924, p. 183) mean when in reference to police matrons, she wrote, "The policewoman has been likened to the mother. Hers is the strong arm of the law as it is expressed in a woman's guiding hand." Was she endorsing the role of matron as nurturing social worker? Or suggesting that because women possess the capacity to be nurturers, they can also provide strong abilities as law enforcers? This example is a bit unfair since the quote is taken somewhat out of the context of Hamilton's writings. However, it should serve to illustrate the sometimes difficult task faced by historical researchers when they attempt to consider the internal validity of documents.

Another example of this task of assessing internal meanings is determining what the decision in a Supreme Court case means. What does the text of the court's decision convey in terms of the court's intent? What will the meanings culled from the high court's decision do in terms of policies or people or agencies affected by it? When you are making these kinds of internal meaning criticisms, the actual question becomes, what do the words mean?

These issues of external and internal criticism are very important for ascertaining the quality of the data and, in turn, the depth of the interpretation or analysis. Rigorous evaluations of the external and internal value of the data ensure valid and reliable information.

These external and internal evaluations also tend to separate historical research from most other forms of archival unobtrusive measures. Traditional archival methods also use secondary source material, such as medical history files, court records, or even arrest reports. However, these are treated as primary data sources and are seldom checked by external or internal evaluations. Instead, there is the tacit assumption of authenticity and accuracy and, therefore, validity and reliability of these data.

During the analysis phase of historical research, data are interpreted. The researcher will review the materials he or she has been so carefully collecting and evaluating. Data will be sorted and categorized into various topical themes (more fully described in Chapter 11). This *content analysis* strategy will allow the researcher to identify patterns within and between sources. Additional sources may be required in order to further explain these patterns as they arise. Any research questions that are proposed will be explained, supported, or refuted only insofar as the data can successfully argue such positions. If the data are faulty, so too will the analysis be weak and unconvincing.

The analysis and synthesis of the data allow the researcher to return to the original literature review and compare commentaries with the researcher's own observations. Thus, the analysis in historical research is deeply grounded in both the data and the background literature of the study. Exposition involves writing a narrative account of the resulting patterns, connections, and insights uncovered during the process of the research. These may extend well into the external and internal criticism you made on data, as well as the patterns identified through content analysis.

Historiographers view history as a field of human action and action as the result of individual and collective reasoning (Roberts, 1996). This reasoning is understood as mediated through various circumstances and impacted by a variety of social, political, economic, ideological, and cultural influences. The actual task of historical researchers, then, is to reconstruct the reasons for past actions. They accomplish this by identifying evidence of past human thinking, which are established as valid and meaningful data. These, in turn, are interpreted with regard to how and why decisions and actions have occurred.

WHAT ARE ORAL HISTORIES?

From the historiographic approach offered in this chapter, historical documentary evidence is taken to include both written and oral sources. As suggested above, the term *written document* may include personal documents such as letters, journals, diaries, poems, autobiographies, and even plays. However, novice researchers should be aware that historical researchers use a wide range of data sources and combine numerous methodologies.

The written sources of documentary evidence are indeed varied. Even when one is examining the history of some local event, person, or phenomenon, there is a wide range of written documents available. However, whether for local studies or larger ones, the documents available to a researcher will influence the perspective that he or she takes. As Samuel (1975, p. xiii) has commented, "It is remarkable how much history has been written from the vantage point of those who have had the charge of running—or attempting to run—other people's lives, and how little from the real life experience of people themselves." As a result, claims Samuel (1975), researchers often obtain only one perspective on the past—namely, that which is represented in official or residual documents of leaders, administrators, or other dignitaries.

Oral histories allow you to escape some of the deficiencies of residual and official presentations in documentary records (Samuel, 1991). This is true at least insofar as moderately recent histories are concerned—those limited to the time within living memories. But this still provides researchers with a means of reaching as far back as perhaps 100 years.

Older people hold a gamut of facts and memories, and this information may be unavailable anywhere else. There may have been no reason for anyone to have recorded these treasures of knowledge or explanations. Were it not for the memories of people, these nuggets of information might vanish. Furthermore, as extremely important as written documents are, they cannot answer questions directly put to them. Nor can they be asked what they mean or to offer greater details than appear on the recorded page. Oral evidence, on the other hand, is ongoing and relentless. The information that is available from oral histories is limited solely by the number of survivors and the resourcefulness of the researcher.

Oral histories also can be useful for providing background and social texture to your research. It provides increased understanding and a living context to the otherwise one-dimensional information frequently offered by documents alone. It is, consequently, very dynamic.

Written documents sometimes create the structure of a research project. In other words, the limitations on the documents are imposed upon the research. If these documents have filtered through officials in agencies or organizations, they may reflect only front-stage information. Facts critical for understanding research questions or hypotheses may have been combed out of the written documents (see Chapter 8 on archival data). The real-life experiences and memories of people cannot so easily be omitted, edited, erased, shredded, or swept away.

Oral histories also offer access to the ordinary unreported interests and tribulations of everyday life along with the better documented occurrences of floods, earthquakes, and other natural disasters (Burgess, 1991; Samuel 1991). Oral histories allow researchers to investigate ordinary people as well as exceptional ones whose life and work may find their way into written documents (see for examples Blythe, 1973; Harkell, 1978; Newby, 1977; Terkel, 1970, 1974).

Single oral histories as well as sets have been written up and published as both analyzed and unanalyzed documents (Reinharz, 1992). Collections of these published oral histories have been accumulated and stored in archives across the country. They can be used as sources of data in historical research.

Frequently, these archived oral histories are biographical in nature. Biography has always been an important aspect of social science research. This is because biographies draw people and groups out of obscurity; they repair damaged historical records, and they give powerless people a voice. The use of oral histories and biographical data recently has become popular among women in feminist literature (Reinharz, 1992). For example, Griffith (1984, p. xix) details the usefulness of biographical data in understanding the women's movement in the United States:

> *Initial efforts to record the lives of eminent American women were made in the 1890s, as the first generation of college-educated women sought to identify women of achievement in an earlier era. [These women] established archives for research and wrote biographies of colonial and contemporary women, like Abigail Adams and Susan B. Anthony. Organizations like the Daughters of the American Revolution related their members to the past that provided proud models of accomplishment. The second surge of biographies came with the renaissance of women's history in the late 1960s.*

As suggested by Griffith's (1984) comments, first-person accounts such as oral histories and biographies are necessary if a researcher is to understand the subjectivity of a social group that has been "muted, excised from history, [and] invisible in the official records of their culture" (Long, 1987, p. 5).

The historical method can be used to access information otherwise simply unavailable to researchers. It provides a means for answering questions and offering solutions that might otherwise go unmentioned and unnoticed. Using a historical method to answer questions or examine problems in one area also facilitates answers to questions and problems in other areas. For example, examination of correctional officers historiographically will necessarily draw in consideration of social reforms, role development, institutional development, questions about education, and numerous other areas. The strength of historical research rests on its applicability to diverse areas and the enormity of information and knowledge it can uncover.

TRYING IT OUT

Suggestion 1

In the library or in a local newspaper's morgue, locate the obituaries of 10 public figures (famous actors, political figures, etc.). Next, locate at least one newspaper story about their deaths.

Suggestion 2

Obtain an oral history from an elderly person in your family. Have him or her tell you about his or her life as a child, an adolescent, an adult, and now as an older adult. You might want to consult Chapter 4 before you begin. Record the oral history on audio- or videotape.

Suggestion 3

Locate four different pieces of primary data (e.g., a diary, an original song or poem, a letter). Consider each item for internal and external critical value. Do not use data of your own creation.

REFERENCES

Babbie, E. (1995). *The Practice of Social Research* (7th ed.). Belmont, CA: Wadsworth Publishing.

Berg, B. L. (1992). *Law Enforcement: An Introduction to Police in Society*. Boston: Allyn and Bacon.

Berg, B. L., & Budnick, K. J. (1986). Defeminization of women in law enforcement: A new twist in the traditional police personality. *Journal of Police Science and Administration 14*, 314–319.

Blythe, R. (1973). *Akenfield: Portrait of an English Village*. New York: Dell.

Brink, P. J., & Wood, M. J. (1989). *Advanced Design in Nursing Research*. Newbury Park, CA: Sage.

Burgess, R. G. (1991). Personal documents, oral sources and life histories. In R. G. Burgess (Ed.), *Field Research: A Sourcebook and Field Manual* (pp. 131–135). New York: Routledge.

Burns, N., & Grove, S. K. (1993). *The Practice of Nursing Research* (2nd ed.). Philadelphia: W. B. Saunders.

Denzin, N. K. (1978). *The Research Act*. Chicago: Aldine.

Elman, R. A. (1996). Triangles and tribulations: The politics of Nazi symbols. *Journal of Homosexuality 30*(3), 1–11.

Encyclopaedia Britannica (Vol. 14, pp. 135–138). (1987). Chicago: University of Chicago Press.

Feinman, C. (1986). *Women in the Criminal Justice System*. New York: Praeger.

Frankfort-Nachmias, C., & Nachmias, D. (1996). *Research Methods in the Social Sciences* (5th ed.). New York: St. Martin's Press.

Gilgun, J. F., Daly, K., & Handel, G. (Eds.). (1992). *Qualitative Methods in Family Research*. Newbury Park, CA: Sage.

Glass, L. (1989). Historical research. In P. J. Brink & M. J. Wood (Eds.), *Advanced Design in Nursing Research*. Newbury Park, CA: Sage.

Griffith, E. (1984). *In Her Own Right: The Life of Elizabeth Cady Stanton*. New York: Oxford University Press.

Hamilton, D. B. (1993). The idea of history and the history of ideas. *Image: Journal of Nursing Scholarship 25*, 45–48.

Hamilton, M. (1924). *The Policewoman: Her Service and Ideas*. New York: Arno Press and the New York Times (Reprinted 1971).

Harkell, G. (1978). The migration of mining families to the Kent coalfield between the wars. *Oral History 6*, 98–113.

Hitler diaries trial stirs judge to disbelief and ire. (1985, January 6). *New York Times*, p. A14.

Jaroff, L. (1993, July 5). Phony arkaeology: In a pseudo documentary, CBS falls victim to a hoaxer. *Time*, 51.

Leedy, P. D. (1993). *Practical Research: Planning and Design* (5th ed.). New York: Macmillan.

Long, J. (1987). *Telling women's lives: The new sociobiography*. Paper presented at the Annual Meeting of the American Sociological Association, Chicago.

Marshall, C., & Rossman, G. B. (1989). *Designing Qualitative Research*. Newbury Park, CA: Sage.

Matejski, M. (1986). Historical research: The method. In P. Munhall & C. J. Oiler (Eds.), *Nursing Research: A Qualitative Perspective* (pp. 175–193). Norwalk, CT: Appleton-Century-Crofts.

Newby, H. (1977). *The Deferential Worker*. London: Allen Lane.

Notter, L. (1972). The case for historical research in nursing. *Nursing Research 21*, 483.

Reinharz, S. (1992). *Feminist Methods in Social Research*. New York: Oxford University Press.

Roberts, G. (1996). Narrative History as a Way of Life. *Journal of Contemporary History 31*, 221–228.

Salkind, N. J. (1991). *Exploring Research*. New York: Macmillan.

Samuel, R. (1975). *Village Life and Labour*. London: Routledge and Kegan Paul.

Samuel, R. (1991). Local history and oral history. In R. G. Burgess (Ed.), *Field Research: A Sourcebook and Field Manual* (pp. 136–145). New York: Routledge.

Sarnecky, M. T. (1990). Historiography: A legitimate research methodology for nursing. *Advances in Nursing Science 12*(4), 1–10.

Shaughnessy, J. J., & Zechmeister, E. B. (1990). *Research Methods in Psychology* (2nd ed.). New York: McGraw-Hill.

Talney, R. (1969). Women in law enforcement: An expanded role. *Police 14*, 49–51.

Taylor, R. B. (1994). *Research Methods in Criminal Justice*. New York: McGraw-Hill.

Terkel, S. (1970). *Hard Times: An Oral History of The Great Depression*. New York: Pantheon.

Terkel, S. (1974). *Working: People Talk about What They Do All Day and How They Feel about It*. New York: Pantheon.

Two charged in Hamburg in "Hitler diary" fraud. (1984, March 23). *New York Times*, p. A4.

Wells, H. G. (1895). *The Time Machine* (Rev. ed., 1977). Edited by F. D. McConnell. New York: Oxford University Press.

Wilson, H. S. (1989). *Nursing Research* (2nd ed.). Reading, MA: Addison-Wesley.

CASE STUDIES

THE NATURE OF CASE STUDIES

Case study methods involve systematically gathering enough information about a particular person, social setting, event, or group to permit the researcher to effectively understand how it operates or functions. It is not actually a data-gathering technique in itself, but a methodological approach that incorporates a number of data-gathering measures (Hamel, Dufour, & Fortin, 1993). The approach of case studies varies significantly from general field studies or from the interview of a single individual or group. Case studies may focus on a single individual, a group, or an entire community. This approach may employ a number of data technologies such as life histories, documents, oral histories, in-depth interviews, and participant observation (Yin, 1984; Hagan 1993).

Given the versatility of the case study method, they may be rather narrow in their focus, or they may take a broad view on life and society. For example, an investigator may confine his or her examination to a single aspect of an individual's life such as a gang member's actions and behaviors in the gang. Or, the investigator might attempt to assess the whole social life of an individual and all of his or her background, experiences, roles, and motivations, which affect his or her behavior in society. Extremely rich, detailed, and in-depth information characterize the type of information gathered in a case study. In contrast to this, even extensive large-scale survey research data may seem somewhat superficial in nature (Champion, 1993).

The case method is not a new style of data gathering and analytic technique. The practice of medicine and psychology, for example, by their very nature have forced physicians and psychologists to examine their patients case by case. The use of diaries and biographies, a popular method among some feminist and other social scientists (Reinharz, 1992), approximate the case study method. In education, the cases of interest include both people and programs examined either for their uniqueness or their commonality (Stake, 1995). In fact, case studies by certain social scientists represent classical research efforts in sociology and criminology. Consider, as examples, Edward Sutherland's (1937) *The Professional Thief*, or Clifford R. Shaw's *The Jack Roller*. More recently, Bogdan's (1974) lengthy life history/autobiography, *Being Different: The Autobiography of Jane Fry*, and Rettig, Torres, and Garrett's (1974) examination of *Manny: A Criminal Addict's Story* stand as notable examples of case studies.

THE INDIVIDUAL CASE STUDY

As in any other research situation, one must determine how broad an area of social life will be covered. In most research this decision is largely dictated by the research question and the nature of the research problem under investigation. When examining an individual case study, a similar type of assessment must be undertaken. In some instances, a single lengthy interview may yield sufficient information to produce answers to the research question(s). In other circumstances, several interviews may be necessary, and these may require supplementation by field notes during direct observation, copies of journal or diary entries from the subject, or other forms of documentation.

Several reasons may make it necessary for a broader, more sweeping investigation. First, the research may itself focus on a broad area such as the subject's relationships in a particular group, necessitating that the group also be examined. It would be unwise, for example, to examine various aspects of changes in the quality of life of hemodialysis patients without also examining how family members perceive changes occurring in the family group itself.

A second reason for broadening a case study is the realization that all the aspects of an individual's social life are interconnected and often one of them cannot be adequately understood without consideration of the others.

The Use of Interview Data

The particular focus of a study might be a woman's adjustment to becoming "the boss" in some predominantly male corporate organization. In order to fully understand this adjustment, it would be helpful to learn how she adjusts to changes in other situations, perhaps adjustments in her home or among friends or in social organizations. These may be accomplished using various standard techniques of interviewing to collect data.

Of these areas of additional study, perhaps the most generally rewarding to the subject is found to be her home and family background. The physical aspects of the home—its size, its neatness or disorder, its furnishings, indications of intellectual, athletic, or aesthetic interests such as books, pictures, records, sporting equipment, and the like—can all be of value in this case study. Even evidence of social support from family members should be observed and included in the research. Obviously to understand the subject's adjustments to the work role, the research must observe the subject in the work site and to speak with various coworkers. It should be likewise obvious that to understand the subject's role in her family, several visits to the home will be necessary. Also. it may be fruitful to speak with (interview) various family members (husband, children, or other relatives in the home) who can provide various pieces of background information and insights.

Unless an individual is exceptionally isolated, he or she is likely to have some role in the neighborhood community. Some people enjoy an elevated position of respect and position in their business, social, or political life. Others may hold no particularly high level of respect, but function as participants in various activities. Still others may actually be social outcasts. This type of information could be very useful for understanding how our woman business executive adjusts to her new position in the company. Visits to neighbors, various social organizations to which the subject may be a member, conversations with local tradespersons, the subject's clergy person, all may supply useful information.

Throughout the preceding paragraphs the chief suggestions for information (data) gathering has been the use of interviews and observation. As implied earlier, however, it is often also useful to supplement this information with various documentary sources. You should, therefore, be familiar with the possible use of records concerning the life course of the subject. These may include birth, marriage, divorce, property ownership, and educational records of the subject. They may additionally include an assortment of other more or less official documents such as police actions, court records, evaluations of work records, and so forth. All of these official documents are potentially valuable sources of information in a case study.

The Use of Personal Documents

The general use of personal documents is discussed in Chapter 8 of this book. As suggested there, personal documents involve any written record created by the subject that concerned himself or herself and his or her experiences. The common types of documents classified under this label include autobiographies, diaries and journals, letters, and memos written by a subject in a research investigation. In addition, and given the extent to which people today use photographic and video equipment, these items may also serve as categories of personal documents.

Autobiographical documents include a considerable variety of written material. They may be published or unpublished documents, cover an entire life span, or focus on only a specific period in a subject's life or even a single event. Even a written confession to a crime may be seen by some researchers as a type of autobiographical document.

Diaries and journals also may arise in a number of varieties. A diary may be kept with no purpose in mind beyond the writer's personal desire to maintain a record of daily events. It may be maintained in order to provide some therapeutic release; or as a kind of log and chronological listing of daily events during new experiences such as an internship. Or, a diary or journal may be created at the specific request of a researcher as a contribution to some study. In the latter case, one may consider the material a solicited document (see Chapter 8).

Letters provide an intriguing view into the life of the author. Typically, letters are not created by the writer with the intention of having them used by a researcher. As a result, they frequently reflect the inner worlds of the writer. They may record the writer's views, values, attitudes, and beliefs about a wide variety of subjects. Or, they may describe the writer's deepest thoughts about some specific event or situation about which they report. Historians have long seen the value of letters to document events during past time periods. Letters written by military figures and politicians, for example, may allow researchers to better understand how and why certain battles have been fought. Letters written by criminals such as serial killers and bombers provide insight into how the culprit thinks and potential explanations for their actions. Letters are simply replete with potentially useful information.

The use of memoranda has become commonplace in virtually all work settings. Memos may contain strictly work-related information, or casual insider jokes and communications. They may reflect the tone and atmosphere of a work setting as well as the potential level of anxiety, stress, and morale of the writer. Moreover, they may even show the research aspects of the workplace culture or work folkways. Also, they may contain information relevant to understanding the general organizational communications network used in the setting, the leadership hierarchy, various roles present in the setting, and other structural elements.

Photographic and video equipment have become so inexpensive that many people now regularly record their lives and the lives of their family members in this manner. It becomes important, therefore, for researchers to consider how these items may illustrate various aspects of the subject's life and relationships. This may involve stepping back and examining the entire photograph in terms of what it shows in general; it may include an examination of the expressions of people shown in the picture; it could involve consideration of where the picture was taken or video recorded such as on a vacation, in the home, or at a party; or it may involve determination of the reason the photograph or video was created—as a simple family record, to commemorate some situation, to have as a keepsake, to document some event or situation, and so forth.

The literal value of personal documents as research data is frequently underestimated in contemporary research texts and courses. While such documents are certainly extremely subjective in their nature, this should not be viewed as a negative or in this case even as some sort of limitation or shortcoming. It is the very fact that these documents do reflect the subjective views and perceptions of their creators that makes them useful as data in a case study. It is precisely through this subjectivity that these documents provide information and insight about the subject that might not be captured through some other more pedestrian data-collection technique.

INTRINSIC, INSTRUMENTAL, AND COLLECTIVE CASE STUDIES

Stake (1994, 1995) suggests that researchers have different purposes for studying cases. He suggests that three different types of cases can be classified: *intrinsic, instrumental,* and *collective* case studies.

Intrinsic case studies are undertaken when a researcher wants to better understand a particular case. It is not undertaken primarily because it represents other cases or because it illustrates some particular trait, characteristic, or problem. Rather, it is because of its very uniqueness or its ordinariness that this case becomes interesting (Stake, 1994). The researcher's purpose is not to understand or test abstract theory or to develop new theoretical explanations; instead, the intention is to better understand intrinsic aspects of the particular child, patient, criminal, organization, or whatever the case may be.

Instrumental case studies are cases examined to provide insight into some issue or to refine some theoretical explanation (Stake, 1994). In these situations, the case actually becomes of secondary importance. It will serve only a supportive role, a background against which the actual research interests will play out. Instrumental case studies often are investigated in depth, and all of its aspects and activities are detailed, but not simply to elaborate the case per se. Instead, the intention is to assist the researcher to better understand some external theoretical question or problem. Instrumental case studies may or may not be viewed as typical of other cases. However, the choice of a particular case for study is made because the investigator believes that his or her understanding about some other research interest will be advanced.

Stake (1994) also points out that since researchers often have multiple interests, there is no solid line drawn between intrinsic and instrumental case studies. In fact, a kind of "zone of combined purpose separates them" (Stake, 1994, p. 237). *Collective case studies* involve the extensive study of several instrumental cases. The selection of these cases is intended to allow better understanding or perhaps an enhanced ability to theorize about some larger collection of cases.

THE SCIENTIFIC BENEFIT OF CASE STUDIES

The scientific benefit of the case study method lies in its ability to open the way for discoveries (Shaughnessy & Zechmeister, 1990). It can easily serve as the breeding ground for insights and even hypotheses that may be pursued in subsequent studies. However, whenever one considers the scientific value of case studies, two points should be addressed. First, does this procedure involve too many subjective decisions made by the investigator to offer genuinely objective results? Second, does this method offer information that can be seen as useful beyond the individual case? In other words, can findings be generalized? Let us consider each of these questions separately.

Objectivity and the Case Method

Objectivity is a somewhat elusive term. For some researchers it involves the creation of analytic strategies in an almost sterile environment. Often, qualitative research of any type is viewed as suspect when questions of objectivity are asked. However, objectivity is actually closely linked with reproducibility (replication). The question is not simply whether or not an individual researcher has made some subjective decision regarding how the researcher should progress or how the study is designed. These types of considerations are regularly undertaken by all who undertake social scientific research—whether quantitatively or qualitatively oriented.

When a quantitative methodologist identifies which level of statistical acceptability he or she will use for some statistical measure, it is often a subjective decision. For example, let's say the researcher sets his or her level at .05. Does that alter the findings when it is statistically significant at the .05 level, but not at the .001 level? Thus, objectivity apparently lies someplace other than in the kinds of decisions made by a researcher regarding various aspects of the research strategy.

For many researchers, objectivity rests on the ability of an investigator to articulate what his or her procedures are so that others can repeat the research if they so choose. It also has the effect of placing the researcher's professional ego on the line. It is akin to saying, "Here is how I did my research, and here are my results. If any reader has questions or challenges, go out and repeat the study to see what you find." From this perspective, case studies, like any other research procedure, require that the investigator clearly articulate what areas have been investigated, and through what

means. If someone has doubts about the findings, he or she is free to replicate the research with a similar case subject.

If the investigator's findings and analysis were correct, subsequent
research will corroborate this. If the research produced from a case study is
faulty, in error, or inaccurate, this too will be shown by subsequent research.
As in any scientific research, findings from a single study are seldom
accepted immediately without question and additional research investigations. In this light, case methods are as objective as any other data-collection-
and-analysis strategies used by social scientists.

Generalizability

The second concern addresses the question of generalizability. For many, the
question is not even necessary to ask. This is because there is clearly a scientific value to gain from investigating some single category of individual,
group, or event simply to gain an understanding of that individual, group,
or event. For those with a more positivist orientation, where concern about
generalizing to similar types of individuals, groups, or events, case methods
are still useful and to some extent generalizable.

When case studies are properly undertaken, they should not only fit the
specific individual, group, or event studied, but generally provide understanding about similar individuals, groups, and events. This is not to say
that an explanation for why one gang member is involved in drug dealing
immediately informs us about why *all* other drug-dealing gang members are
also involved in this activity. It does, however, suggest an explanation for
why some other gang members are likely to be involved in these behaviors.
The logic behind this has to do with the fact that few human behaviors are
unique, idiosyncratic, and spontaneous. In fact, if this were the case, the
attempt to undertake any type of survey research on an aggregate group
would be useless. In short, if we accept the notion that human behavior is
predictable—a necessary assumption for all behavior science research—then
it is a simple jump to accept that case studies have scientific value. "It is the
task of the researcher to determine what it is he or she is studying; that is, of
what is this a case?" (Bogdan & Biklen, 1992, p. 66).

CASE STUDIES OF ORGANIZATIONS

Case studies of organizations may be defined as the systematic gathering of
enough information about a particular organization to allow the investigator
insight into the life of that organization. This type of study might be fairly
general in its scope, offering approximately equal weight to every aspect of
the organization. For instance, you might conduct an organizational case

study on a police department. During this investigation you may examine subunits such as the juvenile division, traffic division, criminal investigations, homicide, and so forth. The results will be a thorough understanding about how the agency operates, and how each subunit fits together and serves the overall objectives of the organization.

On the other hand, you may specialize, during an organizational case study, by placing particular emphasis on a specific area or situation occurring in the organization. For example, you may undertake an examination of how nurses steal drugs and hospital equipment while working in intensive care units. Both focuses can accurately be considered examples of case studies.

There are a number of reasons that a particular organization may be selected for a case study. For example, a researcher may undertake a case study of an organization to illustrate the way certain administrative systems operate in certain types of organizations. Or, the researcher may be interested in accessing how decisions are made in certain types of organizations, or even how communications networks operate. In fact, the case method is an extremely useful technique for researching relationships, behaviors, attitudes, motivations, and stressors in organizational settings.

CASE STUDIES OF COMMUNITIES

A *community* can be defined as some geographically delineated unit within a larger society. Such a community is small enough to permit considerable cultural (or subcultural) homogeneity, diffuse interactions and relationships between members, and to produce a social identification by its members. The literal application of this term *community* is somewhat fluid. However, it does not actually include an entire nation, a state, or even a large city. It would, however, include a particular neighborhood within a city such as a Chinatown, a Little Italy, or the Jewish section, or even an enclave of Amish farmers all residing within a four- or five-mile radius.

Case studies of communities can be defined as the systematic gathering of enough information about a particular community to provide the investigator with understanding and awareness of what things go on in that community; why and how these things occur; who among the community members take part in these activities and behaviors, and what social forces may bind together members of this community. As with other variations of case studies, community case studies may be very general in their focus, offering approximately equal weight in all of the various aspects of community life. Or, community case studies may specifically focus on some particular aspect of the community, or even some phenomenon that occurs within that community. For example, you may consider a community in general, such as examining an Amish farming community. In such an investigation, you may be interested in the various daily routines of members as well as their social interactions. You might consider any political ideologies that predominate among members of the community, and how these affect behaviors among both insiders and outsiders, and so forth. On the other hand, you may be interested in a particular phenomenon occurring within the Amish community. For instance, you may be interested in how social control mechanisms operate in the community. Will the community handle an errant youth who may have shoplifted some petty item such as a magazine, or will the outside, non-Amish community's laws apply? Of course, if you investigate the latter phenomenon, to remain a community case study, this exploration would have to be undertaken against the backdrop of the life of the community. While there are other styles of research that might explore a particular question in isolation from the background of the community, these would not be accurately called case studies.

Robert and Helen Lynd's study of Middletown, first published in 1929, stands as a classic example of how community case studies operate. This research was among the earliest systematic studies of an American community where the purpose was primarily to develop a scientific understanding of community life.

Data Collection for Community Case Studies

The various data collection strategies used in community case studies are, for the most part, those already discussed in this chapter. However, in addition, community case studies frequently make use of maps. These may include existing maps used for various human ecological purposes, as well as maps created by the researcher in order to indicate physical and social proximity of items and events occurring in the community.

Human ecological concerns have long been important foci in community case studies. Human ecology is concerned with the interrelationships among people in their spatial setting and physical environment. An ecological focus might consider how various physical environmental elements shape the lives of people in a community or the life of the community itself. Do rivers block a community's expansion? Are railroad tracks or major highways located close enough to encourage industry in a community? Has a coal mine played out and closed down, sending hundreds of community members to unemployment, and so forth? Maps are frequently the basic tool necessary for a consideration of such ecological concerns in a community case study.

Community Groups and Interests

In a manner similar to how one might break down a community into its constituent physical parts, its human members too can be divided into groups.

These groups may be classified in a number of different ways. For example, there may be different ethnic groups all residing in the same community. While some ethnic groups are sufficiently large enough and homogeneously located to constitute a community in themselves, this is not always the case. In many communities several distinct ethnic groups reside in both physical and social proximity but manage to retain their own individual ethnic identity. In some cases, the ethnic groups may retain certain of their distinctive ethnic features, but merge or assimilate into their surrounding social life. In such a case, one would need to consider this ethnic group both as a thing apart from the community, as well as an element of the larger community.

The study of any group in a community begins much as you would begin any research study, namely, in the library (see Chapter 2). The logical place to begin considering community groups is in published sources. In addition, community case studies may include an examination of census data, local histories, newspaper accounts of group activities and events, any official records of various organizations related to the group or community, etc. As with other variations of case studies, interviews may provide useful information or even historical explanations for various groups, or the presence of certain conditions in the community. Researchers even use fairly traditional strategies of observation to learn about groups in a community. Observations may include consideration of the types of homes and housing in the community, places used for leisure or amusement, schools and religious institutions in the community, and so forth.

Interest groups are another way you might divide up the inhabitants of a community. In this case, you may include street gangs, various social clubs or organizations in the community (Boy and Girl Scouts, YMCAs, Little Leagues, Bowling Leagues, and so forth), lodges and fraternal organizations, political clubs, business associations, and the like. Membership in many of these interest groups is rather ephemeral and transient. Even the more stable of interest groups are likely to lack the continuity of ethnic or religious groups. Direct observation of these interest groups, along with interviews with members, is probably the best general method for studying these kinds of groups.

Social classes may also be viewed as a type of grouping that allows the researcher to divide up a community. While you might argue about what division labels to actually use as categories of class, some categorical labeling schema can be conceived. In keeping with the community case study mode, you could consider how members of each social class operates in the community, and how these categories fit together to form the entire community.

In essence, there are numerous ways of grouping together people of a community for the purpose of systematically exploring life in that community. Community case studies are large-scale undertakings. They may be time-consuming and expensive if they are to be comprehensive. The community is a sufficiently large segment of society that it permits a wide and diverse array of social phenomena to occur and to be observed. While not as popular in recent years as it was during the 1930s and 1960s, especially in areas of urban sociology and urban ecology, community case studies continue to offer an important and valuable means to understanding communities and community members.

TRYING IT OUT

Suggestion 1

Using available archival information located in your school's library and various administrative offices, conduct an organizational case study of your college or university. This will involve using at least some historical tracings (see Chapter 9).

Suggestion 2

Select an adult relative, and conduct a modified case study. For this project, examine only the roles and behaviors of the individual during some aspect of his or her life. This may be during school activities, work life, home life, and so forth. Limit the time on this project to one week of data collection. Remember, this is simply practice, not actual research.

REFERENCES

Bogdan, R. (1974). *Being Different: The Autobiography of Jane Fry*. New York: Wiley.

Bogdan, R., & Biklen, S. K. (1992). *Qualitative Research for Education*. Boston: Allyn and Bacon,

Champion, D. J. (1993). *Research Methods for Criminal Justice and Criminology*. Englewood Cliffs, NJ: Prentice Hall.

Hagan, F. E. (1993). *Research Methods in Criminal Justice and Criminology*. New York: Macmillan.

Hamel, J., Dufour, S., & Fortin, D. (1993) *Case Study Method*. Thousand Oaks, CA: Sage.

Lynd, R. S., & Lynd, H. M. (1929). *Middletown*. New York: Harcourt, Brace.

Rettig, R. P., Torres, M. J., & Garrett, G. R. (1977). *Manny: A Criminal Addict's Story*. Boston: Houghton Mifflin.

Shaughnessy, J. J., & Zechmeister, E. B. (1990). *Research Methods in Psychology*. New York: McGraw-Hill.

Shaw, C. R. (1930). *The Jack Roller*. Chicago: University of Chicago Press.

Stake, R. E. (1994). Case studies. In N. K. Denzin & Y. S. Lincoln (Eds.), *Handbook of Qualitative Research*. Thousand Oaks, CA: Sage.

Stake, R. E. (1995). *The Art of Case Study Research*. Thousand Oaks, CA: Sage.

Sutherland, E. H. (1937). *The Professional Thief*. Chicago: University of Chicago Press.

Yin, R. K. (1984). *Case Study Research: Design and Methods*. Beverly Hills, CA: Sage.

AN INTRODUCTION TO
CONTENT ANALYSIS

THROUGHOUT THE PRECEDING CHAPTERS, techniques and strategies for collecting and organizing data have been discussed. With a partial exception for Chapters 4, 6, and perhaps 7, where limited analytic procedures are mentioned, analysis of data has not yet been extensively
discussed. In this chapter the task of analysis is considered at length.

Interviews, field notes, and various types of unobtrusive data are often
not amenable to analysis until the information they convey has been con-
densed and made systematically comparable. An objective coding scheme
must be applied to the notes or data. This process is commonly called *content
analysis.*

The instructions in this chapter are intended to assist novice researchers
in their attempt to learn the methodological technique for standard content
analysis. First, a brief discussion of some general concerns and debates
regarding content analysis is presented. Then a number of procedures for
analyzing content are discussed. These include consideration of what to
count and what to analyze, the nature of *levels and units of analysis,* and how
to effectively employ *coding frames.* In the next section, the strength and
weaknesses of content analysis as a research technique are discussed, and
analytic induction is examined in relation to content analysis procedures.
Finally, this chapter will address *word crunching,* the use of computers in
qualitative research.

CONTENT ANALYSIS AS A TECHNIQUE

In content analysis, researchers examine artifacts of social communication.
Typically, these are written documents or transcriptions of recorded verbal
communications. Broadly defined, however, content analysis is "any tech-

nique for making inferences by systematically and *objectively* identifying special characteristics of messages" (Holsti, 1968, p. 608). From this perspective, photographs, videotape, or any item that can be made into text are amenable to content analysis. In this chapter, objective analysis of messages conveyed in the data being analyzed is accomplished by means of explicit rules called *criteria of selection*, which must be formally established before the actual analysis of data.

The criteria of selection used in any given content analysis must be sufficiently exhaustive to account for each variation of message content and must be rigidly and consistently applied so that other researchers or readers, looking at the same messages, would obtain the same or comparable results. This may be considered a kind of reliability of the measures, and a validation of eventual findings (Selltiz et al., 1967). The categories that emerge in the course of developing these criteria should reflect all relevant aspects of the messages and retain, as much as possible, the exact wording used in the statements. They should not be merely arbitrary or superficial applications of irrelevant categories. Holsti (1968, p. 598) explains this type of content analysis procedure: "The inclusion or exclusion of content is done according to consistently applied criteria of selection; this requirement eliminates analysis in which only material supporting the investigator's hypotheses are examined."

CONTENT ANALYSIS: QUANTITATIVE OR QUALITATIVE?

One of the leading debates among users of content analysis is whether analysis should be quantitative or qualitative. Berelson (1952), for example, suggests that content analysis is "objective, systematic, and quantitative." Similarly, Silverman (1993, p. 59) dismisses content analysis from his discussion of qualitative data analysis "because it is a quantitative method." Selltiz et al. (1959, p. 336) however, state that concerns over quantification in content analysis tend to emphasize "the procedures of analysis," rather than the "character of the data available." Selltiz et al. suggest also that heavy quantitative content analysis results in a somewhat arbitrary limitation in the field by excluding all accounts of communications not in the form of numbers and those that may lose meaning if reduced to a numeric form (definitions, symbols, detailed explanations, photographs, and so forth). Other proponents of content analysis, notably Smith (1975), suggest that some blend of both quantitative and qualitative analysis should be used. Smith (1975, p. 218) explains that he has taken this position "because qualitative analysis deals with the forms and antecedent-consequent patterns of form, while quantitative analysis deals with duration and frequency of form."

Abrahamson (1983, p. 286) suggests that "content analysis can be fruitfully employed to examine virtually any type of communication." As a consequence, content analysis may focus on either quantitative or qualitative aspects of communication messages.

Recently, some authors of methods books have begun writing about the procedure of *narrative analysis* as distinguishable from the procedure of content analysis (see, for example, Silverman, 1993; Manning & Cullum-Swan, 1994). In narrative analysis, the investigator typically begins with a set of principles and seeks to exhaust the meaning of the text using specified rules and principles, but maintains a qualitative textual approach (Boje, 1991; Heise, 1992; Manning & Cullum-Swan, 1994; Silverman, 1993). In contrast to this allegedly more textual approach, content analysis is suggested to be limited to counts of textual elements. Thus, the implication is that content analysis is more reductionistic and ostensively a more positivistic approach. I argue here that content analysis can be used effectively in qualitative analysis—that "counts" of textual elements merely provide a means for identifying, organizing, indexing, and retrieving data. Analysis of the data once organized according to certain content elements should involve consideration of the literal words in the text being analyzed, including the manner in which these words have been offered. In this way, content analysis provides a method for obtaining good access to the words of the text or transcribed accounts offered by subjects (Glassner & Loughlin, 1987). This offers, in turn, an opportunity for the investigator to learn about how subjects or the authors of textual materials view their social worlds.

From this perspective, content analysis is not a reductionistic, positivistic approach. Rather, it is a passport to listening to the words of the text, and understanding better the perspective(s) of the producer of these words.

This chapter strives for a blend of qualitative and quantitative emphasis. Quantitatively, this chapter describes how researchers can create a series of tally sheets to determine specific frequencies of relevant categories (described in detail later). Qualitatively, this guide describes how researchers can examine ideological mind-sets, themes, topics, symbols, and similar phenomena, while grounding such examinations to the data.

Manifest versus Latent Content Analysis

Another controversy concerning the use of content analysis is whether the analysis should be limited to *manifest content* (those elements that are physically present and countable) or extended to more *latent content*. In the latter case, the analysis is extended to an interpretive reading of the symbolism underlying the physically presented data. For example, an entire speech may be assessed for how radical it was, or a novel could be considered in terms of how violent the entire text was. Stated in different words, manifest content is comparable to the *surface structure* present in the message, and latent content is the *deep structural* meaning conveyed by the message.

Holsti (1969, p. 598) has tried to resolve this debate: "It is true that only the manifest attributes of text may be coded, but this limitation is already implied by the requirement of objectivity. Inferences about latent meanings of messages are therefore permitted but . . . they require corroboration by independent evidence." One reasonable interpretation of this passage, and a similar statement made by Berelson (1952, pp. 488ff), suggests that although there are some dangers in directly inferring from latent symbolism, it is nonetheless possible to use it (see also Merton, 1968, pp. 366–370, on the use of content analysis in examining propaganda). To accomplish this sort of "deciphering" (Heilman, 1976) of latent symbolic meaning, researchers must first incorporate independent corroborative techniques (for example, agreement between independent coders concerning latent content or some non-content analytic source). Finally, and especially when latent symbolism may be discussed, researchers should offer detailed excerpts from relevant statements (messages) that serve to document the researchers' interpretations. A safe rule of thumb to follow is the inclusion of at least three independent examples for each interpretation.

Blending Manifest and Latent Content Analysis Strategies

Perhaps the best resolution of this dilemma about whether to use manifest or latent content is to use both whenever possible. In this case, a given unit of content would receive the same attention from both methods—to the extent that coding procedures (discussed presently) for both the manifest and latent content are reasonably valid and reliable (Babbie, 1992). By reporting the frequency with which a given concept appears in text, researchers suggest the magnitude of this observation. It is more convincing for their arguments when researchers demonstrate the appearance of a claimed observation in some large proportion of the material under study (e.g., 20 percent, 30 percent, 40 percent, and so on).

Researchers must bear in mind, however, that these descriptive statistics—namely, proportions and frequency distributions—do not necessarily reflect the nature of the data or variables. If the theme "positive attitude toward shoplifting," appears 50 times in one subject's interview transcript and 25 times in another subject's, this would not be justification for the researchers to claim that the first subject is twice as likely to shoplift as the second subject. In short, researchers must be cautious not to take or claim magnitudes as findings in themselves. The magnitude for certain observations is presented to demonstrate more fully the overall analysis.

COMMUNICATION COMPONENTS

According to Holsti (1969) and Carney (1972), communications have three major components: the message, the sender, and the audience. The message should be analyzed in terms of explicit themes, relative emphasis on various topics, amount of space or time devoted to certain topics, and numerous other dimensions. Occasionally, messages are analyzed for information about the sender of the communication. According to Chadwick et al. (1984), the linkages between the message content and attributes of the sender are often slight. Nonetheless, some characteristics of the sender may be discernible, especially if numerous examples are available, audible (recorded) messages are examined, or verbatim transcriptions from recordings are used (including literal representations of pauses, mispronounced words, grammatical errors, slang, and other language styles).

Strauss (1987, p. 33) similarly differentiates between what he calls *in vivo codes* and *sociological constructs*. *In vivo codes* are the literal terms used by individuals under investigation, the terms used by the various actors themselves. "In vivo codes tend to be the behaviors or processes which will explain to the analyst how the basic problem of the actors is resolved or processed" (Strauss, 1987, p. 33). In contrast, *sociological constructs* are formulated by the analyst. Terms and categories such as *professional attitude, family oriented, obsessive workaholic,* and *educationally minded* might represent examples of sociological constructs. These constructs, of course, need not derive exclusively from sociology and may come from the fields of education, nursing, psychology, and the like. Strauss (1987, p. 34) explains that these constructs "are based on a combination of the researcher's scholarly knowledge and knowledge of the substantive field under study." The result of using constructs is the addition of certain social scientific meanings that might otherwise be missed in the analysis. Thus, sociological constructs add breadth and depth to observations by reaching beyond local meanings to broader social scientific ones.

Researchers may additionally use content analysis to assess a message's effects on the audience. The Pornography and Television Violence Commissions tried, for example, to assess the impact of sexual or violent material on television and in movies on those who watched this genre of entertainment (Commission on Obscenity and Pornography, 1970; Comstock & Rubinstein, 1972). However, making accurate inferences about either the characteristics of the sender or the effects of the message on the audience is often tenuous at best.

WHAT TO COUNT: LEVELS AND UNITS OF ANALYSIS

When using a content analysis strategy to assess written documents, researchers must first decide at what level they plan to sample and what units of analysis will be counted. Sampling may occur at any or all of the following levels: words, phrases, sentences, paragraphs, sections, chapters, books, writers, ideological stance, subject topic, or similar elements relevant to the context. When examining other forms of messages, researchers may use any of the preceding levels or may sample at other conceptual levels more appropriate to the specific message. For example, when examining television programs for violent content, researchers might use segments between commercials as the level of analysis, or they might choose to use the entire television program (excluding commercials) as the level (see, for example, Fields, 1988).

SAMPLING STRATEGIES

Any of the many conventional sampling procedures used in other data-collection techniques may be used in content analysis. Some of the more commonly cited techniques include simple random sampling, systematic sampling, stratified sampling, and purposive sampling. Each of these strategies is briefly described below.

- *Simple Random Sampling.* Typically, this procedure is intended to produce a representative sample. The process draws subjects from an identified population in such a manner that every unit in that population has precisely the same chance (probability) of being included in the sample (Kish, 1965).
- *Systematic Sampling.* The use of a systematic sample provides a convenient way to draw a sample from a large identified population when a printed list of that population is available. In systematic sampling, every *n*th name is selected from the list. Usually the interval between names on the list is determined by dividing the number of persons desired in the sample into the full population. For example, if a final sample of 80 were desired, and the population list contained 2,560 names, the researchers would divide 2,560 by 80. The resulting 32 becomes the interval between names on the list. It is important, how-

ever, to begin on the list at some random starting place. Frequently, researchers select a number between 1 and 20 (usually taken from a random numbers table) and begin at that location on the list and then stop at every *n*th name—in our example, at every thirty-second name on the list.

- *Stratified Sampling.* A stratified sample is used whenever researchers need to ensure that a certain segment of the identified population under examination is represented in the sample. The population is divided into subgroups (strata), and independent samples of each stratum are selected. Within each stratum, a particular sampling fraction is applied in order to ensure representativeness of proportions in the full population. Thus, sampling fractions in some strata may differ from those of others in the same sample. Stratified samples can be used only when information is available to divide the population into strata.

- *Purposive Sampling.* When developing a purposive sample, researchers use their special knowledge or expertise about some group to select subjects who represent this population. In some instances, purposive samples are selected after field investigations of some group, in order to ensure that certain types of individuals or persons displaying certain attributes are included in the study. Despite some serious limitations (for instance, the lack of wide generalizability), purposive samples are occasionally used by researchers. Delinquent youths, for example, who might not appear in sufficient numbers to be meaningful under more traditional random techniques, might be purposively sampled (Glassner et al., 1983).

CATEGORY DEVELOPMENT:
BUILDING GROUNDED THEORY

Strauss (1987) describes the considerable misconception surrounding the development of grounded theory. The term *misconception*, as Strauss (1987, p. 55) points out, seems more appropriate than *criticism*. *Misconception* implies an inaccurate reading of material pertaining to building grounded theory. On the other hand, *criticism* connotes more of a challenge to or detraction from the benefits of this process. Central to the misconception are the notions that grounded theory is an entirely inductive process, that it does not verify findings, and that it somehow molds the data to the theory (rather than the reverse).

Strauss (1987, p. 55), in a lengthy note, singles out Miles and Huberman (1983) as illustrating several instrumental misconceptions (brackets in original text contain Strauss's responses):

In Miles and Huberman (1983, p. 57) there is also a misunderstanding about grounded theory technology. The material in my book, written before their pub-lication appeared, runs directly counter to some of their remarks, that: the grounded theory approach has a lot going for it. Data get well molded to the codes that represent them, and we get more of a code-in-use flavor than the generic code-for-many-uses generated by prefabricated start lists. . . . The trade-off here is that earlier segments may have different codes than later ones. [They may, in part, of course.] Or to avoid this everything may have to be recorded once a more empirically sculpted scheme emerges. [No.] This means more over-all coding time, and longer uncertainty about the coherence of the coding frame. [Probably, but deliberate, in part].

In addition, Miles and Huberman (1983, pp. 63–64) promote the worri-some notion that coding is not an enjoyable task, which suggests that other aspects of the research enterprise are more fun. This text as well as Strauss (1987) strongly disagree. Coding and other fundamental procedures associ-ated with grounded theory development are certainly hard work and must be taken seriously, but just as many people enjoy finishing a complicated jig-saw puzzle, many researchers find great satisfaction in coding and analysis. As researchers move through the coding process and begin to see the puzzle pieces come together to form a more complete picture, the process can be downright thrilling. Time consuming, tiring, and even laborious as the process is, it is seldom boring!

The categories researchers use in a content analysis can be determined inductively, deductively, or by some combination of both (Strauss, 1987). Abrahamson (1983, p. 286) indicates that an inductive approach begins with the researchers "immersing" themselves in the documents (that is, the various mes-sages) in order to identify the dimensions or *themes* that seem meaningful to the producers of each message. In a deductive approach, researchers use some cate-gorical scheme suggested by a theoretical perspective, and the documents pro-vide a means for assessing the hypothesis. In many circumstances, the relation-ship between a theoretical perspective and certain messages involves both inductive and deductive approaches. However, in order to present the percep-tions of others (the producers of messages) in the most forthright manner, a greater reliance upon induction is necessary. Nevertheless, as will be shown, induction should not be undertaken to the exclusion of deduction.

The development of inductive categories allows researchers to link or *ground* these categories to the data from which they derive. Certainly it is reasonable to suggest that insights and general questions about research derive from previous experience with the study phenomena. This may rep-resent personal experience, scholarly experience (having read about it), or previous research undertaken to examine the matter. Researchers, similarly, draw on these experiences in order to propose tentative comparisons that assist in creating various deductions. Experience thus underpins both inductive and deductive reasoning.

From this interplay of experience, induction, and deduction, Glaser and Strauss formulate their description of grounded theory. According to Glaser and Strauss (1967, pp. 2–3):

> To generate theory . . . we suggest as the best approach an initial, systematic discovery of the theory from the data of social research. Then one can be relatively sure that the theory will fit the work. And since categories are discovered by examination of the data, laymen involved in the area to which the theory applies will usually be able to understand it, while sociologists who work in other areas will recognize an understandable theory linked with the data of a given area.

What to Count

Seven major elements in written messages can be counted in content analysis: words or terms, themes, characters, paragraphs, items, concepts, and semantics (Berelson, 1952; Berg, 1983; Merton, 1968; Selltiz et al., 1959).

Words

The *word* is the smallest element or unit used in content analysis. Its use generally results in a frequency distribution of specified words or terms.

Themes

The *theme* is a more useful unit to count. In its simplest form, a theme is a simple sentence, a string of words with a subject and a predicate. Because themes may be located in a variety of places in most written documents, it becomes necessary to specify (in advance) which places will be searched. For example, researchers might use only the primary theme in a given paragraph location or alternatively might count every theme in a given text under analysis.

Characters

In some studies, *characters* (persons) are significant to the analysis. In such cases, you count the number of times a specific person or persons are mentioned rather than the number of words or themes.

Paragraphs

The *paragraph* is infrequently used as the basic unit in content analysis chiefly because of the difficulties that have resulted in attempting to code and classify the various and often numerous thoughts stated and implied in a single paragraph.

Items

An *item* represents the whole unit of the sender's message—that is, an item may be an entire book, a letter, speech, diary, newspaper, or even an in-depth interview.

Concepts

The use of *concepts* as units to count is a more sophisticated type of word counting than previously mentioned. Concepts involve words grouped together into conceptual clusters (ideas) that constitute, in some instances, variables in a typical research hypothesis (Sanders & Pinhey, 1959, p. 191). For instance, a conceptual cluster may form around the idea of deviance. Words such as *crime, delinquency, kiting,* and *fraud* might cluster around the conceptual idea of deviance (Babbie, 1983). To some extent, the use of a concept as the unit of analysis leads toward more latent than manifest content.

Semantics

In this type of content analysis, *semantics,* researchers are interested not only in the number and type of words used but also in how affected the word(s) may be—in other words, how strong or weak a word (or words) may be in relation to the overall sentiment of the sentence (Sanders & Pinhey, 1959).

Combinations of Elements

In many instances, research requires the use of a combination of several content analytic elements. For example, in my (Berg, 1983) attempt to identify subjective definitions for Jewish affiliational categories (Orthodox, Conservative, Reform, and Nonpracticing), I used a combination of both item and paragraph elements as a content unit. In order to accomplish a content analysis of these definitions (as items), I lifted every respondent's definitions of each affiliational category verbatim from an interview transcript. Each set of definitions was additionally annotated with the transcript number from which it had been taken. Next, each of the definitions (as items) was separated into its component definitional paragraph for each affiliational category. An example of this definitional paragraphing is shown below (Berg, 1983, p. 76):

Interview #60: Orthodox

Well, I guess, Orthodox keep kosher in [the] home and away from home. Observe the Sabbath, and, you know . . . , actually if somebody did [those] and considered themselves an Orthodox Jew, to me that would be enough. I would say that they were Orthodox.

Interview #60: Conservative

Conservative, I guess, is the fellow who doesn't want to say he's Reform because it's objectionable to him. But he's a long way from being Orthodox.

Interview #60: Reform

Reform is just somebody that, they say they are Jewish because they don't want to lose their identity. But actually I want to be considered a Reform, 'cause I say I'm Jewish, but I wouldn't want to be associated as a Jew if I didn't actually observe any of the laws.

Interview #60: Nonpracticing

Well, a Nonpracticing is the guy who would have no temple affiliation, no affiliation with being Jewish at all, except that he considers himself a Jew. I guess he practices in no way, except to himself.

Units and Categories

Content analysis involves the interaction of two processes: specification of the content characteristics (basic content elements) being examined and application of explicit rules for identifying and recording these characteristics. The *categories* into which you code content items vary according to the nature of the research and the particularities of the data (that is, whether they are detailed responses to open-ended questions, newspaper columns, letters, television transcripts, and so on).

As with all research methods, conceptualization and operationalization necessarily involve an interaction between theoretical concerns and empirical observations. For instance, if researchers wanted to examine newspaper orientations toward changes in a state's seat-belt law (as a potential barometer of public opinion), they might read newspaper articles and/or editorials. As they read each article, the researchers could ask themselves which ones were in favor of and which ones were opposed to changes in the law. Were the articles' positions more clearly indicated by their manifest content or by some undertone? Was the decision to label one article pro or con based on the use of certain terms, on presentation of specific study findings, or because of statements offered by particular characters (for example, celebrities, political figures, and so on)? The answers to these questions allow the researchers to develop inductive categories in which to slot various units of content.

As previously mentioned, researchers need not limit their procedures to induction alone. Both inductive and deductive reasoning may provide fruitful findings. If, for example, investigators are attempting to test hypothetical propositions, their theoretical orientation should suggest empirical indicators of concepts (deductive reasoning). If they have begun with specific empirical observations, they should attempt to develop explanations grounded in the data (grounded theory) and apply these theories to other empirical observations (inductive reasoning).

There are no easy ways to describe specific tactics for developing categories or to suggest how to go about defining (operationalizing) these tactics. To paraphrase Schatzman and Strauss's (1973, p. 12) remark about methodological choices in general, the categorizing tactics worked out—some in advance, some developed later—should be consistent not only with the questions asked and the methodological requirements of science but also with a relation to the properties of the phenomena under investigation. Stated succinctly, categories must be grounded in the data from which they emerge (Denzin, 1978; Glaser & Strauss, 1967). The development of categories in any content analysis must derive from inductive reference (to be discussed in detail later) concerning patterns that emerge from the data.

For example, in a study evaluating the effectiveness of a Florida-based delinquency diversion program, I (Berg, 1986) identified several thematic categories from information provided on intake sheets. By setting up a tally sheet, I managed to use the criminal offenses declared by arresting officers in their general statements to identify two distinct classes of crime, in spite of arresting officers' use of similar-sounding terms. In one class of crime, several similar terms were used to describe what amounted to the same type of crime. In a second class of crime, officers more consistently referred to the same type of crime by a consistent term. Specifically, I found that the words *shoplifting, petty theft,* and *retail theft* each referred to essentially the same category of crime involving the stealing of some type of store *merchandise,* usually not exceeding $3.50 in value. Somewhat surprisingly, the semantically rather similar term *petty larceny* was used to describe the taking of cash whether from a retail establishment, a domicile, or an auto. Thus, the data indicated a subtle perceptual distinction made by the officers reporting juvenile crimes.

Recently, Dabney (1993) examined how practicing nurses perceived other nurses who worked while impaired by alcohol or drugs. He developed several thematic categories based on previous studies found in the literature. But Dabney (1993) was also able to inductively identify several classes of drug diversion described by subjects during the course of interviews. For instance, many subjects referred to *stockpiled drugs* that nurses commonly used for themselves. These drugs included an assortment of pain killers and mild sedatives stored in a box, a drawer, or some similar container on the unit or floor. These stockpiled drugs accumulated when patients died or were transferred to another hospital unit and this information did not immediately reach the hospital pharmacy.

Classes and Categories

Three major procedures are used to identify and develop classes and categories in a standard content analysis and to discuss findings in research that use content analysis: common classes, special classes, and theoretical classes.

Common Classes

The first are the *common classes* of a culture in general. These classes are used by virtually anyone in society to distinguish between and among persons, things, and events (for example, age, gender, mother, father, teacher, and so on). These common classes, as categories, provide for lay people a means of designation in the course of everyday thinking and communicating, and to engender meaning in their social interactions (see Duncan, 1962; Schatzman & Strauss, 1973; Strauss, 1959). These common classes are essential in assessing whether certain demographic characteristics are related to patterns that may arise during a given data analysis.

Special Classes

Special classes are those labels used by members of certain areas (communities) to distinguish among the things, persons, and events within their limited province (Schatzman & Strauss, 1973). These special classes can be likened to jargonized terms used commonly in certain professions but not by lay people. Alternatively, these special classes may be described as *out-group* versus *in-group* classifications. In the case of the *out-group*, the reference is to labels conventionally used by the greater (host) community or society; as for the *in-group*, the reference is to conventional terms and labels used among some specified group or that may emerge as theoretical classes.

Theoretical Classes

The *theoretical classes* are those that emerge in the course of analyzing the data (Schatzman & Strauss, 1973). In most content analysis, these theoretical classes provide an overarching pattern (a key linkage) that occurs throughout the analysis. Nomenclature that identifies these theoretical classes generally borrows from that used in special classes and, together with analytically constructed labels, accounts for novelty and innovations.

According to Schatzman and Strauss (1973), these theoretical classes are special sources of classification because their specific substance is grounded in the data. Because these theoretical classes are not immediately knowable or available to observers until they spend considerable time going over the ways respondents (or messages) in a sample identify themselves and others, it is necessary to retain the special classes throughout much of the analysis.

The next problem to address is how to identify various classes and categories in the data set, which leads to a discussion of open coding.

OPEN CODING

Inexperienced researchers, although they may intellectually understand the process described so far, usually become lost at about this point in the actual process of coding. Some of the major obstacles that cause anguish include the so-called true or intended meaning of the sentence and a desire to know the real motivation behind a subject's clearly identifiable lie. If the researchers can get beyond such concerns, the coding can continue. For the most part, these concerns are actually irrelevant to the coding process, particularly with regard to *open coding*, the central purpose of which is to open inquiry widely. Although interpretations, questions, and even possible answers may seem to emerge as researchers code, it is important to hold these as tentative at best. Contradictions to such early conclusions may emerge during the coding of the very next document. The most thorough analysis of the various concepts and categories will best be accomplished after all the material has been coded. The solution to the novice investigators' anguish, then, as suggested by Strauss (1987, p. 28) is to "believe everything and believe nothing" while undertaking open coding.

Strauss (1987, p. 30) suggests four basic guidelines when conducting open coding. These are (1) ask the data a specific and consistent set of questions, (2) analyze the data minutely, (3) frequently interrupt the coding to write a theoretical note, and (4) never assume the analytic relevance of any traditional variable such as age, sex, social class, and so forth until the data show it to be relevant. A detailed discussion of each of these guidelines follows.

1. *Ask the data a specific and consistent set of questions.* The most general question researchers must keep in mind is, What study are these data pertinent to? In other words, what was the original objective of the research study? This is not to suggest that the data must be molded to that study. Rather, the original purpose of a study may not be accomplished and an alternative or unanticipated goal may be identified in the data. For example, in Pearson's (1987) evaluation of a New Jersey intensive problem supervision program, the original aim was to demonstrate cost effectiveness. Although objective indicators failed to support the cost effectiveness of the experimental program, several indirect indicators suggested that the program nonetheless was fairly successful. These other measures involved repeated reports from relatives of probationers about changes in attitudes demonstrated by the program participants. For instance, the wife of one participant reported that her husband had begun to send the child-support payments in full and on time. Parents of another program participant reported that their child had begun to show personal responsibility by doing household chores around the home—something the individual had previously never undertaken.

Thus, Pearson (1987) points to an unanticipated benefit from the program. This illustration demonstrates the need both to keep the original study aim in mind and to remain open to multiple or unanticipated results that emerge from the data.

2. *Analyze the data minutely.* Strauss (1987) cautions that researchers should remember that they are conducting an initial coding procedure. As such, it is important to analyze data minutely. Students in qualitative research should remind themselves that in the beginning, more is better. Coding is much like the traditional funnel used by many educators to demonstrate how to write papers. You begin with a wide opening, a broad statement; narrow the statement throughout the body by offering substantial backing; and finally, at the small end of the funnel, present a refined, tightly stated conclusion. In the case of coding, the wide end represents inclusion of many categories, incidents, interactions, and the like. These are coded minutely during open coding. Later, this effort ensures extensive theoretical coverage that will be thoroughly grounded. At a later time, more systematic coding can be accomplished, building from the numerous elements that emerge during this phase of open coding.

The question that arises, of course, is when to stop this open coding process and move on to the speedier, more systematic coding phase. Typically, as researchers minutely code, they eventually saturate the document with repetitious codes. As this occurs and the repetition allows the researchers to move more rapidly through the documents, it is usually safe to conclude that the time has come to move on.

3. *Frequently interrupt the coding to write a theoretical note.* This third guideline suggested by Strauss (1987) directs researchers closer to grounded theory. Often, in the course of coding, a comment in the document triggers ideas. Researchers should take a moment to jot down a note about these ideas, which may well prove useful later. If they fail to do so, they are very likely to forget the idea. In many instances, researchers find it useful to keep a record of where in each document similar comments, concepts, or categories seem to convey the same elements that originally triggered the theory or hypothesis. For example, during the coding process of a study on adolescents' involvements with alcohol, crime, and drugs, interview transcripts revealed youths speaking about drugs and criminal activities as though they were almost partitioned categories (Carpenter et al., 1988). Notes scribbled during coding later led to theories on drug-crime event sequences and the nexus of drug-crime events.

4. *Never assume the analytic relevance of any traditional variable such as age, sex, social class, and so on until the data show it to be relevant.* As Strauss (1987, p. 32) indicates, even these more mundane variables must "earn their way into the grounded theory." This assumes that these variables are necessarily contributing to some condition, but it does not mean you are prohibited from intentionally using certain variables deductively. The first guideline, What are the study data pertinent to? is germane to the coding process. Consequently, if researchers are interested in gender differences, naturally, they begin by assuming that gender might be analytically relevant, but if the data fail to support this assumption, the researchers must accept this result.

CODING FRAMES

Content analysis is accomplished through the use of *coding frames.* The coding frames are used to organize the data and identify findings after open coding has been completed. The first coding frame is often a multileveled process that requires several successive sortings of all cases under examination. Investigators begin with a general sorting of cases into some specified special class. In many ways, this first frame is similar to what Strauss (1987, p. 32) describes as axial coding. According to Strauss (1987) *axial coding* occurs after open coding is completed and consists of intensive coding around one category. The first sorting approximates Strauss's description of axial coding. An example may better illustrate this process.

I (Berg, 1983) began my first sorting by separating all cases into Jewish affiliational categories declared by respondents during an initial telephone contact. Subjects' responses came after being asked in a screening question: "With which of the following do you most closely associate yourself: Reform, Orthodox, Conservative, or Nonpracticing?" (Subjects were consistently asked this question using the preceding affiliational ordering in an attempt to guard against certain acquiescent response sets.)

This procedure separated my sample (cases) into four groupings bearing the conventional affiliational titles listed above. After completing this sorting, I carefully read the responses to the identical question asked in the course of each respondent's depth interview. Subsequently, each affiliational grouping was subdivided into three groups using the following criteria of selection:

1. The first subdivision in each category consists of all cases in which respondents' answers to the interview version of the question, "With which of the following . . ." (1) were consistent with the response given during the telephone screening and (2) were offered with no qualification or exception.

2. The second subdivision in each category consists of cases in which respondents qualified their responses with a simple modifier (usually a single adjective), but were otherwise consistent with the response offered on the telephone screening question (for example, "I am a *modern* Orthodox Jew.").

3. The third subdivision consists of all cases in which the respondents offered detailed explanations for their affiliational declarations that were also consistent with their telephone screening response. For example, one male respondent explained that just as his father had switched from being an Orthodox to a Conservative affiliate, so too did he make a switch from being a Conservative to a Reform affiliate. His declaration of *Reform*, however, was consistent with what he had originally declared during the telephone screening.

4. The fourth subdivision consists of all cases in which the respondents contradicted their original telephone screening question response or indicated that they simply could not determine where they fit in terms of the four conventional affiliational categories.

Using the above criteria, I sorted my cases into the indicated subdivisions. Following this, and using a sorting process similar to the preceding one, I again subdivided each newly created subgroup to produce a typological scheme containing 16 distinct categories, the overarching or key linkage in every case being the subjective declaration of each respondent (at two distinct iterations of the same question).

Having sorted and organized my data, I was ready to interpret the patterns apparent from both the organizational scheme and the details offered in response to interview questions. At this juncture in my analysis, relevant theoretical perspectives were introduced in order to tie the analysis both to established theory and to my own emerging grounded theory (Glaser & Strauss, 1967). These theoretical considerations and sociological constructs led me to analyze several other detailed responses to interview questions. These other questions concerned respondents' involvement in and knowledge of religious symbols and ceremonies. In order to preserve the key linkage throughout the entire analysis process, each subsequent analysis of responses was performed against the newly created typological scheme of subjective identification labels (the 16-category scheme mentioned previously).

Another example of this axial coding or sorting process is offered by Bing (1987), who examined plea bargaining by using an archival strategy. He created a master list containing over 400 articles that examined plea bargaining as represented in 12 major social science journals during the past 5 years (Bing, 1987, pp. 50ff).

Following the creation of his master list, Bing sorted his articles, first by *manifest theoretical orientation* and second by *methodological approach*. After eliminating categories that contained only a single article and collapsing fundamentally similar theoretical orientations, Bing identified 12 distinct theoretical categories (for example, labeling theory, organizational theory, crime control/due process theory, economic theory, dramaturgical theory, and so forth). The second coding resulted in six distinct methodological approaches, which Bing used to subdivide each of the theoretical categories. Bing established objective criteria for each of the possible theoretical categories. As Bing (1987, pp. 72–73) explains his criteria: "The general focus of the article was used to determine the theoretical orientation [of each article]. In some instances, the author would clearly state the theory; on other occasions, the theoretical approach was lifted based upon statements [offered by the author and] used to characterize the study." In essence, Bing sought to identify theoretical approaches by examining the expression by each author (either directly or indirectly) of a theoretical declaration.

Strauss similarly outlines the coding process. According to Strauss (1987, p. 28), the analyst begins with a procedure he calls *open coding*. This procedure is described as an unrestricted coding of the data. With open coding, you carefully and minutely read the document line by line and word by word to determine the concepts and categories that fit the data. These concepts, once uncovered, are entirely tentative. As you continue working with and thinking about the data, questions and even some plausible answers also begin to emerge. These questions and answers should lead you to other issues and further questions concerning "conditions, strategies, interactions and consequences" (Strauss, 1987, p. 28).

A Few More Words on Analytic Induction

As Robinson (1951) suggests, "Since Znaniecki stated it in 1934, the method of analytic induction has come into important use." The use of analytic induction, however, also has involved a number of refinements—including several variations on its style and purpose. For example, Sutherland and Cressey (1966) refined the method and suggest that it be used in the study of causes of crime. Even before Sutherland (1950), Lindesmith (1947) had discovered the usefulness of an analytic inductive strategy in a study of opiate users. Lindesmith (1952, p. 492) describes analytic induction as follows:

> *The principle which governs the selection of cases to test a theory is that the chances of discovering a decisive negative case should be maximized. The investigator who has a working hypothesis concerning the data becomes aware of certain areas of critical importance. If his theory is false or inadequate, he knows that its weakness will be more clearly and quickly exposed if he proceeds to the investigation of those critical areas. This involves going out of one's way to look for negative evidence.*

Adding further refinements to the method, Glaser and Strauss suggest that analytic induction should combine analysis of data after the coding process with analysis of data while integrating theory. In short, analysis of data is grounded to established theory and is also capable of developing theory. Glaser and Strauss (1967, p. 102) describe their refinements as follows:

We wish to suggest a third approach to the analysis of qualitative data—one that combines, by an analytic procedure of constant comparison, the explicit coding procedures of the first approach [analysis of data after coding] and the style of theory development of the second [the integration of data and theory]. The purpose of the constant comparative method of joint coding and analysis is to generate theory more systematically than allowed by the second approach, by using explicit coding and analytic procedures. While more systematic than the second approach, this method does not adhere completely to the first, which hinders the development of theory because it is designed for provisional testing and not discovering hypotheses.

Glaser and Strauss (1967) suggest that such a joint coding and analysis of data is a more honest way to present findings and analysis. Similarly, Merton (1968, pp. 147–148) discusses the "logical fallacy underlying post factum explanations" and hypothesis testing. Merton states:

It is often the case in empirical social research that data are collected and only then subjected to interpretative comment. . . . Such post factum explanations designed to "explain" observations, differ in logical function from speciously similar procedures where the observational materials are utilized in order to derive fresh hypotheses to be confirmed by new observations.

A disarming characteristic of the procedure is that the explanations are indeed consistent with the given set of observations. This is scarcely surprising, in as much as only those post factum hypotheses are selected which do accord with these observations. . . . The method of post factum explanation does not lend itself to nullifiability.

Researchers should make extensive use of Glaser and Strauss's (1967) style of analytic induction and, perhaps more directly, of Strauss's (1987) rearticulation of their position. According to Strauss (1987, p. 12):

Because of our earlier writing in Discovery (1967) where we attacked speculative theory—quite ungrounded in bodies of data—many people mistakenly refer to grounded theory as "inductive theory" in order to contrast it with say, the theories of Parson or Blau. But as we have indicated, all three aspects of inquiry (induction, deduction, and verification) are absolutely essential. . . . In fact, it is important to understand that various kinds of experience are central to all these modes of activity—induction, deduction, and verification—that enter into inquiry.

Throughout the analysis, researchers should incorporate all appropriate modes of inquiry. Thus, both logically derived hypotheses and those that have "serendipitously" (Merton, 1968) arisen from the data may find their way into the research.

Interrogative Hypothesis Testing

In order to verify and assess the applicability of a given hypothesis, researchers should use a style of *negative case* testing suggested by Robinson (1951), Lindesmith (1952), Manheim and Simon (1977), and Denzin (1978). This process of negative case testing essentially involves the following steps:

1. Make a rough hypothesis based on an observation from the data.
2. Conduct a thorough search of all cases to locate negative cases (that is, cases that do not fit the hypothesized relationship).
3. If a negative case is located, either discard or reformulate the hypothesis to account for (or exclude) the negative case.
4. Examine all relevant cases from the sample before determining whether "practical certainty" (Denzin, 1978) in this recommended analysis style is attained.

For example, based on a reading of responses to the open-ended question, "With which of the following do you most closely associate yourself: Conservative, Orthodox, Reform, or Nonpracticing?" I (Berg, 1983) hypothesized that certain groups of persons offered instrumentally oriented answers (that is, oriented to achievement and goals) while other groups offered expressively oriented answers (that is, sentimental, feeling oriented, and symbolic). I further hypothesized that these styles of responses could be linked to particular categories relevant to the analysis of differential involvement with religious activities and subjective affiliational identification. However, after carefully reexamining each case, with these hypotheses in mind, I found many negative cases. At each negative juncture, I attempted to reformulate the hypotheses to account for the cases that did not fit. Unfortunately, I soon realized that my hypotheses had become artificial and meaningless. Consequently, I soon abandoned them. None of the successive formulations were constructed de novo but were based on some aspect of the preceding hypothetical relationship (see Denzin, 1978, pp. 193–194; Lindesmith, 1947, pp. 9–10).

It may be argued that the search for negative cases sometimes neglects contradictory evidence (that is, when a case both affirms and in some way denies a hypothetical relationship) or distorts the original hypothetical relationship (that is, when the observers read into the data whatever relationship they have hypothesized—a variation on post factum hypothesizing). To accomplish content analysis in the style recommended here, researchers must use several safeguards against these potential flaws in analysis. First, whenever numbers of cases allow, examples that illustrate a point should be lifted at random from among the relevant grouped cases. Second, every assertion made in the analysis should be documented with no fewer than three examples. Third, analytic interpretations should be examined carefully by an independent reader (someone other than the actual researchers) to ensure that their claims and assertions are not derived from a misreading of the data and that they have been documented adequately. Finally, whenever inconsistencies in patterns do emerge, these too should be discussed in order to explain whether they have invalidated overall patterns. Failure to mention these inconsistencies in pattern is a less than forthright presentation of the data and analysis.

In effect, the use of the above safeguards avoids what Glaser and Strauss (1967, p. 5) describe as *exampling*. According to Glaser and Strauss, exampling is finding examples for "dreamed-up, speculative, or logically deducted theory after the idea occurred," rather than allowing the patterns to emerge from the data. For instance, in the course of analyzing responses to the question, "How do you celebrate Chanukkah, if at all?" during an early analysis of the data, I (Berg, 1983) suggested that gift giving was emphasized to a greater extent by some affiliational groups than by others. However, when this section was read by an independent reader, the reader noticed that several negative cases had been presented in evidence of this assertion. What I had originally missed was that the more traditional affiliational group members had described their style of gift giving in the midst of a number of traditional (religious) rituals. On the other hand, many of the nonpracticing affiliational group members had described gift giving as being in competition with an observance of Christmas and thus actually fused their observance of Chanukkah with an observance of Christmas.

STRENGTHS AND WEAKNESSES OF THE CONTENT ANALYSIS PROCESS

Perhaps the most important advantage of content analysis is that it can be virtually unobtrusive (Webb et al., 1981). Content analysis, although useful when analyzing depth interview data, may also be used nonreactively: no one needs to be interviewed, no one needs to fill out lengthy questionnaires, no one must enter a laboratory. Rather, newspaper accounts, public addresses, libraries, archives, and similar sources allow researchers to conduct analytic studies.

An additional advantage is that it is cost effective. Generally, the materials necessary for conducting content analysis are easily and inexpensively accessible. One college student working alone can effectively undertake a content analysis, whereas undertaking a national survey, for instance, might require enormous staff, time, and expense.

A further advantage to content analysis is that it provides a means by which to study processes that occur over long periods of time or that may reflect trends in a society (Babbie, 1992). As examples, you might study the portrayal of women in the media from 1800 to 1993 or you might focus on changing images of women in the media from 1982 to 1992. For instance, McBroom (1992) recently examined women in the clergy as depicted in the *Christian Century* between 1984 and 1987. McBroom (1992, p. 208) reports:

> *1984 was a year when the issue of women's ordination gained support in the news media, as indicated by the number of positive references, especially articles, during the year. . . . The next year, 1985, was a year of transition, as few references were recorded for that year. The data for the years 1986 and 1987 indicate a growing negative response to the issue of the ordination of women, especially in the negative news reports.*
>
> *The data . . . indicate that, in general, conditions and opportunities for women in the clergy in the United States deteriorated rather than improved during these years.*

Thus, using content analysis, McBroom (1992) was able to examine data during individual years as well as over the span of all years under study.

The single serious weakness of content analysis may be in locating unobtrusive messages relevant to the particular research questions. In other words, content analysis is limited to examining already recorded messages. Although these messages may be oral, written, graphic or videotaped, they must be recorded in some manner in order to be analyzed.

Of course, when you undertake content analysis as an analysis tool rather than as a complete research strategy, such a weakness is minimal. For example, if researchers use content analysis to analyze interview data or responses to open-ended questions (on written questionnaires), this weakness is virtually nonexistent.

Another limitation (although some might call it a weakness) of content analysis is that it is ineffective for testing causal relationships between variables. Researchers and their audiences must resist the temptation to infer such relationships. This is particularly true when researchers forthrightly present the proportion or frequency with which a theme or pattern is observed. This kind of information is appropriate to indicate the magnitude of certain responses; however, it is not appropriate to attach cause to these presentations.

As with any analytic method, the advantages of content analysis must be weighed against the disadvantages and against alternative research strategies. Although content analysis may be appropriate for some research problems and designs, it is not appropriate in every research situation. It is a particularly beneficial procedure for assessing events or processes in social groups when public records exist. It is likewise helpful in many types of exploratory or descriptive studies. But if you are interested in conducting experimental or causal research, content analysis is virtually useless.

COMPUTERS AND QUALITATIVE ANALYSIS

It is now nearly 30 years since General Inquirer, the first software program designed to assist in the analysis of textual data, became public (Stone et al., 1966; Tesch, 1991). Of course, when General Inquirer came out, small affordable personal computers did not exist. To use General Inquirer, one needed access to a large mainframe computer and sufficient time to read and digest its book-length instructions. This program still largely operated on the basis of counting and numerous calculations. Yet it did work exclusively with textual data (Tesch, 1991).

In today's "Star Wars," supersonic, hypertechnology age, most academics have or have access to personal computers—at least for word processing. In fact, die-hards who cling to their Smith Coronas and IBM Selectric typewriters are likely to be viewed by colleagues as somewhat strange.

Most experienced qualitative researchers are aware that a number of computer programs for qualitative data exist, even if they do not use them. Each year, more and more qualitative researchers *do* begin trying and using these programs. Throughout the 1980s, many academic journals began publishing articles directing considerable attention toward commercially available software designed specifically for qualitative analysis (Conrad & Reinharz, 1984; Drass 1980; Gerson, 1984; Heise, 1981; Jacobs, 1987; Seidel, 1984).

In 1987, Brent, Scott, and Spencer reported that 77 percent of the qualitative researchers they surveyed on computer use said they used computers in their research. More recently, in 1991, Tesch reported that over 3,000 people had purchased a single dedicated qualitative analysis software package called The Ethnograph (Tesch, 1991). Furthermore, in a 1991 survey of qualitative researchers by Miles and Huberman (1994), three quarters of respondents reported using computer software for data entry, coding, searching and retrieval, display, and concept building. Miles and Huberman also found that satisfaction with computer software was mixed among these researchers.

It would be impossible to estimate how many qualitative researchers today use either such dedicated software packages or word processing programs in their analysis.

To be sure, the potential for using computers in qualitative research for analytic purposes or, as Dennis (1984) calls it, *word crunching,* is enormous. Some researchers have adapted commercial software packages to their personal qualitative sorting or data management needs. For example, Lotus 1-2-3 and similar spreadsheets can be applied to a wide assortment of tasks common in content analysis. You can, for instance, create fields to contain shorthand versions of themes, classes, or categories and corresponding fields to indicate tallies of these categorical containers. After you sort textual data into these fields, calculations of the magnitude (how many times a theme has been placed in a given thematic category) can be automatically determined.

Commercial computer utility programs such as Gofer, HyperCard, and Super-HyperCard have been used by some qualitative researchers (Gerson, 1984). Additionally, most modern word processing programs have Find, Go To, Locate, and indexing capabilities. These provide a wide assortment of functions useful for sorting, managing, and coding qualitative textual data and word crunching (Dabney, 1993). Norman (1989) describes the use of the WordStar word processing program and, to a lesser extent, WordPerfect and XYWrite, to locate words, move sections of text, and sort and rearrange textual materials for nurse researchers conducting content analysis.

Recently, Weitzman and Miles (1995) produced a sourcebook on computer software for qualitative data analysis. In this book, they review 24 different programs that might be useful to qualitative researchers. As Weitzman and Miles (1995) caution readers, "There is no computer program that will 'analyze' your data. . . . Computers don't analyze data; people do." Weitzman and Miles (1995) also explain that choosing the right software package depends not only on the nature of your data—interview transcripts, field notes, or other documents—but on how you desire to approach and analyze these data. In other words, what exactly do you want to accomplish with the analysis?

In addition, Weitzman and Miles (1995) suggest that choosing a software program to assist in qualitative analysis depends on what I will call a computer comfort level. If a researcher is new to computers, or not very comfortable using them, it is probably better to begin with a simple word processing program. This will provide an opportunity for the novice to learn about and explore the computer operating system and become more comfortable with creating files, moving text and, in general, more confident about computers. If, on the other hand, the researcher is fairly well acquainted with computers and computer operating systems, he or she might want to explore one or another of a number of more dynamic database management programs.

As Weitzman and Miles (1995) outline, there are approximately six general types of functions available in software programs used in qualitative analysis. In many cases, multiple functions are available in a given program. These functions include: word processors, text retrievers, textbase managers, code-and-retrieve programs, code-based theory builders, and conceptual network-builders.

Word Processors

Word processors allow you to create text-based files and to effectively find, move, reproduce, and retrieve sections of the text in each file. These provide a means for transcribing interviews or audio portions of video, writing up or editing field notes, coding text for indexing and retrieval purposes, and even writing up findings in reports.

Text Retrievers

Software packages such as Metamorph, Orbis, Sonar, Professional, The Text Collector, WordCruncher, or ZyINDEX are dedicated text search programs (Weitzman and Miles, 1995). These programs specialize in locating every instance of a specified word, phrase, or character string. As well, these programs are able to locate combinations of these items in one of several files.

Textbase Managers

Although similar in basic function to text retrievers, textbase managers provide a greater capacity for organizing, sorting, and making subsets of the textual data. Several examples of these programs include askSam, Folio VIEWS, Tabletop, and MAX. Some of these programs are intended to manage fairly structured text organized into records or specific case files and fields or specified areas in a given case. Other programs are capable of dealing with more free-flowing forms of text and in some cases, even certain quantitative information.

Code-and-Retrieve Programs

Code-and-retrieve programs, according to Weitzman and Miles (1995) are often developed by qualitative researchers rather than commercial software developers. These programs are intended to assist the researcher in dividing text into segments or chunks, attach codes, and find and display these coded sections. These programs tend to fill in for the kind of cutting, pasting, and sorting of hard copy data qualitative researchers once used. HyperQual2, Kwalitan, QUALPRO, Martin, and The Ethnograph are all examples of code-and-retrieve types of programs.

Code-Based Theory Builders

These types of programs are also frequently developed by researchers. Usually, these programs include the capacity to code and retrieve and also offer special features that assist you in developing theoretical connections between coded concepts. As a result, higher-order classifications and connections can be formulated. Weitzman and Miles (1995) list AQUAD, ATLAS/ti, HyperRESEARCH, NUD.IST, and QCA as examples.

Conceptual Network Builders

Programs designed for conceptual network-building are intended to assist the researcher in building and testing theory. These programs provide the capacity to create graphic networks. Variables are displayed as nodes (usually rectangles or ellipses) linked to other nodes by lines or arrows representing relationships. These networks represent various types of semantic networks that evolve from the data set and the concepts used by the researcher. Examples of these programs include ATLAS/ti (which is also a code-based theory builder), MECA, and SemNet.

While new computer programs and applications for qualitative research arise nearly daily, computer use in qualitative research remains in its infancy. For some researchers, it makes no difference whether they use a dedicated qualitative analysis program or apply some utility or word processing program to the task. This is because, clearly, qualitative researchers have not yet adequately figured out how best to use computers in their research work! In part, this may be because none of the tasks currently accomplished by computers and used in qualitative research really move beyond data organization and management. Any computer program or adaptation still requires that the researcher think through the analytic and theoretical relationships between original conceptualizations and eventual empirical evidence. Quantitative application of computers, which is enormously fast, largely makes hand calculation obsolete. Computers make it easy for researchers to take hundreds of thousands of cases and quickly determine a vast number of statistical aspects of the data set. Yet even quantitative computer programs cannot by themselves (at least not yet) extrapolate on or beyond the statistical manipulations made on the data.

In the case of qualitative analysis, this problem of extrapolation is made even more difficult. Analysis of data is often intertwined in the presentation of findings and the explanation of results. Creating an apparatus that can simultaneously present the findings and describe their analytic importance would require perfection of artificial computer intelligence—a step into the future at least several decades away.

As a result, the use of computers by qualitative researchers remains, for now, an attempt to locate "chunks of technology" (Gerson, 1990) that are available, affordable, and seem to work for the present. It is important, however, to remember that computers are intended to reduce the amount of overall time a researcher spends in the data organization and analysis phase of research. If you spend enormous amounts of time trying to locate, learn how to use, and enter data into a computer program, this process may defeat the original time-saving purpose of computers. Nonetheless, the use of computers in qualitative research can significantly assist novice researchers. This is because programs such as The Ethnograph provide clear directions on how to begin organizing data into a usable structure. As you become more experienced and adept at both data analysis and computer operations, you may feel more confident and try other computer applications or adaptations.

TRYING IT OUT

Suggestion 1

Select a topic of interest to you, such as crime, medical advances, ecology, technology, or another broad concern. Next, using your school library's collection of the *New York Times,* locate 10 consecutive weeks of the Sunday Week in Review section. Now see if you can locate articles with headlines that relate to your topic of interest. If you accomplish these tasks, you have actually conducted a rudimentary form of thematic content analysis. Your topic served as the theme and the newspaper story headlines as your units of analysis.

Suggestion 2

Without writing their names on the paper, have everyone in your class write a response to the following question: If you could change one thing in the world today, what would it be?

Ask each classmate to write his or her gender and age at the bottom of the response, but remind them not to write their names. Have each person make enough photocopies to distribute one copy to every person in the class. Now everyone has a set of data to work with.

Next, go through the responses and see if you can locate any patterns of similarity or difference. Sort the responses into groups according to the patterns or themes that emerge as you read through the responses. Try to make the following assessments:

1. How many times have students identified the same (or very similar) things they would change if they could?

2. What proportion of the class used identical words to describe what they would change?
3. Are patterns any different if you first sort them according to gender?
4. Are patterns any different if you first sort them into the following age groupings: *young* (under 20 years old), *older* (21–25 years old), *oldest* (over 25 years old)?

REFERENCES

Abrahamson, M. (1983). *Social Research Methods*. Englewood Cliffs, NJ: Prentice Hall.

Babbie, E. (1983). *The Practice of Social Research* (3rd ed.). Belmont, CA: Wadsworth Publishing.

Babbie, E. (1992). *The Practice of Social Research* (6th ed.). Belmont, CA: Wadsworth Publishing.

Berelson, B. (1952). *Content Analysis in Communications Research*. Glencoe, IL: Free Press.

Berg, B. L. (1983). *Jewish identity: Subjective declarations or objective life styles*. Doctoral dissertation, Syracuse University, Syracuse, NY.

Berg, B. L. (1986). Arbitrary arbitration: Diverting juveniles into the justice system. *Juvenile and Family Court Journal 37*(5), 31–42.

Berg, B. L. (1988). The Chanukkah bush: Chanukkah and Christmas celebration among Jews. *Free Inquiry in Creative Sociology 16*(2), 143–148.

Bing, R. L., III. (1987). *Plea bargaining: An analysis of the empirical evidence*. Doctoral dissertation, Florida State University, Tallahassee.

Boje, D. (1991). The story telling organization: A study of story performance in an office supply firm. *Administrative Science Quarterly 36*, 106–126.

Brent, E., Scott, J., & Spencer, J. (1987). The use of computers by qualitative researchers. *Qualitative Sociology 10*(3), 309–313.

Carney, T. F. (1972). *Content Analysis*. Winnipeg: University of Manitoba Press.

Carpenter, C., Glassner, B., Johnson, B., & Loughlin, J. (1988). *Kids, Drugs, and Crime*. Lexington, MA: Lexington Books.

Chadwick, B. A., Bahr, H. M., & Albrecht, S. L. (1984). *Social Science Research Methods*. Englewood Cliffs, NJ: Prentice Hall.

Commission on Obscenity and Pornography. (1970). *The Report of the Commission on Obscenity and Pornography*. New York: Bantam Books.

Comstock, G. A., & Rubinstein, E. A. (1972). *Television and Social Behavior*. Technical Reports to the Surgeon General's Scientific Advisory Committee on Television and Social Behavior. Washington, DC: U.S. Government Printing Office.

Conrad, P., & Reinharz, S. (Eds.). (1984). Computers and qualitative data. *Qualitative Sociology 7*(1/2).

Dabney, D. A. (1993). *Impaired nursing: Nurses' attitudes and perceptions about drug use and drug theft*. Master's thesis, Indiana University of Pennsylvania, Indiana, PA.

Dennis, D. L. (1984). Word crunching: An annotated bibliography on computers and qualitative data analysis. *Qualitative Sociology 7*(1/2), 148–156.

Denzin, N. K. (1978) *The Research Act*. New York: McGraw-Hill.

Drass, K. A. (1980). The analysis of qualitative data: A computer program. *Urban Life 9*, 322–353.

Duncan, H. D. (1962). *Communication and Social Order*. New York: Bedminster Press.

Fields, E. E. (1988). Qualitative content analysis of television news: Systematic techniques. *Qualitative Sociology 11*(3), 183–193.

Gerson, E. M. (1984). Qualitative research and the computer. *Qualitative Sociology 17*(1/2), 61–74.

Glaser, B., & Strauss, A. (1967). *The Discovery of Grounded Theory: Strategies for Qualitative Research*. Chicago: Aldine.

Glassner, B., Ksander, M., Johnson, B., & Berg, B. L. (1983). The deterrence effects of juvenile versus adult jurisdiction. *Social Problems 31*(2), 219–221.

Glassner, B., & Loughlin, J. (1987). *Drugs in Adolescent Worlds: Burnouts to Straights*. New York: St. Martin's Press.

Heilman, S. (1976). *Synagogue Life: A Study in Symbolic Interaction*. Englewood Cliffs, NJ: Prentice Hall.

Heise, D. R. (Ed.). (1981). Microcomputers and social research. *Special Issue of Sociological Methods and Research*.

Heise, D. (1992). *Ethnography* (2nd ed.). Chapel Hill: University of North Carolina Press.

Holsti, O. R. (1968). Content analysis. In G. Lindzey & E. Aaronson (Eds.), *The Handbook of Social Psychology*. Reading, MA: Addison-Wesley.

Holsti, O. R. (1969). *Content Analysis for the Social Sciences and Humanities*. Reading, MA: Addison-Wesley.

Jacobs, E. (1987). Qualitative research traditions: A review. *Review of Educational Research 57*(1), 1–50.

Kish, L. (1965). *Survey Sampling*. New York: Wiley.

Lindesmith, A. R. (1947). *Opiate Addiction*. Bloomington: Indiana University Press.

Lindesmith, A. R. (1952). Comment on W. S. Robinson's The Logical Structure of Analytic Induction. *American Sociological Review 17*, 492–493.

Manheim, H. L. & Simon, B. A. (1977). *Sociological Research*. Homewood, IL: Dorsey Press.

Manning, P. K., & Cullum-Swan, B. (1994). Narrative, content, and semiotic analysis. In N. K. Denzin & Y. S. Lincoln (Eds.), *Handbook of Qualitative Research*. Thousand Oaks, CA: Sage.

McBroom, J. R. (1992). Women in the clergy: A content analysis of the *Christian Century*, 1984–1987. *Free Inquiry in Creative Sociology 20*(2), 205–209.

Merton, R. K. (1968). *Social Theory and Social Structure*. New York: Free Press.

Miles, M. B., & Huberman, M. A. (1983). *Qualitative Data Analysis*. Beverly Hills, CA: Sage.

Miles, M. B., & Huberman, M.A. (1994). *Qualitative Analysis: An Expanded Sourcebook* (2nd ed.). Thousand Oaks, CA: Sage.

Norman, E. (1989). How to use word processing software to conduct content analysis. *Computers in Nursing 7*, 127–128.

Pearson, F. (1987). Taking quality into account: Assessing the benefits and costs of New Jersey's intensive supervision program. In B. R. McCarthy (Ed.), *Intermediate Punishment*. Monsey, NY: Willow Tree Press.

Robinson, W. S. (1951). The logical structure of analytic induction. *American Sociological Review 16*, 812–818.

Sanders, W., & Pinhey, T. K. (1959). *The Conduct of Social Research*. New York: Holt, Rinehart & Winston.

Schatzman, L., & Strauss, A. (1973). *Field Research: Strategies for a Natural Sociology.* Englewood Cliffs, NJ: Prentice Hall.

Seidel, J. (1984). The Ethnograph. *Qualitative Sociology* 7(1/2), 110–125.

Selltiz, C., Jahoda, M., Deutsch, M., & Cook, S. W. (1959). *Research Methods in Social Relations.* New York: Holt, Rinehart & Winston.

Selltiz C., Jahoda, Deutsch, M., & Cook, S. W. (1967). *Research Methods in Social Relations* (2nd ed.). New York: Holt, Rinehart & Winston.

Silverman, D. (1993). *Interpreting Qualitative Data.* Thousand Oaks, CA: Sage.

Smith, H. W. (1975). *Strategies of Social Research.* Englewood Cliffs, NJ: Prentice Hall.

Stone, P. J., Dunphy, D. C., Smith, M. S., & Ogilvie, D. M. (1966). *The General Inquirer: A Computer Approach to Content Analysis.* Cambridge, MA: MIT Press.

Strauss, A. L. (1959). *Mirrors and Masks.* Glencoe, IL: Free Press.

Strauss, A. L. (1987). *Qualitative Analysis for Social Scientists.* New York: Cambridge University Press.

Sutherland, E. H. (1950). *Principles of Criminology* (2nd ed.). Philadelphia: J. B. Lippincott.

Sutherland, E. H., & Cressey, D. (1966). *Principles of Criminology* (7th ed.). New York: J. B. Lippincott.

Tesch, R. (1991). Introduction. *Qualitative Sociology* 14(3), 225–243.

Webb, E. J., Cambell, D. T., Schwartz, R. D., Sechrest, L., & Grove, J. B. (1981). *Nonreactive Measures in the Social Sciences.* Boston: Houghton Mifflin.

Weitzman, E. A., & Miles, M. B. (1995). *Computer Programs for Qualitative Data Analysis.* Thousand Oaks, CA: Sage.

WRITING RESEARCH PAPERS: SORTING THE NOODLES FROM THE SOUP

M Y CHILDREN, ALEX AND KATE, were eating alphabet soup for lunch one Sunday afternoon. Kate, then about four years old, was stirring her soup with great care and deliberation. She managed to capture several of the letters on her spoon, carefully spill off the liquid, and spell out her name. "Look, Daddy, I wrote my name with my noodles!" She held her spoon up for my inspection. She had arranged the letters to spell "KATIE." Alex, seeing the attention his sister had received, pulled his dripping spoon from his soup, and, spilling much of it onto the floor, exclaimed, "Me too!" Unfortunately, his letters spelled out "XCYU," a unique spelling of "Alex," or simply failure to sort the noodles from the soup in a fashion that made his noodles mean something to others.

Qualitative methods similarly can result either in improved social scientific understanding or in meaningless gibberish. This last chapter is designed to enable inexperienced researchers to offer up their noodles for inspection by others in an understandable fashion—in other words, to write up the research so that it will be disseminated.

IDENTIFYING THE PURPOSE OF THE WRITING: ARRANGING THE NOODLES

When preparing to report information obtained from research, investigators should begin by considering the purpose of the study. If you want, as some sociological researchers do, to advance theory and conceptualization about certain patterns of behaviors, this is the goal you must aim for (see Burns, 1980; Glassner & Berg, 1980; Humphreys, 1975). A slightly different goal may be necessary if the purpose is to improve some particular component of

253

the practice of a particular discipline, such as nursing (see Ipema, 1979; Jacobsen, 1979; Leininger, 1982; Peterson, 1985). Similarly, as seen in much of the literature in criminology, corrections, the justice community, and other political spheres, researchers may focus upon policy issues (see Adler & Adler, 1983; Berg, 1987; Johnson et al., 1985; Skibinski & Koszuth, 1986; Michalowski, 1996). Naturally, yet another purpose may be intended when educators examine the interactions of children at play or activities associated with administrative roles in education (see Hart & Sheehan, 1986; Peshkin, 1986; Spindler, 1988).

In part, identification of the purpose goes hand in hand with understanding the audience. For effective written dissemination of research information, the character of the reading audience is as important to the writer as the character of the listening audience is to the speaker when presenting an oral presentation (Frankfort-Nachmias & Nachmias, 1996). If the researcher is interested in reaching a selected audience, their reports must speak to issues and concerns relevant to that particular community. If, on the other hand, they want to reach a broader, more general audience, the researcher must take care to address larger, more general concerns. A common mistake made by inexperienced researchers is coining terms to accommodate a given discipline—audience. One may "sociologize," for example, nursing issues, believing this will make them more understandable to sociologists. Conversely, one may "nursiologize"—to coin a phrase—sociological terms in order to make these more understandable to nurses (terms like *ethnonursing, transcultural nursing,* and so forth). Both efforts are mistakes. Clear, concise writing and avoiding all unnecessary jargon from any particular social scientific discipline are the best tactics. In the remainder of this chapter, major sections and components of social scientific reports are described.

DELINEATING A SUPPORTIVE STRUCTURE: VISUAL SIGNALS FOR THE READER

Generally speaking, written reports can be conceptually divided into several different segments, each of which contributes some element necessary for the reader to understand fully what the researchers say. In essence, these elements form the skeleton or *supportive structure* of the report. *Supportive structure,* as it is used here, refers to a number of major headings that give order to the research report.

Many of the sections are requisites of all research reports regardless of what specific label is used. The sections typically consist of:

1. *An abstract:* a brief explication of the entire report
2. *An introduction:* a section that introduces key terms and research foci

3. *A literature review:* a detailed examination of the extant research literature relevant to the report's topic
4. *A methodology section:* a comprehensive description of how the researchers gathered data and analyzed it
5. *Findings or results:* the presentation of information uncovered during the research process
6. *Discussion and/or implications:* an examination of these findings and consideration of how they may impinge on relevant groups, communities, or agencies
7. *References, notes, and/or appendices:* a section that contains the evidence that supports the research report

Let us consider each of these sections in detail.

The Abstract

An abstract is a brief summary (50–200 words) of the most important (and interesting) research findings of a study. In addition, abstracts usually contain some mention of key methodological features of the study and relevant implications of the major findings.

Abstracts are always found in the beginning of a research report, but given their contents, they cannot be created until after the report has been written. The major function of an abstract is to provide potential readers with sufficient information both to interest them and to help them determine whether to read the complete article. Often, researchers scan collections of abstracts (for example, journal indexes of abstracts) in order to identify potentially useful elements for their own literature reviews (to be considered presently). It is therefore critical that an abstract be both concise and precise.

As a broad guide to writing an abstract, regardless of the researchers' particular substantive interests, the following three key facets should be included:

1. A statement identifying the key focus or issue considered in the study.

   Example: This is the first study of drug trafficking in the United States to penetrate the echelons of the marijuana and cocaine business—[it concerns] the smugglers and their primary dealers.

2. The nature of the data analyzed in the study.

   Example: We spent six years observing and interviewing these traffickers and their associates in southwestern California and examining their typical career paths.

3. The major finding or result examined in the report.

   Example: We show how drug traffickers enter the business and rise to the top, how they become disenchanted because of the rising social and legal costs of upper-level drug trafficking, how and why they either voluntarily or involuntarily leave the business, and why so many end up returning to their deviant careers, or to other careers within the drug world.[1]

In some instances, you may want to include a fourth element that suggests the relevance of the research to a given agency, policy, or discipline:

4. Potential use or implication of the reported finding.

   Example: The findings of the current study outline the multiple conflicting forces that lure drug dealers and smugglers into and out of drug trafficking.[2]

These four elements should more or less suit virtually any research enterprise and may adequately produce an abstract consisting of as few as four sentences.

The Introduction

An introduction orients the reader to the study and the report. It should acquaint the reader with the basic research question or problem (Leedy, 1993). Introductions should be written in statement sentences that are clear and concise, and describe the type of writing that will follow (e.g., a descriptive report, an ethnographic narrative, a research proposal, etc.). Sometimes, introductions are referred to as *maps for the report*. Ideally, in addition to stating the research problem and placing it into theoretical and/or historical context, an introduction offers a sequential plan of presentation for the report. The reader is thus informed about what headings will be included and what each identified section will address.

It is additionally important to recognize that introductions can entice readers to continue reading, or turn them off so that they don't bother. The main attention-getting device, beyond the report title, is the opening sentence to an introduction (Meyer, 1991). A number of strategies are available to the writer. You might use a startling finding from the research, suggest some interesting problem from literature, or relate some relevant recent news event. Whatever you choose, it should be as interesting as possible. The introduction may be a distinct section complete with heading or it may be combined with a literature review.

Literature Review

The basic intention of a literature review is to give a comprehensive review of previous works on the general and specific topics considered in the report. At least to some extent, the literature review foreshadows the researcher's own study. Chapter 2 has already elaborated on the procedures usually surrounding the development of a literature review. During the writing stage of your research, you describe for the readers the state of the literature: its limitations and research directions.

For example, the researchers may want to challenge previously accepted ideas or findings. It is important, therefore, that these competing conceptualizations be presented and errors or fallacies identified. In some situations, researchers might be attempting to replicate previous studies and improve on their use of theory or methods. In such cases, it is necessary to illustrate how these previous studies examined their subject matter.

To a large measure, the literature review may also serve as a kind of bibliographic index and guide for the reader, not only by listing other studies about a given subject but also by demonstrating where the current study fits into the scheme of things.

Literature reviews should certainly include reference to classic works related to the investigation and should also include any recent studies. Omission of some relevant recent study may leave researchers open to criticism for carelessness—particularly if omitted studies have more exhaustively examined the literature, identified or conducted research in similar areas, or pointed out theoretical and methodological issues the current study overlooks. The more thorough the literature review, the more solid the research report's foundation becomes.

It is important to remember that not all sources of information are considered equal or can be legitimately used in writing literature reviews. Moreover, there is a kind of accepted hierarchy of informational sources. As I see this hierarchy, there are certain pieces of information that are better accepted by the scientific community than others. My version of this informational hierarchy is as follows:

1. Scholarly empirical articles, dissertations, monographs, and the like
2. Scholarly non-empirical articles
3. Texts
4. Certain nationally and internationally recognized news magazines (e.g., *Time, Newsweek*)
5. Certain nationally and internationally recognized newspapers (e.g., *The New York Times, The Washington Post, The Times* [of London])
6. Lower order but acceptable newspapers (e.g., *The Boston Globe, USA Today*)
7. Only when all other sources are unavailable should one use a local newspaper
8. Written personal communications
9. Oral personal communications

The elements listed in 1–3 offer the strongest documentary support in scholarly writing. Items listed in 4 and 5 offer moderately viable, and useful documentary sources of information. As one moves down the list, one should realize there is considerable loss of scientific confidence in the information obtained from these sources. These lower-order sources should be used only when noting some event or highlighting some already well-documented piece of information.

Like everything else, of course, too much of a good thing ruins the experience. Although certain types of research reports, such as a thesis or dissertation, expect lengthy (10–20 pages) literature reviews, reports and articles do not. Just as omitting a recent relevant article creates problems for a report, so too can an overdone literature review. The basic rule of thumb in writing literature reviews is to keep them long enough to cover the area, but short enough to remain interesting.

Methodology

Inexperienced researchers often think the methodology section is the most difficult section to write. It need not be so. In fact, since methodology sections typically report what you did during the course of a research project, it may well be one of the easiest sections to produce. The central purpose of a methodological section is to explain to readers how the research was accomplished—in other words, what the data consist of and how data were collected, organized, and analyzed. It is actually quite interesting; yet people who have little trouble describing intricate instructions for operating complicated medical equipment or repairing cars and electrical appliances pale at the thought of describing research methods.

The simplest, most straightforward way to write up the methodology section is to imagine explaining the process to a friend. Explaining the details about how the research was conducted is reasonably similar to telling a story. The points of detail most important to the researchers may vary from study to study, just as certain details in classic tales vary from storyteller to storyteller. Nonetheless, certain salient features of research methods tend to be present in most, if not all, methods sections. These features include considerations of subjects, data, setting, and analysis techniques.

Subjects
Methodology sections should include references to whom the subjects are, how they have been identified (selected), what they have been told about their participation, and what steps have been taken to protect them from harm. Ancillary concerns connected to discussions about the subjects may include how many are included, what determined their numbers, and how many refused to take part in the research and why (if it is known).

Data

In addition to identifying the nature of the data (for example, interviews, focus groups, ethnographies, videotapes, and so on), researchers should explain to readers how data were collected. Details about data collection have several important purposes. First, they allow readers to decide how much credence to attach to the results. Second, they provide a means for readers to replicate a research study, should they desire to do so. This notion of *replication* is very important to establishing that your research endeavor is objective. If someone else can replicate your study, then the original premises and findings can be tested in the future.

Finally, data-collection sections frequently are among the most interesting aspects of a research report—particularly when the researchers include details about problems and how they were resolved. Some self-reflection and disclosure may be necessary to offer what the literature sometimes calls *subjective views of the researcher*. In addition to offering interesting and vivid experiences, these subjective offerings may allow future researchers a way around problems in their own research studies.

Setting

Descriptions of the setting can be important in reporting an ethnographic study or a door-to-door interviewing project. The reliability of the research data, for example, may depend on demonstrating that an appropriate setting for the study has been selected. In some instances, settings are intricately related to the data and the analytic strategies and may possibly contaminate the research. A failure on the part of researchers to consider these elements during the study may weaken or destroy their otherwise credible arguments.

Analysis Techniques

Even when data are to be analyzed through generally accepted conventional means, a discussion and justification of the analytic strategy should be offered. It is not good procedure to assume anything regarding a research report. Researchers should never assume that the readers will immediately understand what is meant by such vague terms as *standard content analysis techniques*. As suggested in Chapter 11, even so-called standard content analysis may have many possible analytic alternatives depending on which unit of analysis is selected and whether the approach is inductive or deductive.

Findings or Results

In quantitative research reports, the findings or results section commonly presents percentages and proportions of the data in the form of charts, tables, and graphs. Quantitative methodologists often use the two terms synonymously, although in fact, there is a slight distinction between them. *Findings* quite literally refer to what the data say, whereas *results* offer interpretations of the meaning of the data. In short, *results* offer an *analysis* of the data.

In the case of qualitative research reports, however, the findings or results section is not as easily explained. For example, in qualitative research reports, the analysis section often follows the methods section. Sometimes, however, the researchers forthrightly explain that data will be presented throughout their analysis in order to demonstrate and document various patterns and observations (see Berg, 1983, Bing, 1987; Dabney, 1993). Sections of qualitative reports are also often organized according to conceptual subheadings (often arising from the terms and vocabularies of the subjects).

When ethnographic research is reported, the findings are more accurately presented and labeled an *ethnographic narrative,* followed by a separate *analysis* (Berg & Berg, 1988; Burns, 1980). Of course, there may be occasions when weaving the ethnographic observations throughout the analysis seems an effective presentation strategy (Cabral, 1980).

Reporting observations from a content analysis of interview data or other written documents may similarly be accomplished either by separately presenting the findings or by interweaving findings and analysis. What should be clear from the preceding presentation is that with regard to qualitative research reports, several options are available for writing about the findings (data) and results (interpretation of the data).

Discussion

The basic content of the discussion section will vary depending on whether the researchers have presented an analysis section or a findings section. In the former case, when an analysis section is included in a report, the discussion section frequently amounts to reiteration and elaboration of key points and suggestions about how the findings fit into the extant literature on the topical study area.

In the case of a separate findings section, the discussion section provides researchers with an opportunity to elaborate on presented observations. Frequently, in either case, after completing a research project, the social scientists realize they have gained both greater knowledge and insight into the phenomenon investigated. The discussion section provides a canvas on which the researchers may paint their insights. Occasionally, researchers gain Socratic wisdom—that is, they begin to realize what they—and the scientific community—still do not know about some substantive area. The discussion section allows the researchers to outline the areas requiring further research.

The discussion section also provides an opportunity to reflexively consider the research study and the research results. More and more these days, researchers are being acknowledged as active participants in the research process and not passive observers or mere scribes (Hertz, 1996). It becomes essential, therefore, to indicate the researcher's location of self within the constellations of gender, race, social class, and so forth (Edwards, 1990; Williams & Heikes, 1993; DeVault, 1995). Through reflexive personal accounts researchers should become more aware of how their own positions and interests affected their research. In turn, this should produce less distorted accounts of the social worlds about which they report.

References, Notes, and Appendices

Throughout the sections of a research report, references should document claims, statements, and allegations. Although a number of style texts recommend various ways of referencing material, there are chiefly two broad options: *notes* or *source references*. Superscript numerals can be placed in the text to correspond to notes, located either at the bottom of the page on which they appear (footnotes) or at the conclusion of the report (endnotes). The second broad option is source references, which appear immediately following the point in the text where a quote, paraphrase, or statement in need of documentation is made (the style used in this text). Source references are identified by the last name of a referenced author, the date of publication, and in the case of a direct quotation, the page(s) from which the quote has been taken.

In the social sciences, source references are more often used for documenting statements made in the text, and notes generally give further explanation to the text rather than cite source references. The following points concerning source references should be observed:

1. If the author's name appears in the text, only the date of the publication appears in parentheses.

   Example: According to Burns (1980) . . .

2. If the author's name is not used in the text, both the last name and the date of publication appear in parentheses.

   Example: The use of ethnographic narratives offers details of social discourse (Burns, 1980).

3. When a reference has two or three authors, the last name of each author is included in text. For reference material with more than three authors, the first author is shown in text followed by "et al."

   Examples: Link and Cullen (1987) and Johnson et al. (1985) have examined various aspects of deviant behavior.

4. For institutional authorship, the agency that produced the document is considered to be the author.

Example: Information on Index crimes suggests an increase (F.B.I. Uniform Crime Report, 1985).

5. When several sources are offered to document one claim or statement, each complete citation is separated by a semicolon and presented in chronological order.

   Example: This has been suggested throughout the literature, especially by Glassner and Berg, 1980; Cullen, 1982; Johnson et al. 1985; and Beschner, 1986.

6. When quoting directly, it is important to offer the page reference as well as the author's name and publication date in one of two forms.

   Examples: Doerner (1983, p. 22) states, ". . ." or Doerner (1983, p. 22) states, ". . ."

References are listed alphabetically by the first author's last name, in a separate section entitled "References." A reference section must include all source references included in the report. As a matter of practice, the abbreviation "et al.," which is appropriate for citations in text, is unacceptable in a reference section. The first names of authors may be either indicated in full or by initial, unless you are writing for some particular publication that specifies a preference.

The better academic journals of each discipline differ somewhat in the format for writing up full citations in the reference section. These specifications are generally given in the first few pages of the journals and may change slightly from time to time. It is thus advisable to consult the particular journals associated with your discipline to ascertain the proper form for the reference citations. To get inexperienced researchers going, however, what follows is the format recommended in the American Sociological Review as of 1986:

1. *Books:*

   Guy, Rebecca F., Charles E. Edgley, Ibtihaj Arafat, and Donald E. Allen. 1987. *Social Research Methods.* Boston: Allyn and Bacon.

2. *Periodicals:*

   Berg, Bruce L. 1986. "Arbitrary Arbitration: Diverting Juveniles into the Justice System." *Juvenile and Family Court Journal* 37:31–42.

3. *Collections:*

   Peterson, Blythe H. 1985. "A Qualitative Clinical Account and Analysis of a Care Situation." Pp. 267–281 in *Qualitative Research Methods in Nursing,* edited by Madeleine M. Leininger. Orlando, Florida: Grune & Stratton.

PRESENTING RESEARCH MATERIAL

The purpose of social research is to locate answers to social problems or questions. However, this is not enough: Once a possible solution is identified, it remains worthless until it has been presented to others who can use the findings. Social scientists have a professional responsibility to share with the scientific community (and the community at large) the information they uncover, even though it may be impossible for researchers to predict in advance what impact (if any) their research will have on society. To a large measure, how the research is used is a different ethical concern from whether it is used at all. How research is implemented is discussed in Chapter 3. This section concerns the dissemination of information obtained in research.

Disseminating the Research: Professional Meetings and Publications

There are at least two major outlets for social scientific research: professional association meetings and professional journals. Although the social science disciplines have less formal situations for sharing research (for example, staff meetings, colloquia, training sessions, and so forth) these gatherings are often very small and for limited audiences (four or five people). Professional meetings, however, have the potential of reaching far greater numbers of persons from many different facets of the same discipline.

It is common, for example, for the American Sociological Association to have 2,000 or more people attend a conference. The American Society of Criminology has, at each of the past several years' meetings, recorded more than 1,000 people in attendance. Although nursing conferences are not quite as well attended, several hundred people do attend the annual gatherings of the American Association of Nursing. Professional meetings provide opportunities for researchers to present their own work, as well as to hear about the work of colleagues working in similar areas. Particularly for inexperienced researchers, such meetings can be very edifying—not only with regard to the content of the papers but also for building confidence and a sense of competence. Graduate students attending professional meetings and listening to established scholars present papers can often be heard to mumble, "I could have written that." Most professional association meetings now regularly include student sessions designed to allow student researchers to present their work in a less frightening and less intimidating forum than the main sessions but to present their work nevertheless.

The saying that academics need to publish or perish is still true today—only more so! The academic standards, for example, in nursing have risen to a level such that it is no longer sufficient for a person who wants to teach to hold a graduate degree in nursing. More and more nursing programs are requiring of potential teachers doctorates in nursing—and *publications.* Publishing articles both strengthens the social science disciplines and improves the chances of being hired in a vastly competitive academic market.

Getting published, however, is partly a political matter, partly a matter of skill and scholarship, and partly a matter of timing and luck. It is not, as some quantitative purists might have you think, a matter of having large aggregate data sets and sophisticated multivariate analysis (Cullen, 1989). Often, such orientations move so far from reality that the findings offer little of practical value and, even in statistical terms, have little practical validity.

Good research is simply that! It does not matter in terms of publishability whether the approach is quantitative or qualitative (Berg, 1989). However, new researchers should be aware that a kind of bias does exist in the world of publishing. This bias tends to favor quantitative research for publication. Thus, in some journals, you may find no qualitative empirical research published at all. Yet this does not automatically mean that all the studies the journal publishes are especially good. Neither the word *quantitative* nor the word *published* immediately translates into the term *high quality.*

The process of getting published is further complicated by the *blind referee system* that better journals rely on. This system involves having a manuscript reviewed by two to four scholars who have expertise in the subject of the paper and who do not know the author's identity. Based upon their recommendations, the journal will either publish or reject the manuscript.

Pragmatically, this process can be very disheartening to inexperienced researchers, who probably have invested considerable effort in their research. It is important not to take personally a rejection of a manuscript by a journal. There are countless war stories about attempts to have some piece of research published. Many excellent scholars have experienced split decisions when two reviewers have disagreed, one indicating that the manuscript is the finest piece of work since Weber's *Economy and Society* and the other describing the manuscript as garbage.

Particularly when attempting to have qualitative research published, researchers can anticipate certain problems. It is fairly common, for example, to find that an ethnographic account or life history case study has been rejected because the authors failed to provide *quantified* findings. In some cases, this may result because the journal sent your manuscript to a reviewer who does not understand qualitative research. In other cases, however, this may occur because the reviewer honestly felt your manuscript was not ready for publication. It is important not to always assume that the former explanation applies.

Inexperienced researchers should not become too discouraged about publishing their research. It is quite like any other game: To win, you need to know the rules, including the recognition that reviewers often have a variety of hidden reasons for rejecting a manuscript. For example, the reviewer may also be attempting to publish an article on the same subject and simply wants to kill off some of the competition. Of course, some pieces of research should not be published. As the old saying goes, "If seven people tell you you're drunk, perhaps you should lie down!" Yet you should not give up too quickly on a piece of research. Becoming familiar with the publication process from start to finish helps researchers gain perspective.

When a research project has been completed, the next step is to do some research in the library. Although experienced researchers often write their reports with a particular journal in mind, inexperienced researchers frequently do not. All journals in a given discipline are not directed toward the same audience. In fact, several social science journals are explicitly for quantitative research, while others are devoted to qualitative studies.

A perusal of the periodical stacks will sometimes reveal to inexperienced researchers several possible publication outlets. Researchers should carefully note which journals appear to publish which types of studies. Often, a declaration of a journal's purpose is included on the inside of the front cover or on the first few pages. Next, researchers should identify what particular writing style and format the journal requires. This information is typically listed under the headings, "Notice to Contributors" and "Submission and Preparation of Manuscripts." Writing up a manuscript in the correct form the first time around often saves considerable time and lamentation later.

Once the manuscript has been written, it is time to make a final assessment. Perhaps the hardest decision to make honestly is how good the manuscript really is. This critical concern is necessary for several reasons. First, it is always wise to send a manuscript to the best journal in which the researchers realistically believe they can be published. An underestimate may result in publication, but one of less prestige than might have been afforded in a better journal. On the other hand, sending a manuscript of lesser weight to a high-powered journal simply increases the time it may take to get the article in print; there will be enough time lags as it is without such misjudgments. Although many journals indicate that manuscript review time varies from five to twelve weeks, researchers often wait eight or ten months merely to hear that their manuscript has been rejected.

A second reason for carefully choosing a journal to which to send your manuscript is the academic restriction against multiple submission. Because it is considered unethical to submit article manuscripts to more than one journal at a time, these time lags can be a considerable problem. Choosing the wrong journal may literally mean missing an opportunity to have a timely subject published.

Although inexperienced researchers are often hesitant to call a journal to check on the status of a manuscript, they should not be. After patiently waiting a reasonable time (perhaps 12 to 15 weeks), it is not only acceptable but recommended to telephone the journal to check on the status of your manuscript. Journals are busy enterprises and like any other enterprise can make mistakes. Sometimes when researchers call, they are informed that some error has been made and the manuscript has not been sent out for review. On other occasions, editors explain that they have been chasing after reviewers to make a decision. In yet other situations, editors may simply have no news about the manuscript. It is not likely, although inexperienced researchers may fear this, that a journal will suddenly reject a paper simply because the author called. In short, authors have nothing to lose and everything to gain by calling.

As the library research may indicate, and as Zurcher (1983, p. 204) explicitly states, "Some journals are more likely than others to publish papers reporting qualitative studies." Some of the journals that have traditionally published qualitative research and have continued to do so during recent years include *Journal of Contemporary Ethnography* (previously *Urban Life*), *Symbolic Interaction, Qualitative Sociology, Human Organization, Human Relations, Journal of Creative Inquiry, Journal of Social and Behavioral Sciences, Heart and Lung, Western Journal of Nursing, American Educational Research Journal, Journal of Popular Culture, Sociological Perspectives, Journal of Applied Behavioral Science, Signs, International Review of Sport Sociology, Journal of Voluntary Action, American Behavioral Scientist, Journal of Police Science and Administration, American Journal of Police, International Journal of Offender Therapy and Comparative Criminology, Journal of Marriage and the Family, Teaching Sociology, Criminal Justice Policy and Review, Nursing Research, Holistic Nursing Practice, Sociological Quarterly, Sociological Spectrum,* and to a slightly lesser extent during recent years, *Social Problems and Social Forces*. As even this brief and incomplete list suggests, there are numerous outlets for publishing qualitative research.

A WORD ABOUT THE CONTENT OF PAPERS AND ARTICLES

Although it may go without saying that researchers must include in their reports accurate, truthful, and documented information, it may not be as obvious that it should be interesting as well. As Leedy (1985, p. 246) states, "There is no reason why a report should be dull—any more than there is a reason why a textbook should be dull. Both of them deal with the excitement of human thinking prompted by the fascination of facts in the world around us." I cannot count the number of times I have attended a professional conference and listened to a boring presentation. I can only assume that the pained expressions on the faces of others in the audience reflected opinions similar to my own.

When you listen to a quantitative, statistical, and perhaps convoluted report or wade through an article full of regression equations and path diagrams, you may reasonably expect a certain amount of dullness. But when you hear or read dull qualitative research reports, there is no reasonable excuse. Qualitative research reflects the real world. In its purest form, it reveals elements previously unknown and/or unnoticed by others. It can be as creative a contribution to human knowledge as the Mona Lisa is a contribution to art. There are no dull facts about social life, only dull ways of presenting them!

WRITE IT, REWRITE IT, THEN WRITE IT AGAIN!

Experienced researchers realize that writing a research report is a multiple-level process. During those carefree high school days, many students could stay up late the night before a paper was due, writing the whole paper, and still receive a good grade. Unfortunately, in the so-called real world (which incidentally should include college) the submission of such a first draft is not likely to get the same results.

Becker (1986) has asserted that one possible explanation for "one-draft writing" is that teachers do not tell the students how the textbooks they read actually are written. Most students never have an opportunity actually to see either their teachers or professional writers or researchers at work and thus do not realize that more than one draft is necessary.

Most textbooks on writing have chapters on revising and recomposing (Walker, 1987), but students often think these chapters recommend merely editing for typographical and spelling errors. The notion of rewriting substantive portions of the report or adding interesting information learned after the first draft is complete may never occur to inexperienced researchers/writers.

Many inexperienced researchers/writers are simply unaware that virtually all effective writing goes through a series of revisions. Most research goes through many stages of development, versions of presentation, and editions before it ever reaches its intended audience.

For example, I was once asked to write a brief essay on politically correct behavior in criminology (Berg, 1991). After completing several drafts, I asked a few of my male colleagues to read it. They thought it was great. They told me it was hard hitting and shot from the hip. Next, I asked several female colleagues to read the essay. Both of these women describe themselves as *feminist criminologists.* They saw my essay through very different eyes than my male colleagues.

The first thing they asked me was what audience I wanted to reach. They explained that if my purpose was to reach a general audience, the essay as it was then written failed. Yes, it was hard hitting, but it was also too angry. If, on the other hand, I had a target audience of males upset with the way politically correct behavior was emerging in criminology, I was told, the piece might work. Four drafts later, my feminist colleagues agreed that the essay was ready for a general audience—although they both made it clear that they disagreed with my equalitarian position.

The important lesson here is not merely to have others read your drafts. It is important to *hear* what they have to say and to use this advice to improve the eventual final draft.

Certainly, there is no single all-purpose way to compose a research report. In fact, in the social sciences, researchers may want to write for several distinct audiences. In such cases, it may be necessary to write both multiple drafts and multiple drafts of different versions. For example, researchers may write at one level when the audience is their academic colleagues, for example, attending a conference. But this academic level of writing may be unacceptable if the audience is more diverse, as in the case of a report to a governmental funding agency that would be reviewed by professionals from several different backgrounds,

Agar (1986, p. 15) similarly suggests that ethnographies may be written up differently for different audiences, "In my own work the presentation of the same chunk of ethnographic material takes different forms depending on whether I write for clinicians, drug policymakers, survey sociologists, or cognitive anthropologists." When researchers write for their own disciplines, they write for a limited audience that is thoroughly familiar with the particular field of study and shares similar educational backgrounds. In contrast, when the audience consists of different kinds of readers, special limitations must be set on the form the written report should take.

Beyond the realities of different audiences requiring different types or levels of language, there is no single right way to say something. Often one way of saying something may be correct but uninteresting. Another way may be interesting but inexact. After three, or four, or more attempts, the authors may finally find an acceptable way to express themselves, but even that is not necessarily the only good way to phrase their ideas.

A fairly common problem all writers have occasionally is trouble getting started (Becker, 1986). Often, after having written a rather weak beginning, researchers suddenly find the words begin to flow with ease. When the writers reread the weak opening section, they will likely notice that they must rewrite, but if they do not bother to reread and rewrite the opening material, readers will probably not read beyond the poor beginning and get to those wonderful later sections.

Similarly, distance from their own writing frequently allows authors to see their presentations from a different perspective. Many researchers have experienced the phenomenon of reading a research paper they wrote several days earlier and then wondering, How on earth could I have written such drivel? On other occasions, many authors have reread something written a few days earlier and thought, I can hardly believe I actually said that—it's great! These self-reflective examinations of your own writing require some time between the actual penning of the words and the revisions. Usually several days is sufficient, although the actual time required may vary for different pieces of work.

Because of the advances in computer technology and software, it is now easy to rewrite, correct, and edit papers. Many word processing programs now offer extensive spelling and thesaurus programs, further aiding researchers/writers in their quest to find and use just the right word. The advantages to using computers in both research itself and report writing simply cannot be overstated.

A FINAL NOTE

Throughout this book, qualitative techniques and analytic strategies, rather than quantitative ones, have been the focus. Although questionnaires and quantification procedures are probably the most extensively used techniques in the social sciences, they have tended to become inhuman and reductionistic. This criticism is not so much against the procedures, which certainly could enhance understanding in the social sciences, as it is against their indiscriminate application. As Coser (1975, p. 691) warned more than two decades ago, "The fallacy of misplaced precision consists in believing that one can compensate for theoretical weakness by methodological strength." Application of sophisticated statistical procedures frequently seems akin to hunting rabbits with a cannon.

As suggested throughout this book, no single measurement class—quantitative or qualitative—is perfect. But neither is any data-collecting procedure scientifically useless (Webb et al., 1981). Some may have been amused by Jelenko's (1980) description of the Wayne State rock (see Chapter 8), and others may even have caught themselves smiling at the thought of Sawyer (1961, cited in Webb et al., 1981) sifting through the garbage of Wellesley, Massachusetts (see Chapter 8). Yet each of these studies suggests ways of accessing relevant and useful information. As a group, many of the nonreactive techniques described in this text are not as adequate in themselves as a well-constructed interview or ethnographic field study, but each of these strategies can be improved significantly through triangulation of methods.

The flexibility of the qualitative research approach permits exactly this combined use of innovative data-collection and -analysis strategies. Conversely, many of the highly sophisticated quantitative data-manipulation strategies can become stilted because they require information in a limited specialized form and format. For better or worse, however, quantitative techniques are more quickly accomplished than qualitative ones, produce what is presumed by many social scientists to be more reliable conclusions, and offer what many public agencies consider truly reportable findings (percentages of variable occurrences).

That quantitative procedures remain predominant in the social sciences is not in itself a problem or a question. What must be questioned, however, is the preoccupation of so many quantitative social scientists with methods, often at the expense of both theory and substance. Qualitative strategies on the other hand are intricately intertwined with both the substance of the issues they explore and theories grounded in these substantive issues. If social science is to sort the noodles from the soup, it must do so in a substantively meaningful manner.

NOTES

1. The abstract shown is reprinted from *Social Problems* 31(2), December 1983, p. 195.

2. This last statement is my own creation and does not appear in the original abstract. It is included, of course, in order to demonstrate the use of an implications statement.

REFERENCES

Adler, P. A., & Adler, P. (1983). Shifts and oscillations in deviant careers: The case of upper-level drug dealers and smugglers. *Social Problems* 31(2), 195–207.

Agar, M. H. (1986). *Speaking of Ethnography*. Beverly Hills, CA: Sage.

Becker, H. S. (1986). *Writing for Social Scientists*. Chicago: University of Chicago Press.

Berg, B. L. (1983). *Jewish identity: Subjective declarations or objective life styles*. Doctoral dissertation, Syracuse University.

Berg, B. L. (1987). The privatization of medical systems in correctional settings: The case of Florida. *International Journal of Offender Therapy and Comparative Criminology* 31(1), 21–30.

Berg, B. L. (1989). A response to Frank Cullen's "Having trouble getting published?" essay. *The Criminologist* 14(6), 7–9.

Berg, B. L. (1991). The progress of PC behavior in criminology. *International Journal of Offender Therapy and Comparative Criminology* 35(2), iii–vi.

Berg, B. L., & Berg, J. P. (1988). AIDS in prison: The social construction of a reality. *International Journal of Offender Therapy and Comparative Criminology* 32(1), 17–28.

Bing, R. L., III. (1987). *Plea bargaining: An analysis of the empirical evidence*. Doctoral dissertation, Florida State University, Tallahassee.

Burns, T. F. (1980). Getting rowdy with the boys. *Journal of Drug Issues* 80(1), 273–286.

Cabral, S. L. (1980). Time-out: The recreational use of drugs by Portuguese-American immigrants in southeastern New England. *Journal of Drug Issues 80*(1), 287–300.

Coser, L. (1975). Presidential address: Two methods in search of a substance. *American Sociological Review 40*(6), 691–700.

Cullen, F. (1989). Having trouble getting published? *The Criminologist 14*(4), 1–4.

Dabney, D. A. (1993). *Impaired nursing: Nurses' attitudes and perceptions about drug use and drug theft.* Masters thesis, Indiana University of Pennsylvania, Indiana, PA.

DeVault, M. (1995). Ethnicity and expertise: Racial-ethnic knowledge in sociological research. *Gender and Society 9*, 612–631.

Edwards, R. (1990). Connecting method and epistemology: A white woman interviewing black women. *Women's Studies International Forum 13*, 477–490.

Frankfort-Nachmias, C., & Nachmias, D. (1996). *Research Methods in the Social Sciences* (5th ed.). New York: St. Martin's Press.

Glassner, B., & Berg, B. L. (1980). How Jews avoid alcohol problems. *American Sociological Review 45*(1), 647–664.

Hart, C. H., & Sheehan, R. (1986). Preschoolers' play behavior in outdoor environments: Effects of traditional and contemporary playgrounds. *American Educational Research Journal 23*(4), 668–678.

Hertz, R. (1996). Introduction: Ethics, reflexivity and voice. *Qualitative Sociology 19*, 3–9.

Humphreys, L. (1975). *Tearoom Trade: Impersonal Sex in Public Places* (Enl. ed.). Chicago: Aldine.

Ipema, O. K. (1979). Rape: The process of recovery. *Nursing Research 28*, 272–275.

Jacobsen, M. (1979). Qualitative data as a potential source of theory in nursing. *Image 4*, 10–14.

Jelenko, C., III. (1980). The rock syndrome: A newly discovered environmental hazard. *Journal of Irreproducible Results 26*, 14.

Johnson, B. D., Goldstein, P. J., Preble, E., Schmeidler, J., Lipton, D. S., Spunt, B., & Miller, T. (1985). *Taking Care of Business.* Lexington, MA: Lexington Books.

Leedy, P. D. (1985). *Practical Research.* New York: Macmillan.

Leedy, P. D. (1993). *Practical Research: Planning and Design* (5th ed.). New York: Macmillan.

Leininger, M. M. (1982). Caring: A central focus for nursing and health care services. *Nursing and Health Care 1*(3), 135–143.

Meyer, M. (1991). *The Little, Brown Guide to Writing Research Papers.* New York: HarperCollins.

Michalowski, R. (1996). Ethnography and anxiety: Fieldwork and reflexivity in the vortex of U.S.-Cuban relations. *Qualitative Sociology 19*(1), 59–82.

Peshkin, A. (1986). *God's Choice.* Chicago: University of Chicago Press.

Peterson, B. H. (1985). A qualitative clinical account and analysis of a care situation. In M. Leininger (Ed.), *Qualitative Research Methods in Nursing.* Orlando, FL: Grune & Stratton.

Skibinski, G. J., & Koszuth, A. M. (1986). Getting tough with juvenile offenders: Ignoring the best interests of the child. *Juvenile and Family Court Journal 37*(5), 45–50.

Spindler, G. (1988). *Doing the Ethnography of Schooling*. Prospect Heights, IL: Waveland Press.

Walker, M. (1987). *Writing Research Papers* (2nd ed.). New York: Norton.

Webb, E. J., Campbell, D. T., Schwartz, R. D., Sechrest, L., & Grove, J. B. (1981). *Nonreactive Measures in the Social Sciences*. Boston: Houghton Mifflin.

Williams, C., & Heikes, E. (1993). The importance of researcher's gender in the in-depth interview: Evidence from two studies of male nurses. *Gender and Society* 7, 280–291.

Zurcher, L. A. (1983). *Social Roles*. Beverly Hills, CA: Sage.

NAME INDEX

SUBJECT INDEX

Abstract concepts
  edited autobiographies and, 189
  ethnography and, 121, 128
  interviewing and, 57
  intrinsic case studies and, 216
  qualitative research and, 2
  sociometric techniques and, 167
  in textbooks, 1
Abstracts (of reports), 254, 255–256
Accessibility
  of data, 46, 244
  of settings, 133, 186, 193
  of subjects, 48, 58, 129, 133, 145
Accountability (of public officials), 45
Accounts (personal)
  case studies and, 221
  commercial media, 179–180
  content analysis and, 224–225
  ethical issues and, 183–184
  ethnographic, 145, 151–152. See also
    Ethnography/Ethnographers
  first-person, 209
  gaining entry and, 130–134
  historical research and, 199, 202, 209
  interviewing and, 67, 86
  observations and, 121
  as secondary sources, 202
  types of, 7, 12, 145, 179, 199, 243, 261
Accretion measures, 191, 192–193
Accuracy
  in communication, 63
  in field notes, 142, 145–146
  in qualitative data, 5, 152, 203–207,
    227, 266
  in social interpretations, 79–80
Acquiescent response sets, 238
Acquired immune deficiency syndrome
  (AIDS), 32, 94, 102, 118, 124, 156, 270

Actors (interviewers as), 79–83. See also
  Dramaturgical interviews/
  interviewing
Actuarial records, 179, 180, 181, 182
Affect (and interview questions), 69–70
Affirmative responses (on consent
  forms), 48
Aggregated data, 45, 181
AIDS. See Acquired immune deficiency
  syndrome (AIDS)
Alcohol consumption (research on)
  cigarette smoking and, 41, 131, 136
  crime and, 62, 125, 131, 136, 140, 237
  gambling and, 39
  hypothetical, 15, 18–19, 24
  by Jewish people, 82–83
  by juveniles, 62, 125, 131, 136, 140, 237
  by nurses, 234
  other drug use and, 82–83, 136, 140, 237
  by researchers conducting research, 139
Altruism, 37, 40, 45, 187
Alzheimer's disease, 102, 118
American Society of Criminology, 44, 253
American Sociological Association, 263
Analysis (data)
  archival strategies for, 178–191
  case studies and, 218
  classes of, 235
  content analysis and. See Content
    analysis
  ethical issues and, 31, 49
  ethnography and, 121–122, 128, 146,
    151–153
  field research and, 58
  historical research and, 198–202, 206–207
  interviewing and, 70, 90–94, 105, 108,
    111. See also Dramaturgical inter-
    views/interviewing; Focus groups